WHAT THE TALIBAN TOLD ME

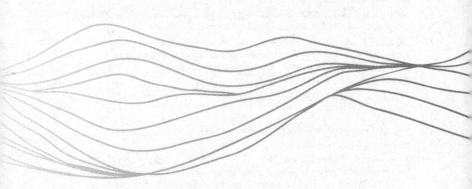

IAN FRITZ

SIMON & SCHUSTER

New York   London   Toronto   Sydney   New Delhi

Simon & Schuster
1230 Avenue of the Americas
New York, NY 10020

First Simon & Schuster hardcover edition November 2023

SIMON & SCHUSTER and colophon are registered trademarks of Simon & Schuster, Inc.

The views expressed in this publication are those of the author and do not necessarily reflect the official policy or position of the Department of Defense or the U.S. government. The public release clearance of this publication by the Department of Defense does not imply Department of Defense endorsement or factual accuracy of the material.

This book grew from the essay "What I Learned While Eavesdropping on the Taliban," © 2021 by Ian Fritz, as first published in the *Atlantic*. Portions of the essay are reproduced throughout the book.

"Baby We'll Be Fine." Words and Music by Matthew D. Berninger and Aaron Brooking Dessner. Copyright © 2005 Val Jester Music and ABD 13 Music. All Rights Administered by BMG Rights Management (US) LLC. All Rights Reserved. Used by Permission. *Reprinted by Permission of Hal Leonard LLC.*

For information about special discounts for bulk purchases, please contact Simon & Schuster Special Sales at 1-866-506-1949 or business@simonandschuster.com.

The Simon & Schuster Speakers Bureau can bring authors to your live event. For more information or to book an event, contact the Simon & Schuster Speakers Bureau at 1-866-248-3049 or visit our website at www.simonspeakers.com.

Interior design by Wendy Blum

Manufactured in the United States of America

10 9 8 7 6 5 4 3 2 1

Library of Congress Cataloging-in-Publication Data

Names: Fritz, Ian, 1990– author.
Title: What the Taliban told me / Ian Fritz.
Description: First Simon & Schuster hardcover edition. | New York : Simon and Schuster, 2023. | "This book grew from the essay 'What I Learned While Eavesdropping on the Taliban,' first published in the *Atlantic*. Portions of the essay are reproduced throughout the book."
Identifiers: LCCN 2023010727 (print) | LCCN 2023010728 (ebook) | ISBN 9781668010693 (hardcover) | ISBN 9781668010679 (paperback) | ISBN 9781668010686 (ebook)
Subjects: LCSH: Fritz, Ian, 1990– | Operation Enduring Freedom, 2001—Personal narratives, American. | United States. United States. Air Force—Biography. | Military linguists—Afghanistan—Biography. | Afghan War, 2001–2021—Aerial operations, American. | Special operations (Military science)—United States—History—21st century. | United States. Air Force. Intelligence Squadron, 25th—Biography. | Taliban.
Classification: LCC DS371.413 .F75 2023 (print) | LCC DS371.413 (ebook) | DDC 958.104/7480973 [B]—dc23/eng/20230425
LC record available at https://lccn.loc.gov/2023010727
LC ebook record available at https://lccn.loc.gov/2023010728

ISBN 978-1-6680-1069-3
ISBN 978-1-6680-1068-6 (ebook)

به نیپون

ممکن گدو

If I could tell you of its beauty
this place that I once loved
you'd ask me where I'd been
hoping that one day you might see it too

Where we were is no secret
I can point it out to you on a map
But it is not somewhere that you can go
It is not a place that you can be

If I could tell you how I miss it
this land that I still love
you'd ask me how to get there
saying, "that's a place I'd like to visit"

And I'd tell you that
I can't go somewhere
that obviates the need for me

I'm no e e
I can't carry it in my heart

Afghanistan is not a place
anyone can take

It isn't the(i)r/e(s) to steal

But I can tell you of this place
this land that I will love
if only so that
you know

Where we have been

CONTENTS

Listen   1

Flying, or The Valley of Death   7

Before, or How to Become a Linguist   24

Sapir-Whorf, or Next to My Heart   41

Pashto, or Experienced Linguists   62

Bullshit, or You'll Only Die Tired   73

Threats, or It's Too Cold to Jihad   93

Griffin, or You Keep Flying   110

Home, or You Look Like More of a Man   126

Kandahar, or Listening to Afghans   150

Fear, or You Can't Go Home Again   180

Anger, or You Can't Kill an Idea   199

Infinity, or What I Wish I Hadn't Heard   222

Tinnitus, or You Seem Fine Now   238

Reaping, or Fuck 'em   252

After, or You Can't Unkill Them   264

Acknowledgments   279
Notes   281

WHAT THE TALIBAN TOLD ME

LISTEN

TO BE ON A GUNSHIP is to be a god. This is not to say that flying in these magnificent monstrosities provided me with some sort of spiritual moment or religious exaltation. This is to say that to be on a gunship, to carry out its mission, is to feel as powerful as any deity from the pantheons of old. But these gods, like all gods, are not interested in creation. To use the 105, a gun that is loaded with forty-five-pound bullets, a gun that, when fired, causes the 155,000-pound plane it's mounted on to buck so far to the right that the pilot must actively correct the flight path, is to be Zeus hurling Hephaestus's bolts. To fire a Griffin missile from an altitude so great that the men on the ground could only know of it in the same moment that it kills them is to be Mars flinging his spear.

And while the old gods may have died, they were profligate with their genes, leaving their sons and daughters, we Nephilim, to carry on their legacy. Some of us use our eyes to find those who have sinned, scanning the earth below for evidence of their crimes, a hot spot of soil here, a silhouette of a gun there. We are called sensor operators. Some of us aim the guns at the targets the sensor operators have found, carefully correcting for height and angle, terrain, and nearby friendlies. We are called fire control officers. And some of us load these guns, the last people to touch the bullets that will go on to end existences. We are called gunners. These are the greater gods, the ones who are known and worshipped by many.

But there is a lesser god, known to few, understood by fewer, even these other divinities. You cannot see what this god does, as he sits there (overwhelmingly *he*), cocooned in his headset, eyes closed, manipulating energy, listening to invisible messages. They are called direct support operators, or DSOs. You could listen to what they are hearing, but you wouldn't understand it, as it is not the language of mortals. Or of the living. For they hear the dead.

This is the story the United States Air Force, and many a DSO, want to tell. Call it the DSO as deity. This is not a true story. It isn't even a good one; that shit sounds like a rough draft of a freshman creative writing prompt. But this is the story I was told, and it is the story I believed for a time. The truth, or at least a truth, is a little more grounded. Because man wasn't meant to be deified. Our minds aren't ready for it. So very few of us can be trusted with power of the mortal variety, so what are we supposed to do when we're given the mythical version?

A DSO (pronounced "dizzo") is just an airborne cryptologic linguist by another name. Historically, there weren't very many DSOs, mostly because the Air Force didn't want or need that many, and partly because DSOs like feeling special, so they artificially limited the number of spots available to other non-DSO linguists. And because there were so few DSOs, it was that much easier to craft an image as badass "operators," the best of the best, the only people who could do what they do. This was plausible; there are those elite groups within the military who have been selected for their talent, grit, and exceptionalism. And, like those elite groups, if you pushed the DSOs on it, they would be able to credibly say that because their job was highly classified (true) they couldn't tell you specifically what they did (untrue).

A DSO does what all airborne linguists do. They "translate intelligence communications or data received or intercepted while in the air," aka listen to what the bad guys (usually) are saying in another language and turn it into English (that quote is from the USAF's Quincy, Massachusetts, recruiter's Facebook page). Most airborne linguists do this aboard a jumbo jet, the RC-135 Rivet Joint, or RJ, flying thirty thousand or so feet above the ground at four or five hundred miles an hour, in an orbit that encompasses a few hundred miles. This is strategic work; the communications they receive or interpret rarely have an immediate impact on something actively happening on the ground. But it is important, at least according to the military, as "a lot of the things we do might end up on the desk of the president" (ibid., and a little misleading, though technically not a lie if you note the usage of "might").

The primary difference between these linguists and DSOs is one of location. DSOs don't fly on RC-135s, or any similar massive aircraft. DSOs fly exclusively on the planes that are utilized by Air Force Special Operations Command, or AFSOC. For the most part, these are C-130s that have been modified for various purposes. Some of these, like the AC-130s, or gunships, have been changed so much from their original cargo-carrying mission as to be unrecognizable; the only cargo a gunship carries is bullets. Others, like the MC-130s, still can and do carry cargo, but they've been made to be better at doing it. AFSOC has other aircraft that DSOs are trained to fly on, but in my time in Afghanistan, we almost exclusively flew on C-130s.

Timing is the other thing that makes a DSO's work different from that of other linguists. AFSOC doesn't do strategic work all that often, and so neither do DSOs. In Afghanistan, our job was to "provide real-time threat warning" to the planes we were on and to the people on the ground that these planes were supporting. How we did this work is unimportant, and honestly quite boring.

I don't know if they still think of themselves as badasses, but when I was a DSO, that was the ethos of the community. We (not all, but most of us) felt that we were the best of the best: better than other linguists, cooler than other linguists, more important than other linguists. Once upon a time, some of this may have been true. Long before I did it, in order to be a DSO you had to be very good at the language(s) you spoke, and you had to be handpicked by other DSOs, interviewed, and tested; it was a whole process. And there were those DSOs who flew scary, complex missions in dangerous places. But by 2010 the Air Force just randomly assigned new linguists to become DSOs, and the thing most likely to take down the aircraft a DSO was in was a drone (seriously, they have a bad habit of losing connection and orbiting at preselected altitudes that are, let's say, inconvenient for other, human-containing aircraft).

But the DSO told himself that he was a badass. An elite, specialized, and superior human who had earned the right to do what he did purely on merit, and to shit on others who hadn't earned the same opportunity. You may recognize this story, as it's the same story most small men tell themselves. The DSO, for obvious reasons, did not realize this.

If I sound petulant, obstreperous, dismissive, arrogant, or, you know, just like a fucking *dick*, that's fair. I have a strong dislike of those who consider themselves Better Than, and that dislike turns into utter contempt when this shameless self-promotion is founded on false pretenses that rely on the diminishment of others. This is somewhat a reaction formation, given that I spent my childhood, adolescence, and a decent amount of my young adulthood committing this very sin, and I continue to feel great shame about it. That doesn't mean that I'm not right. I am. Being a DSO does not make you particularly special. It doesn't make you better than anyone else, especially other linguists. And ultimately, like most things, it isn't all that important.

But it really is spectacularly, mind-blowingly, worldview-changingly awesome. I mean like, biblically awesome. A DSO is no god (the new gods are as dead as the old), but he is sometimes powerful beyond comprehension. Providing "real-time threat warning" is a very bland way of saying that I listened to the Taliban as they were talking (essentially with no delay), translated it from Pashto to English, and relayed that information to my crew, to other planes, or to forces on the ground, often within seconds. If I was on a gunship, what I heard would be used to decide whether we killed those Talibs. If I was on a different type of C-130, what I heard could force us to take evasive maneuvers, to try and keep us from getting shot by those Talibs. Either way, I would temporarily be responsible for a hundred-million-dollar war plane.

Being a DSO in Afghanistan meant making life and death decisions (*and* not *or*). We could decide who lived, and who died. When we had flown a mission, and done our job right, it was no lie or even an exaggeration to say we had done something that very few other people were capable of doing. When I did it, I was one of only two DSOs who spoke both Dari and Pashto; there was only one other person on Earth who had received the training I had, who could do the work I did.

Because I experienced all of the things I did in the Air Force at a young age, it might have been impossible for them to be anything but formative. Because very little else that followed was imbued with the same amount of life and death, other things will always pale in comparison. Or maybe it really was the most important thing I've ever done, or will ever do. And so, though everything in this book is true, and most of it is about me, it is not a memoir, as I don't know how to tell you who I am. Nor is it a war book, as I don't know how to make you understand war. All this book can do—all I can do—is show you what I was.

I was a DSO.

And this is what I heard.

FLYING, OR THE
VALLEY OF DEATH

I LEARNED HOW TO BE a crewmember of an AC-130 over the course of two months in early 2011. I'd spent some time before that in a classroom learning the basics of DSOing, a little general radio theory here, some specific stuff about walkie-talkies there. I'd walked around a gunship parked out on the flight line a few times, had studied the layout of the plane, and knew where all the exits and fire extinguishers were. But I hadn't actually flown a training mission. And somehow, in eight weeks, less than fifty hours of time in the air, I learned how to fly.

First things first, all the crew positions: pilot, copilot, FCO, Nav, EWO, flight engineer, loadmaster, sensor (TV), sensor (IR), gunners.

The pilot and copilot were pretty straightforward. The rest, though, needed some familiarizing. The FCO (pronounced foco), or fire control officer, is responsible for calibrating and aiming the massive guns attached to the plane, and for sort of overseeing and directing the sensor operators. The navigator, or Nav, not only does what the job title explains, but also talks to other aircraft and troops on the ground, coordinating airspace and movements within it in real time. The EWO, or electronic warfare officer, knows everything there is to know about enemy fighters, radars, and surface-to-air missiles, and has to be able to tell the pilots how to evade incoming attacks.

You have to be an officer to be in any of those positions, aka have a college degree. You get to wear shiny stuff on your collar, instead of stripes on your sleeves, and everyone has to call you sir or ma'am.

The rest of the crew is enlisted. The flight engineer is like a super mechanic who knows everything about the plane and tells the pilots what to do if some mechanical or electrical or hydraulic thing fails. The loadmaster does the math to figure out how to balance the multiple tons of ammunition that get loaded onto the plane. The sensor operators, TV (television) and IR (infrared), operate the cameras mounted on the side of the plane. The gunners (all four of them) maintain the bullets and the guns in the back half of the plane, when not busy giving out naked gunner hugs or just generally goofing off. (A naked gunner hug is exactly what it sounds like; a gunner strips down to little to no clothing and gives you a big ol' bear hug.)

I also learned about mission planning and checklists and safety. I learned how to talk on a plane, how you always address someone by their crew position, and name yourself by yours, like:

"EWO, DSO, I'm hearing chatter about a possible surface-to-air missile."

Or "Nav, DSO, I'm picking up a couple guys coordinating movement toward the objective."

And, most importantly, I learned that together the fourteen of us would find the enemy, and we would kill them.

Ten flights later, I was qualified as a DSO, which meant I could, three years after joining the Air Force, finally do the work of an airborne cryptologic linguist. I just had to get over to Afghanistan to do it. My squadron wasted no time arranging the trip, and I was scheduled for the next flight east, a couple weeks later. My last meal stateside was with my buddy Quinn at a Longhorn Steakhouse. I ate entirely too much shitty food, confident that it would be better than what I'd be able to get in Afghanistan.

There were two main bases in Afghanistan: Bagram, in the north, and Kandahar, in the south. Bagram was the OG, but it was also a shithole. Good old-fashioned bunk beds set up in a giant tent with curtains that were supposed to provide enough privacy to rub one out (they didn't, but that didn't stop anyone), inadequate heat, and little to do on base. Being up north also meant that the missions were often less exciting, as the brunt of the battles were in the southern and eastern parts of the country. Kandahar, in the south, was the place to be; the place I was assigned for my first deployment.

It was a massive base, with troops from dozens of countries stationed at it. Over time, a sort of town square, affectionately known as the boardwalk, had been built. Every country contributed: the French had a nice little shop with all sorts of bonbons; the Germans had a duty-free where you could get a carton of cigarettes for twenty-five bucks (a steal); the Dutch even had a discotheque. At least I think it was the Dutch. There was definitely a discotheque, country of origin uncertain. But it was the Americans that really transformed the place. I arrived in 2011, at the height of our occupation of Afghanistan, joining over one hundred thousand other American service members in the country (in addition to all the contractors and members of other militaries). We did our best to make the base feel like home. You could get a can of Coke and some mozzarella sticks at the TGI Fridays on the boardwalk, or some fried chicken at the KFC.

The other major upside to Kandahar was that you didn't have to share a big-ass tent with twenty other horned-up airmen. Instead, you got a nice freight container, individual AC unit included, and you only had to share it with one other guy (occasionally two). If you were lucky, you were on opposite flight schedules, and you could jerk it in peace. And even if you weren't, 'bating with one other guy in the room was far preferable to flogging yourself in the vicinity of a dozen others.

The downside to going to Kandahar was that it meant you stood a chance of flying on the Whiskeys instead of real gunships. At the time, the Air Force had two gunships in service: AC-130Us (known as the U-boat, or their official call sign, Spooky) and AC-130Hs (H-model, or Spectre). These had been around since Vietnam, when the Frankensteined imaginations of artillery-loving madmen had determined that not only was it possible to attach a 105mm howitzer—aka the gun that tanks use against other tanks—to the side of a cargo plane, but that it was in fact also a good idea to do so. Once a fever dream like this begins to take shape, it builds on itself with ever more frightening results. The 105 wasn't enough, as a gun that big can only fire so fast. No, there must be other guns that, though they provide less damage per bullet, can hit more targets at once with a greater rate of fire. For medium damage and medium speed, there's a 40mm Bofors cannon. For light damage and massive speed, a 25mm Gatling gun. If you are someone who has the slightest appreciation of mechanical engineering and the building of things that simply aren't supposed to exist, it's difficult not to love gunships. Inversely, when it registers that these impossibly real monstrosities have no purpose but killing, it can be difficult to love gunships.

Then there are the Whiskeys. The MC-130Ws, call sign Recoil, were the prototype of what would eventually replace the aging Spooky and Spectre fleets. The Whiskeys had access to Griffin and Viper missiles, which some thought were improvements over the 105. This might be true. But it seems worth noting that a single 105 round costs $400. Each Griffin is $127,333. Raytheon, the company who makes these missiles, knew what they were doing when they pitched them to the DoD. (The Whiskeys would eventually get a smaller gun, a 30mm Bushmaster II that was purported to be far more accurate than the Gatling gun and Bofors cannon on the ACs.)

In part because they were less capable of mass destruction, but more because men will always find reasons to shit on other men, the Whiskeys were not only Other, they were also Lesser Than. The crew of a Whiskey were seen as transporters, guys who just flew shit from point A to point B. They also flew during the day, which had the double downside of not being vampirically sexy and being tasked to missions that were, so it was said, less likely to involve schwacking some Afghans. Real gunships, AC-130U/Hs, didn't fly during the day, as they had to be much closer to the ground than a Whiskey. This was deemed too risky, especially after *Spirit 03*, an AC-130H, was shot down in broad daylight in Iraq in 1991.

I knew before I left that I would be flying on Whiskeys for at least some of my deployment, and maybe even the whole thing. Despite the Whiskey's less virile image, commanders across Afghanistan were excited to have a gunship, any gunship, overhead during the day. The fact that I had never seen an MC-130W, much less flown or even trained on one, wasn't important. DSOs are unique in that they can get qualified on another aircraft with just one or two flights, either stateside or in a combat zone. This may sound irresponsible, and it might be, but our job doesn't really require all that much knowledge about a given plane beyond basic safety rules, escape routes, and the location of the pisser. That said, I still had to be trained on the Whiskey, which meant I had to fly with an instructor. Fortunately, there was an instructor already deployed to Kandahar: Ed.

Ed was a little high-strung, kind of twitchy. He was on his second marriage—which didn't appear to be going much better than the first—on deployment number whatever-the-fuck doing a job that he had been poorly trained for, a combination that helped further his progression into an ebulliently stressed-out bundle of nerves. He talked too fast, expected too much, and, as near as I could tell, hated most everything, including, but very much not limited to, his marriage, Afghanistan, Afghans, deployments, and existence. Ed was a nice enough guy, and he usually meant well. He wasn't necessarily disliked, but he wasn't popular, partly due to his anxiety and self-seriousness, partly by virtue of being an instructor, as it's sort of hard to like the person grading you.

Once you get to Afghanistan, you get one day or so to adjust to the new time zone. And so my first combat mission wound up being at the tail end of March 2011. Ed felt that it was going to be a good first mission, easy, just circling overhead a forward operating base (FOB). This would give me time to adjust to the new plane and let Ed teach me the few differences that mattered. I couldn't ask for a better way to ease into finally doing the job for real.

We went to our mission brief, and stepped to the plane a little earlier than the rest of the crew. Along the way, Ed told me some of the differences between the gunships and the Whiskeys. How I wouldn't have to worry about naked gunner hugs, as there were no gunners, just two loadmasters. How I wouldn't be talking to the EWO and Nav, but instead to the CSOs (sizzos), or combat systems officers, the Whiskey's hybrid FCO/Nav/sensor operators. How I wouldn't have to turn around to see what the CSOs were looking at, as my seat was right in front of the monitors they used. He said that the cameras were incredible, basically HD, but given my experience with the gunships' ancient and grainy black-and-white CRTs, I figured he just meant they were HD in comparison.

The base radio station was playing "Asshole" by Denis Leary, a favorite of Ed's I had never heard, so he had me listen to the whole thing. He showed me around; taught me how to set up my equipment on a Whiskey; showed me where to piss, where to shit (the Whiskeys had this on the U-boats, an actual can). All the important stuff. The flight over to Kunar took a while, so we bullshitted about this and that and lamented the Kunari accent (in most Pashto, the word "yes" is either *balay* or *balay ho* or just *ho*. In Kunar, *ho* becomes something like "hhhhnyeah." Dialects are weird.) Mostly, we just hoped that there wouldn't be anything all that important waiting for us.

This was wishful thinking, as Kunar is an infamous part of an infamous country. Kunar is one of the N2KL provinces—Nuristan, Nangarhar, Kunar, and Laghman in the northeastern corner of Afghanistan—the area that has been host to most of the worst battles in modern Afghanistan's history, at least on the U.S. side; twelve of the fourteen Medals of Honor awarded to American military in Afghanistan were for actions carried out in these four provinces. Kunar might or might not be the most dangerous of the four. It's the most recognized, though, as it's home to the Korengal Valley, known widely as "The Valley of Death."

This name makes sense from the American point of view, given how many of our soldiers have died there. But the area is full of life.

Eastern Afghanistan is mountainous in a way that's hard to explain if you haven't seen it. It's not dissimilar to the Rockies, in that there are seemingly countless peaks, rugged and rough. But the valleys between the mountaintops are unlike any other place I've seen. They're so deep that it's hard not to envision an ancient god astride the planet, driving his world-sized pickaxe thousands of feet into the earth, jaggedly scraping out the land in one fell swoop, replacing what was once lifeless rock with seemingly endless life. The valleys, ten thousand feet and more above the sea, are lush and vibrant, often verdant beyond belief; the idea that so much life can flourish at such heights almost requires these divine descriptions, as it's hard to believe that nature and time alone could result in such extravagant beauty.

The beauty of this landscape was brought to incredible life by the new cameras on the Whiskeys. As the precursors to the next-generation gunships, they'd had their sensors upgraded. These cameras are connected to high-definition, full-color monitors, making watching the world through the eyes of the Whiskey like something out of the future compared to what I was used to on U-boats. So I was not a little distracted while we were in transit, trying to process everything I was seeing, along with what I was hearing over the radios, as we started getting updates en route. A TIC—troops in contact—had been called.

"Hey Ed, uh, that means there's like, actual fighting, right?"

"Eh, it means there's shooting, but by the time we get there it could be over."

This was meant to reassure me. Ed was calm and collected (I quickly learned that flying Ed was a much more controlled person than on-the-ground Ed), but I was pretty wet with flop sweat. And my dampness wasn't being helped by the increasingly intense radio calls we were hearing directing more assets in the same direction as us. Soon, we knew we were close, and the CSOs started scanning the ground with the Whiskey's cameras. But in those mountains, even if you're flying at twenty-five thousand feet above sea level, you aren't all that high above the ground, so you can't really see down into a given valley until you're directly overhead. When we finally cleared the last crest and got directly overhead Barawala Kalay Valley, there was plenty of life. And a lot of it was moving.

I looked at Ed, hoping to gain some reassurance that the madness below was just a product of my greenness, that because this was my first real flight I was just overwhelmed. But even Ed wasn't calm anymore. Wide-eyed, almost a little slack-jawed, his forehead now glistening with the same sweat I felt streaming over my entire body, he made it clear that the madness was real.

"Yeah. It's not over."

Our wishful thinking had been in vain. The valley was swarming with men. With Talibs. Hundreds of them. At our altitude, we could see almost everything. Usually, this meant that we had a better understanding of the battlefield than the guys on the ground. But with this many enemies running around, it was more like sensory overload.

No one will ever be able to say with any certainty, but it's estimated that there were three hundred or more Talibs fighting that day in Barawala Kalay. If we assume that only 10 percent of them were actively communicating over radios—think walkie-talkies, also called push-to-talk radios, the Taliban's preferred method of communication—that's thirty voices all trying to talk over each other while we listened. Under the best of circumstances, the Taliban doesn't generally have the same level of radio discipline that we do. This was not the best of circumstances, not for them, not for us. When we started listening, it was just an onslaught of noise; Ed and I were inundated. It was eventually possible to focus in on a single voice or conversation, and hear things like:

> "God is great, brother! We are killing them! We are killing them! Move forward, move forward!"
>
> "Keep shooting keep shooting, we will go around!"

But we faced the same problem that the guys scanning visually did: There was just too much going on in the battle below. Even if we told someone that a group of Talibs were going to move up, it would be meaningless, as there were so many of them moving up all the time.

As the battle progressed, more aircraft were called in. The ground team undoubtedly would have preferred a "real" gunship, but because there was daylight, they only had us. But some fighter jets and their bombs came. Helos too, both Pave Hawks for medevacs and Apaches for attacks. When two of the Apaches arrived, we heard the Taliban yelling:

> "East, brother! They're coming from the east! The dub-dubs are coming! At least two dub-dubs!"

The word for a helicopter in Pashto, or at least the Taliban's Pashto, being دب دب دبوکی or *thing that makes the dub dub sound.*
And as the Apaches carried out their attacks:

> "The demons are firing, brother! Stay safe, brother, we are moving!"

Who knows how many drones were on station (this isn't a rhetorical statement; it's probably not known, what with how often they lose their connections and wind up just circling around at inconvenient altitudes). The battle soon felt like something out of a training simulation. While the men on the ground used their mortars, rockets, and rifles, the Apaches did their gun runs and fired their missiles, and the fighters dropped their bombs. One of the medevacs had to turn back after it took heavy fire.

The fighting continued for hours. Throughout, Ed and I tried our hardest to discern what we could from the voices, struggling to interpret the thick Kunari accent between the sounds of guns firing and bombs exploding, the screaming and yelling that are part and parcel of battle. We passed along any information we could, but truth be told, I don't see how we were of much use. And even if we were, it certainly didn't feel like it.

I watched a five-hundred-pound bomb land, turning what I'd thought looked like twenty men into dust. As I took in the new landscape, full of craters instead of people, there was a lull in the noise, and I thought, *Surely now we've killed enough of them.*

We hadn't.

"Keep shooting! Keep shooting! We will kill them all! God is
   great! Keep shooting! They will retreat!"
"We are killing them! Move the others! They are still coming!"

Throughout the battle they constantly repeated variations on the theme of their success.

"Brothers, we are winning. This is a glorious day!"
"God willing, the monsters will all die today!"
"God is great, brother. God is great! Kill all the demons!"

Even if we couldn't count the bodies just yet, it was obvious that we were killing so many more of them than they were of us. And yet, they kept fighting. More of them appeared on every hillside, our game of schwack-an-Afghan not going very well.

And still:

> "Brothers, we are killing them! Go go go go go! Keep shooting! We will kill all the devils!"
>
> "Keep fighting, brothers! We are killing all the monsters! God is great!"

Eventually, the battle slowed, likely due to a combination of us killing enough Talibs that even they felt it prudent to back off and the waning sunlight. We had to return to base as we were running low on fuel.

This mission, my very first, is the only one I know of that was captured on film, courtesy of a reporter embedded with the army at the time. What a video. It's got it all. Soldiers, heavy and bulbous with their armor and ammo, crouching behind walls as the countless reports of the Taliban's bullets echo all around them, firing back when they can. Medevacs flying in and out. An Apache firing its missiles. And the money shot, a bomb hitting one of the hillsides, the smoke and dust rising in memoriam, accompanied by all the cheering that comes from men being on the right side of such power.

What you don't see is any of the Taliban; the footage is too low-resolution, the camera too far from the men who appear as ants on such massive mountainsides. They also aren't the point of the video, despite their presence being the entire reason the video even exists. You don't see them in their loose-fitting clothes, flitting about, running on rocks, occasionally using trees and brush as cover, but frequently out in the open, firing as often as possible. (If this contrast seems to you like a thinly veiled, sophomoric attempt at an allegory painting the American war machine as a galumphing giant and the Taliban as some lithe leopard, don't worry, I'm not nearly clever enough for all that.)

I'd been "danger close" to 105 rounds. This is pretty far in training situations, a few hundred feet, but the rush of wind from the impact still knocked dirt off the truck I was standing next to. I'd felt the soil vibrate as an A-10 used its GAU-8 Avenger to rip up the earth, and I'd been shot at by SEALs as they drove into a compound (real guns with simulation rounds, think paintball but with automatic rifles). But these were controlled environments, and unless some terrible accident occurred, I had no chance of getting hurt, let alone dying. Despite having witnessed such fatal danger both from the ground and from the safety of my plane on high, and having had the added experience of hearing, via radio, the experience of the Taliban in real time, I still don't understand fully what it was like to be a Talib on the ground that day. I know I don't know, because even through static and fear and thick Kunari accents, they told me, even if indirectly, how they felt. And it was so absurdly removed from anything I could imagine.

How could they not feel like ants under the magnifying glass of our cruel godhood? How could they have even had the nerve to engage in this battle in the first place? What hope did they and their ancient AKs have against our LMGs and Apaches and fucking *gunships*? Yes, we were the invaders, and no, we had never successfully secured a position in this area, but like, wasn't that only because we hadn't really tried? What chance did they have of beating us if we gave it our all?

I knew, of course, that they would fight in the presence of a gunship, despite their name for the gunship being "bogeyman." I knew that they would use their decades-old Russian rifles against our $30-million attack helicopters. I knew because I'd listened to training audio of conversations like these back in Florida, and so I thought I knew what it would be like to hear it in real time.

But while that training audio kept me from being completely overwhelmed during this mission, it was entirely different from the simultaneous hearing and seeing of the real battle. Sure, they were ants, but only insofar as they were swarming. Yes, their guns were old and busted, but they'd still managed to use them to make a helo turn back. And yes, we secured our position in Barawala Kalay, but for how long?

The next day, Ed sent me an email. All it said was "So you know this is real," followed by a line break with a link to a news article and some names below it. They were the names of the Americans who died on our mission.

In the final tally, six Americans died, seven more were wounded, and anywhere from fifty to over one hundred Talibs were killed in action, depending on the source. (One of my enlisted performance reports, the Air Force's annual evaluation form, chose to go with the bigger number. The more enemy combatants I had killed, helped kill, or at least been in the vicinity of when they were killed, the better.) Besides the medevac that was shot—it turned out the pilot was hit—at least six more had followed it in. The commander of the 101st Airborne went on to say it was their biggest battle since Vietnam.

Ed, it would seem, felt I did not appreciate the reality of the situation. At the time, I was insulted. Who was this fucker who spoke Pashto half as well as I did trying to tell me what's real and what's not? I get it, "You're an asshole," but you really think I don't understand that death is *real*? You think I spent three years training for this job and didn't figure out along the way that there are very *real* consequences to war?

I'm still insulted, and Ed is still an asshole, but now I can at least understand why he thought this was something he should do. To him, I must have looked completely unaffected by this utterly insane battle. I didn't ask to talk about it or to take a day off from flying, and I came in the next day perfectly well rested. It wasn't that I'd decided to not think about the mission, I just sort of didn't. This was what I'd been trained to do. The Taliban were supposed to die en masse; some of us would die, hopefully less en masse; and we would facilitate both of these outcomes to the best of our ability.

So it would make sense if Ed felt like my puny virginal brain couldn't fully comprehend the scale of the battle and all that had happened. Maybe he felt that because I didn't have the same reaction he did, I hadn't taken the mission seriously. Maybe he really meant well, and was genuinely worried that because I'd spent so much time in training, I hadn't yet connected all the dots.

My therapist has told me that I shouldn't automatically assume that people's actions are negatively motivated; indeed, I should operate under the assumption that everyone is doing their best (thank you, Brené Brown, for spreading this delightful message). These conjectures are my attempt at this generosity. I must not be doing it right though, as I don't feel any better and I'm still pretty sure Ed was being a dick.

That said, I didn't yet know how troubled Ed was and how

powerless he felt to do anything about his problems. Sure, there was always *that* solution, the one available to all of us, so he might put his 9mm in his mouth on occasion, but it usually wasn't loaded, almost always had the safety on, and he had his kids back home to think about. He wouldn't actually do it; he just wanted to know how it felt to have all that steel in his mouth. Instead, he would dutifully wake up, exercise, fly his missions, and when he felt that too many occupiers and not enough occupants were dying, when the cold steel was starting to taste too good, he'd go through the battle damage assessment (BDA) photos on JWICS, our Top Secret version of the internet, and get his emotional rocks off looking at bloody, holey, half-blown-up Afghans. These pictures are taken after missions and, according to the Chairman of the Joint Chiefs of Staff Instruction (CJCSI) Methodology for Combat Assessment, help to "develop observable, achievable, and reasonable measures and indicators, including targeting measures of effectiveness (MOEs) and targeting measures of performance (MOPs) to assess the outcome of operations." I guess pictures that detail exactly how much of a dead guy's face is missing let you know how effective you were. Fifty percent of head left? Not good enough, aim better next time.

These pictures, this war porn, provided Ed with a catharsis. I don't think he found this behavior all that concerning, at least not at the time. These were bad men, and they had been righteously killed, and as a member of the pantheon that resulted in their just and permanent end, he had every right to revel in their grisly, brutal, futile demise. Because if he didn't, the chances were all too high that he would meet the same fate. A 9mm isn't a big gun, but at close range, it can take off more than half your face.

That first mission was not the easing in we'd both expected.

With so much going on, Ed hadn't really been able to get a feel for my comfort level on this new plane or do the cursory "instructing" he was supposed to (mostly just "Hey, do you know how to get out of this plane if it catches on fire"–type stuff). All of this was reasonable, safety first and all that, so we flew together once more. Ed taught, I listened, and he gave me his blessing. I learned how to be a crewmember of an MC-130W over the course of 15.9 hours. And, finally, 1,120 days after joining the Air Force, two days before I turned twenty-two, I was qualified to fly on my own.

BEFORE, OR HOW TO BECOME A LINGUIST

I MET MY FIRST RECRUITER in tenth grade, in my AP U.S. history class. At this point in my life—it was 2005—I had no knowledge of the military or intention of having anything to do with it. I wasn't necessarily for or against the idea, I simply had no conception of it beyond what I'd been taught about soldiers and wars throughout school. My only direct connection was through my father, who, I was told, had been in the army, but had been unceremoniously booted for "breaking his commanding officer's jaw" after an overly long guard shift or some such nonsense. I only ever heard this story from my mother, who likely misunderstood or embellished (or both) the tale until it stopped resembling the original in any meaningful way, other than the violence (I don't know that it was then, but at some point my father figured out that hitting people in the face doesn't leave much room for deniability; anywhere else, though, was fair game). She still had his dog tags, so I knew the part about him actually having been in the army was true. But beyond that, I'll never know anything else about him or his time in, courtesy of his leaving when I was in fifth grade, and then his dying fifteen years later, a lone, unresponded-to Facebook message (him to me) being the only attempt at communication from those fifteen years.

Other than this more or less tangential relation to the armed forces (the man may have touched the arc of my life, but he most certainly didn't cross it), I didn't know anyone who had been in, and I had never thought of the idea of joining. But then this thin, compact, fit, and really just exuberant recruiter, with a big-ass smile, no small amount of sarcasm, and the surety that comes with not actually having any experience with the thing you're describing, started talking about this linguist gig. I don't know if he changed his presentation for different classroom audiences, but I can't help but wonder if he brought up the position of airborne cryptologic linguist because he was in a room of allegedly smart kids. Or maybe it was good bait for anyone who was considering joining. As he told us that if you joined up as an airborne linguist, you got a fat signing bonus, the Air Force taught you a language of your choice, and then you used that language to spy on people from a jumbo jet, it was easy to see that many of us were at least interested in the idea.

He wasn't pushy, and I suspect now that he knew he didn't have to be, as eventually, one or another poor kid from Lake City, Florida, would realize that they had fuck-all else going for them, figure they may as well join up, and start knocking at his door. I wasn't interested in the position; I was only in tenth grade, and besides, I was convinced of my future in college and beyond. I was, however, interested in getting attention from my classmates, so I piped up with "Yeah, but I'd have to cut my hair, right? Sorry, no deal." I got the laughs I wanted, including his. "You'd have to do a lot more than that, Red. You also gotta be pretty smart. Not too many people pass the tests to qualify for this job."

I have no idea how clever this man was, whether he had figured out this round-faced, floppy-haired, truculent fifteen-year-old, or if this was a generic tactic that recruiters employed, digging at a teenager's pride so that they'd join the illustrious war machine. Clever or not, I suppose I'm evidence that he was pretty good at his job. Even if I didn't decide then and there that I would join—he wasn't that good—I remembered his presentation.

In part this was because I really did think that I wanted to be a linguist, if not by that point, then soon after. My mother and her sisters were trilingual, raised speaking English, French, and Bambara, the national language of Mali. My grandfather was allegedly nonalingual, though I have a hunch that, as was family tradition, this was a bit of an exaggeration. He was at least quadralingual: Tamashek, a language spoken by the Tuareg in Mali, was his first tongue, followed by English, then French, then Bambara. I figure he gained some proficiency in other dialects and even a couple of other languages, but I don't know that it could truthfully be said that he was fluent in an additional five.

I was my grandfather's heir apparent, in no small part because we looked uncannily similar (I once saw a picture of him as a teenager and legitimately wondered when someone had taken a picture of me without my knowledge), but also because I was alleged to be as smart as him. I too enjoyed reading the rest of the page of the dictionary whenever I looked up a word I didn't know. I too had memorized large swaths, or what I and others thought were large swaths, of the Bible, New Testament and Old. And I too would happily disappear into another room for hours on end, more than content with my books and all the friends in them.

With this legacy it was said that I'd be a natural at learning languages—never mind that I only spoke English, and even after multiple years of high school French (and the added benefit of a French-speaking mother) I couldn't readily conjugate *être* or *avoir*, inarguably the most important verbs in the entire language. In my mother's defense, she maintained that my father didn't allow her to teach my brother and me anything other than English, as he didn't want us to be able to conspire against him, which he may not have ever outright admitted, but he didn't have to. The guilty suspect everyone of talking about and plotting against them. By the time he left for good, she probably felt that it was too late to teach us, and it's fairly unlikely we of the short attention spans would have made particularly good students. None of this mattered, because when I got to college I would be able to rely on my natural "giftedness" the same way I had for all academic endeavors my entire life.

The problem with being "gifted," or at least with constantly being told just how "gifted" you are, is that it obviates the need to develop the much more important abilities of hard work and dedication, or any semblance of humility. Instead, I had endless faith, if not necessarily in God, then in myself. So I knew that I would get into college, study linguistics, and at some point in there work out what precisely one does with this esoteric degree.

I did not get into college. My grades from the first two years of high school had been good, math class notwithstanding, but when I turned fifteen I started working, and because my mother (1) made somewhere in the area of ten dollars an hour at her job, and (2) was not good at managing that meager sum, this money was important. My mother rarely outright asked me for my paychecks, as that would be shameful, but when the nice man from Clay Electric showed up to our trailer for the third time to remove our access to the power grid, and I called my mother, unsure, but somehow still hopeful that this was a mistake, only to be told that no, she had in fact not paid the electric bill in three months, resulting in the by now familiar sinking feeling that we would be powerless, both literally and otherwise, yet again, combined with the anger that the cable bill had still been taken care of, so that she could lay in bed for hours each night staring at that numbing screen, somehow unable to see through her depression and narcissism that without electricity the TV would be both moot and mute, even then she wouldn't or couldn't bring herself to ask me to pay the nice man from Clay Electric, some weird quaver in her voice preventing her, as it would have prevented her from asking her husband, or her father, or all the other males in her life that she was still so afraid of that she projected them onto my brother and me, but mostly me, and so to outright ask me would have been to admit that she was so unable to meet the needs of her children that one of said children would, in a fit of selfish-fulfilling prophecy, now inhabit the role of that man she was so afraid of, which maybe is a thing she needed or wanted or craved, or how else do I explain that I still had to pay the nice man from Clay Electric, who was surprised to see me, it being strange to him that I, clearly still of school age, would be home at two in the afternoon, though this was in fact the reason I would be able to pay him, because I had enrolled in my high school's early bird program, such that I went to school from 0645 to 1300, it being important to be out at this lunchtime hour, instead of the traditional 1600, because my shift at the local Chinese restaurant started at 1630, and it didn't matter that it didn't end till 2200, resulting in my getting home at 2230, too keyed up and young and irresponsible to go to bed, such that I then overslept for these early start classes so often that the school nearly kicked me out of early bird, my untold number of tardies and full-on absences of my first, and sometimes even second, classes resulted in my grades plummeting in a perfect inverse relationship with my growing sleep debt, such that even though my teachers often told me that I was smart enough for these AP classes, and always recommended that I stay in them, my grades were terrible, but if I didn't work those hours, far over the state limit of twenty per week for high school students (my bosses were kind enough to fudge said hours but still pay me for all the time worked), then I wouldn't have been home to talk to the nice man from Clay Electric, let alone ask him for the six minutes it would take to drive my 1989 Dodge Ram 50 with the wooden fence for a tailgate over to the S&S convenience store and withdraw the $340 to pay all three of the past due electric bills in full, so that my household and I (for who was the "head of" it in this moment if not me?) could continue to bathe, and eat cooked food, and otherwise be a part of civilized society, thereby proving that whether they were my priorities or not, I had to continue this work, which I did, such that my college application was, shall we say, lacking in evidence of commitment to academic rigor, which maybe would have been okay were it not accompanied by what I thought was a compelling essay about my desire to study linguistics in order to follow in the footsteps of my missionary grandfather and learn how to spread the Word to all those poor, unsuspecting heathens the world round, and while I doubt I was rejected based on any overt stance on the school's part against this profession of such dogmatic religion, I wouldn't be surprised if it played a part, albeit a minor one, demonstrating as it did my utter and complete lack of understanding that linguistics is not, in fact, a matter of learning languages, but understanding how languages work, and providing major evidence that I hadn't bothered to do even the most cursory of investigations into this field that I swore I was such a fervent fan of, though, in my defense, I was a little too tired to take the time. Probably should have written about that instead.

After I was rejected, my mother tried to convince me to move down to Gainesville and enroll at Santa Fe Community College. If I just went there for two years, I'd be able to transfer over to the University of Florida, no problem (and with a lot less debt). But the idea of going to anything other than a real university was insulting. I was gifted! Gifted people are better than community college.

At least I was going to be a high school graduate, this by no means a sure thing in Lake City (the attrition rate between my freshman and senior class was somewhere around 60 percent). I could keep my job waiting tables at the restaurant, as they'd let me work as much as I wanted, and at least the food was free. But then what? Lake City had its own community college, but they'd never even heard of philology, my new favorite synonym for linguistics, which isn't actually a synonym but a topic within the overall field, but how was I to know this when I couldn't be bothered to consult a dictionary to look up the definition of a word I most certainly already knew? Besides, who was gonna call me on it?

I stewed in this aimless post-rejection miasma for weeks that turned into months. I graduated and listened to all of my friends, every single one of them, discuss their plans for college and the big cities they were moving to. While at the time only 4 percent of my high school went on to a four-year university immediately after graduation, I only really knew those who were a part of this upper echelon, the years of AP classes having effectively limited my peer group to a scant thirty people. I knew of people who had graduated before me who had enlisted, but the only ones I knew personally had joined to be a part of the Army or Marine Corps Band, not because they didn't have any other option. At some point, though, I remembered the cocky, charming recruiter, and how he said I could be a linguist, a real one. I figured he would remember me (who could forget me?), and on one of my days off I went to the local mall, where all the recruiters had their offices. I didn't know that recruiters rotate through assignments, so I was surprised when a very different human greeted me.

He wasn't anything like the recruiter from school. He was much calmer, less salesman-like, almost languid in his sense of ease. When I walked in and told him I wanted to enlist as an airborne cryptologic linguist, he didn't scoff or challenge me. He just asked me why, and whether I thought I could pass the tests. I was, clearly, not someone who would have considered the military otherwise, and it seemed that he knew this. Still, he didn't try to sell me on anything.

"Someone told me you can't join if you have asthma. Is that true?"

"Yes. Do you have asthma?"

"I was told I do," I said and gave him the name of the doctor who'd told me this.

"That guy would see a kid not breathing underwater and diagnose them with asthma. Why'd he say you did?"

"I did an experiment in chemistry and inhaled some gas. I had a really bad cough for a long time after. My mom said it was asthma, and so did he."

"Do you think you have asthma?"

"No, not really."

"Okay, good. When you come back in a few months, we'll go on a run and see if you do."

"Okay! Yeah! Wait, why in a few months?"

"How tall are you?"

"Six-two."

"How much do you weigh?"

"Uh, I'm not sure."

"I'll tell you. Too much. Let's see, though. Hop on the scale."

I looked at the doctor's office scale that I had only then noticed, and I must have hesitated, because he said, "Go on. You can take your shoes off if you want, but they won't matter."

He confidently set the base at two hundred, and then jostled the balance up, and up, and up, and finally stopped, right around the forty mark.

"That's why in a few months. You're too fat."

He didn't say this with any cruelty or malice in his voice, only matter-of-factness. Every branch of the military has standards for height and weight. In 2007, the Air Force's limit for a male who stood six feet, two inches tall was 212 pounds. There are exemptions—if you get your body fat measured and it's below a certain amount, then you can be above the weight cutoff, but suffice it to say I would not have qualified for such an exemption, as my extra twenty-eight pounds were not muscle. Between growing up attending Southern Baptist churches (which meant attending Southern Baptist potlucks), having an overweight mother who had tried and failed at every diet fad of the last twenty years, and working more or less full-time the last two years at a restaurant where they felt that food was equally as important as pay, I had not so slowly but oh so steadily gained a lot of weight.

Kindly, the recruiter told me, "You have to lose forty pounds. Thirty isn't enough. You don't want to be near the cutoff. Lose the weight, then come back."

The only thing I thought I knew about dieting was that it didn't work. Everyone I knew who had ever lost weight always gained it back. But I had seen my mother successfully lose a lot of weight, for a time, using the Atkins diet. So I quit carbs. This was not all that easy, given that I worked at a Chinese restaurant and had grown accustomed to eating huge helpings of rice with dinner six nights a week. And at lunch. And for afternoon snacks. Not eating rice was tantamount to not eating period, or so I, and my employers, felt.

Looking back, I'm not sure how I actually managed to lose weight on this "diet" of mine, as I was eating fairly large portions of meat and cheese, not exactly calorically light items, for most meals. They must have amounted to fewer calories than I had been eating, though, as over the next four months it worked. I got down to 205 pounds and figured this was good enough to go back and see the recruiter.

Except he wasn't there. In fact, no one was. Lake City, Florida, had a population of about ten thousand people at the time, and the whole of Columbia County only seventy thousand, so it makes sense that a recruiter wouldn't spend each day at our mall. Disappointed, and hungry, I called the number listed on the office door. No one answered. I left a message and didn't hear back for a week, which, in no-carb time, is an eternity. I called again, left another message. Eventually, I got through, and I was excited to tell Sergeant R. that I had done what he said. But the voice on the other line was different. Said voice informed me that his main office was in Valdosta, but that he would be down in Lake City in a week or two, and that I should see him then.

Here, again, a different recruiter. But this one was less calm, less fit, and far less supportive in person. When I asked where Sergeant R. was, the new guy sort of dismissively said, "He got blood cancer. Stationed him out in Arizona, I think, for treatment."

"Oh, I . . . That sucks."

"Yeah. His wife and kid will be taken care of by the Air Force though."

I didn't understand how fatalistic this proclamation was at the time, and so I just said, "That's good."

"So, you want to do what again?"

"Airborne cryptologic linguist."

He sort of smiled at this, with that same now seemingly standard-issue surety that comes with not actually having any experience with the thing you're so confident about. I can't blame him for this dismissal. To him, I'm sure I was just another redneck kid who thought too highly of himself.

I agreed to take a practice Armed Services Vocational Aptitude Battery, or ASVAB, in his office. Every potential military recruit has to take this multiple-choice test, which "measures developed abilities and helps predict future academic and occupational success in the military." There's a minimum score for joining each branch of the military, but there are other, higher scores that serve as cut-offs for different career fields; I don't think my recruiter expected me to score high enough to even qualify for the other test that all prospective linguists have to take. It turned out that the practice ASVAB was harder than the real thing, so when I scored in the

88th percentile, his tune changed drastically. Gone was his apathy, replaced with hustle and bustle, finding of paperwork, looking up of phone numbers, his excitement to get me to take the real ASVAB and then the follow-up I would have to pass in order to qualify for linguist training almost palpable.

The Defense Language Aptitude Battery, or DLAB, is a test used by the Department of Defense to assess a candidate's ability to learn a language. This is in direct opposition to testing knowledge of any one specific language, as the military most often aims to teach you a new language, not use whatever random one you happen to already know. To this day, this test is spoken and written of in hushed, fearful tones. When I (and all the others before me) took it, before information about it was readily available on the internet, it was even more fabled. Allegedly, the DLAB is written in Esperanto, or at least derived from Esperanto, a synthetic language invented by a Polish ophthalmologist in the late 1800s. If this sounds confusing and slightly silly, you can imagine how I felt when the recruiter told me some of these details (he mentioned the Esperanto part, but either didn't know or care to include the eye doctor detail). There are apparently guides and resources to prepare for the test now; Wikipedia goes so far as to say that without using these materials obtaining a passing score would be well-nigh impossible. Unless the test has changed dramatically, I can assure you this isn't true, as I, and thousands of others that attended language school alongside and before me, didn't have such materials. We just took the test.

As far as I could tell, a strong grasp of English grammar, or, I suppose, any language's grammar, would take you pretty far on much of it. While it is specific to language, the test evaluates a much broader skill, that is, the ability to assimilate unfamiliar, seemingly conflicting information and apply it to novel situations. I, characteristically, believed that this test, like all other (non-math) standardized tests before it, would be a cakewalk. It was not. The DLAB, like other tests based on logic, doesn't have wholly correct answers. Instead, it relies on the test-taker's ability to determine the most likely, or best available answer. This could be, and indeed was, immensely frustrating for someone who had undergone traditional public education (in rural North Florida no less), where tests are multiple choice and simply have one right answer, and three wrong ones.

At the time, the Air Force required a minimum passing score of 100 (out of 164) to be eligible for language school. Through some combination of luck, exposure to the sound of multiple languages, and unalloyed bookwormishness that had provided me with a decent understanding of English grammar, I received a score of 103. Not great, but good enough.

The entire process of enlisting lasted six months, even if we don't count the time it took me to lose enough weight to be eligible. Initially, my recruiter told me that I would likely head to basic training toward the end of November, maybe even the week of Thanksgiving. I wasn't particularly excited to spend the entirety of the holidays (the Air Force's basic training was six and a half weeks long at the time) trapped under the thumb of a drill sergeant, but I was eager to leave my life behind, so I accepted this timeline. I could have asked and would have found out that the Air Force doesn't have drill sergeants, but, again, still me.

November came and went, with no open spots for yet another wannabe linguist to enter the training pipeline. I'll likely never know why, maybe because it was becoming a realer possibility, or maybe because they felt that I was responsible for the delay, but those around me began sharing their misgivings about my decision. My relatives, none of whom were successful (either financially, academically, or interpersonally), felt that this was a waste of my God Given Talents, that I was Too Smart for the military. My work family, who knew far better than my blood family what my true work ethic and grit looked like, or more accurately, didn't look like, routinely made remarks to the effect of "Well, when you come back from boot camp, we'll have a spot for you." Not if, but when. They were entirely sure I wouldn't make it past the first month. I ignored this, mostly out of pride, and my contrary nature, though I see now why they felt this way. I was ill-fit for the military. Arrogant, entitled, lazy, combative, occasionally unreliable, usually fickle, I looked to them like someone I couldn't see: a pent-up boy desperate for something greater than himself, willing to take a step toward it, but probably not capable of pushing through any obstacles.

But the thing about desperation is that it lets you do things that are otherwise impossible. Things that defy your nature. Things that can, ultimately, transform you. My metamorphosis began on February 5, 2008, the day I arrived at basic training.

And so the literary version of the eighties classic training montage begins.

Scene: my first time on a plane—I who signed up to be an *airborne* fucking linguist—is my flight to basic training. Lackland Air Force Base in San Antonio is surprisingly cold in February, and sitting outside some building waiting to complete paperwork at 0200 is unpleasant. Staff Sergeant Raymundo Contreras, my training instructor, or TI, is more unpleasant. With his scarred, permanently frowning face, he asks me where I'm from, and when I, too scared to think about or remember that I was one thousand miles west of my hometown, respond "Lake City," he punches the locker behind me and screams, "Lake City where, Fritz!" I nearly shit myself.

I manage to do only eleven push-ups during our first physical fitness test, immediately qualifying me for remedial physical training. I learn how to make a bed with hospital corners. I try to eat lasagna so fast that I burn my tongue and can't taste anything for days. The weeks pass by in a blur of hunger and exhaustion, until, somehow, seemingly magically, I pass all of the tests, physical fitness included, and I'm marching down the flight line during graduation.

From here, along with one other wannabe linguist from my basic training flight, I travel the two miles across the road to Medina Annex to attend Aircrew Fundamentals, where, we're told, our intelligence will be tested, and, more importantly, we'll be told what languages we're going to learn. I meet other future linguists. Despite falling asleep in class multiple times and receiving a formal Letter of Counseling—exhaustion/boredom being a punishable offense—I pass the class. My basic training flight mate does not. I sit around on casuals, aka scut work, aka sweeping and mopping and picking up rocks on sidewalks and shining the pieces of metal on the floor that separate rooms and any other number of meaningless tasks that the Air Force feels we must complete while we wait for our next set of orders. I get my wisdom teeth removed at some point in there.

The fateful day of language assignments arrives. Hayward gets Chinese. Knight gets something called Pashto. I get . . . Dari? What the fuck is Dari? There's another airman on casuals working the front desk of our dorm who I hear was in Dari. He informs me that it's the language spoken in Afghanistan, and that it's very difficult to learn, as it utilizes the Arabic alphabet, where each letter actually has three forms, but Dari has more letters than Arabic, and I'll have to learn how to say letters like *ayn* and *ghayn* and *kaff* and *qāf* and best of luck dude, it's a bitch.

We, which is to say I and the other linguists at Medina, are informed that the training pipeline is backed up and that we will not be heading to language school now, and will instead be sent to survival school, or SERE (Survival Evasion Resistance Escape), at Fairchild Air Force Base in Spokane, Washington. SERE is mythical, said to involve broken fingers, dogs hunting you, full-on torture. Many of those who have been to it come out changed; my roommate at Medina had just been there and he's, let's say, not quite right. But he won't talk, and the others who have been won't provide details beyond the legends we've already heard.

SERE involves at least one of these mentioned things. It also involves a lot of other things, the details of which aren't important, as they all serve the same purpose, testing our will. I mostly whine throughout the whole process, but, again, somehow make it through. We're told at the end of it that blood tests done on SERE graduates show the same amount of stress hormone as a Navy pilot has on their first nighttime aircraft carrier landing. We are duly impressed by this. Now I just think about how crazy it is that those pilots are as stressed out in ten minutes as I was over nineteen days.

I do non-parachuting water survival training right after SERE. There's a pool, and a raft, and a firehose. It's uncomfortable, but it's also only two days. That side of the base has a great dining facility.

And then, finally, I arrive in Monterey. In the year that I spend there, I will drive down Highway One in a convertible with the top down at sunset, lose my virginity, have my first great beer, and make lifelong friends. It will become, and remains to this day, my favorite place on Earth. It is also where I will learn Dari, and in that process, expand the boundaries of my life in ways I never could have imagined.

SAPIR-WHORF,
OR NEXT TO MY HEART

THERE IS A CONTENTIOUS CONCEPT in the field of linguistics known as the Sapir-Whorf hypothesis. One of the interpretations of this hypothesis roughly states that language, native or acquired, shapes how people understand the world around them. Taken to its logical extreme, this hypothesis says that the language you know dictates not just what, but *how* you think. For some, this means they can differentiate between shades of blue particularly well, as their language has more than one word for the basic color that we English speakers (and many other non-English speakers) perceive as "blue." For others, their sense of direction is spectacular, as their language doesn't utilize ideas like turning left or right to go somewhere, but instead requires constant awareness of the cardinal directions. These examples, and others like them, are used to support the "strong" version of this hypothesis.

I wasn't aware of Sapir-Whorf when I signed up to become a

linguist or when I was learning Dari. In my estimation, a language was no more than a collection of words, discrete facts that simply had to be memorized. Yes, there was the grammar with its rules and exceptions to those rules that required a different organization of information, but again, these were simply more facts used to rein in all the other facts that had to be forced into one's head.

The first time I can remember noticing that I was beginning to think differently was when I sat down to write something in English, and while English came out, I started it on the wrong side of the page. Dari, because its alphabet is based on Arabic, is written and read in the opposite direction of English, that is, from right to left. So the first English words I wrote down, which were some lines of the song "Now That You're Home" by Manchester Orchestra, appeared on the page like this:

Home you're that now

It felt strange while I was writing, like something was off, but it wasn't until I was four words in that I realized why: I'd been doing so much writing in Dari by this point that my brain automatically assumed I should be writing starting on the right side of the page. When I put the words on the left side of the page, in the correct order, they looked weird; when I kept writing in English, it didn't feel natural. So I just decided to stick to the language that started on that side.

حالا که در خانه استی مه را خواهد می‌پوختی؟ جدی کشش میکنم که دوباره خوب بودن باشم

When I say I'd been doing so much writing in Dari, I mean it. The Defense Language Institute (DLI) is probably, on the whole, the best place in the world to learn a new language. Located in Monterey, California, it churns out hundreds of newly fluent speakers of dozens of languages every year. Class is five days a week, seven to eight hours a day, split between the three modalities of reading, listening, and speaking. Nearly all the instructors are native speakers of the language they teach (there are also some obligatory military vocabulary lessons taught by DoD linguists). You can expect at least an hour of homework on weekdays and multiple hours on weekends. And while you are a student, you're also a soldier, sailor, marine, or airman, and the military is paying you to be there (not much, but still, it's something). Sick days require a visit to medical, tardiness is taken seriously, and failure can mean getting kicked out of one's respective branch.

I was, at best, anomalous in my unassigned writing of Dari. Less generously, I was, as always, a big ole nerd; there were enough assignments at school that sitting down to translate song lyrics would have been anathema to most of my classmates, or at least extra work. But everyone practiced their speaking outside of school, whether they thought of it as work or not.

This was in part due to one of the "rules" of DLI: No English in the schoolhouse. This is treated as more of a guideline by students and teachers alike, as when students are first starting out this would essentially demand mutism. But as you get more comfortable with the language you're learning, it's not such a hassle to forsake English. A visitor to downtown Monterey on a weekend night might encounter hundreds of young, white (linguists are overwhelmingly white, even more so than the rest of the military) men (idem) speaking languages from the world over. Sometimes, they're using this newfound skill as way to talk shit about the people standing next to them or to complain about the food without their waiter knowing. Practical things. But most of the time, they're just having *fun*.

It's fun to speak in a secret language known only to you and your friends. While there might be a few hundred Chinese speakers wandering around the bars, the members of a given class, say fifty people, will likely have developed a group dialect. Even if a native Chinese speaker were in earshot of these pullulating polyglots, there's a good chance they wouldn't understand what they were hearing, as all these young men (and a few young women) would be switching back and forth between their native and new languages in fluid patterns that would only make sense to them.

A native speaker who tried to keep track of all this nonsensical shuffling of speech would be further confused by the interjection of seemingly random phrases into the conversations they were eavesdropping on. An Arabic speaker might be sitting there enjoying their dinner, listening to the petty gossip of the soldiers and sailors the next table over, wondering why they kept hearing the words "only discipline" repeated over and over again, accompanied by so many chortles and cackles. There would be no way for them to know that in the Arabic schoolhouses, some of the instructors had turned this phrase into a refrain, reminding the students that Arabic is difficult (and it is, particularly for English speakers), and that only discipline would allow them to succeed (natural ability plays in too, I suspect, but what do I know). Unfortunately for those instructors, "only" in Arabic sounds a whole lot like "fuck it" in English. And "discipline" is all but indistinguishable from "in ze butt." Together, "only discipline" combines into the wondrous command to "fuck it in ze butt." It isn't all that hard to imagine a bunch of drunk twenty-somethings relishing the use of this phrase.

About three months into our school year, my classmates and I had gotten to this point. We routinely spoke in a sort of pidgin conglomerate of Dari and English, creating our own verbs where need be, flouting grammar rules when they were inconvenient, using English for the Dari words we hadn't been taught (or more likely hadn't yet studied hard enough to learn).

This substitution of Dari (or whatever language) for English starts to go both ways. It's initially simple, and purposeful, the peppering of the new tongue into the mother, the substitution of the word *dummy* or *ass* or *gay* (there being an inverse relationship between originality and usage of insults—as well as a direct relationship between offensiveness and usage—among young men). But like most subconscious thought, it eventually becomes more complex and less controlled. In Dari, verbs are more or less obligated to occupy the last spot in a sentence; sentences like "I'm going to the store later" would be literally translated into English as "Later, to the store I'm going." And so, as time went on, my friends and I found ourselves applying Dari grammar to English. This meant that for months, we often spoke our native language like some sorts of young Yodas. This is pretty funny at first, until you're out at a store with a date you like and when she asks you if you like the jeans you're looking at you reply, "Yes, buy them I will." (Okay, still funny, but less so to nineteen-year-old me.)

But these are simple crossed wires and the formation of new habits. The changes were in what I was thinking, not how. I was still learning facts, and facts don't change your mind. It wasn't until I began engaging with the language, trying to understand how it worked, why words meant the things they did, that Dari began to change the way I thought about the world.

At some point, maybe around the four-month mark, I was reading an assigned passage about cars and driving, and I kept coming across the word *soldier* strewn throughout the text. Reading the sentence "We were driving down the road in our soldier, wind blowing in our hair" will make you feel like you're losing your mind, or at least like you're a bad linguist. I kept trying to power through, to make sense of this passage, but I was getting more and more frustrated. I finally had to ask that hour's teacher for help (at DLI you stay put, the teachers rotate through the classrooms).

Professor (*Ustaad* in Dari) Fawad was a marvelous, strange, and kind man. He was always a little late, a little disorganized, and more than a little disheveled. And he was vain, in that charming way a middle-aged man who maybe once upon a time really was handsome—and still feels that way—can be. So though he routinely forgot handouts or assignments that we needed and would have to dash back to his office to grab them halfway through a lesson, he always had his comb on him, ready to touch up his hair as he re-entered the room like some sweeter, (slightly) less crazy version of Cosmo Kramer (these entrances had earned him the nickname of The Tornado). Thinning though it was, Fawad could still construct his hair into a four-inch pompadour.

He also had a different accent than most of our instructors, a little throatier, with a different rhythm to it. This, we later found out, was due to his having lived in France for many years. (Both French and Dari have an innate meter to them, and they had combined in Fawad to form a magnificent melodic mélange.) Like most of our teachers, he had left Afghanistan because of the Taliban. But Fawad was older, which meant he left early, the old-fashioned way, by putting his pregnant wife on a donkey and walking alongside her for three days until they reached Pakistan. How they wound up in France I'm not sure, but it wouldn't surprise me if they only got there because Fawad somehow sweet-talked someone into it.

He was well liked, as he was always kind and generous, ready to offer you some of the walnuts he had just cracked open with his bare hands (Fawad contained multitudes), or an earnest and kind "*Afrein!*" ("Bravo") whenever you got the simplest of questions right. He also talked a lot. His brain seemed to be constantly engaged in some sort of free association, so any simple question, like the one I had about this unknown word, could quickly turn into a lecture on something completely unrelated. But, as he was the only person in the room who could help me figure this word out, I prepared myself for the inevitable outpouring of information.

"Professor, I don't understand this passage. Why is the word *soldier* in here?"

Fawad took out his smudged glasses, set them on his surprisingly (or maybe not so surprisingly, Afghanistan being the world's original melting pot) Roman nose, and bent over to read the passage under his breath.

"Ah! Baktaash (we were given new, non-English names in language school), yes, *sarbaaz* does mean soldier, but here, it means convertible."

"Uh, what?"

"Baktaash, *sar* you already know. What does it mean?"

"Head."

"*Balay* [yes in Dari], or top! And *baaz*?"

"Open."

"*Balay!* Very good. And so, open, top . . . Oh!"

Fawad usually looked a little startled, as a natural consequence of always being in a rush or a reverie, but here he jumped, like literally snapped upright, his mouth initially forming this great "O" shape, eyes wide, eyebrows working their way toward his combover. And then a big, sly smile spread across his face.

"Maybe this is why they call you soldiers, no? Because you have such open tops?"

It took me a second, but once I realized Fawad was basically calling me, and the rest of us, empty-headed dumbasses, I started cackling. From that day on, I was a Fawad fan. So what if he talked too much? I did too! And the way he thought about words was fascinating, and fun. His example of سرباز had introduced me to a whole new way of looking at words, of trying to suss out their hidden meanings.

I had learned a word for favorite, دلچسپ (*dillchaasp*), early on in the school year. I used it for months, asking people what their favorite insert-new-vocabulary-word was. Sometime after Fawad's convertible-soldier joke, I learned the verb *to stick* (as in to stick something to something else), چسپیدن (*chaspeedan*). I already knew that دل meant *heart*, and so the next time I asked someone what their favorite insert-new-word-I-had-just-learned was, it dawned on me that دلچسپ means *heart-sticky*. What poetry! Such meaning! How wondrous! I was enamored of this conceptualization, that one's favorite thing is not simply a preference, but something (or someone) that is stuck to your heart. During our next break I found Fawad and asked him if he had ever thought of this.

"Oh, Baktaash! *Afrein!* Yes, of course, this is a beautiful word. Do you know دلخواه (*dillkhwaa*)?"

"*Heart . . . Heart want?*"

"Yes! *Heart's desire!*"

Fawad had gotten very excited by this point, his head and his pseudo-pompadour bobbing up and down in agreement. So when he reached into his breast pocket, I assumed his comb was coming out.

Instead, he produced a beautiful, small notebook. In his meaty hands (walnut-crackers, remember?) it looked even smaller than it was, and more organized than anything I'd ever seen in Fawad's possession. He opened it, tenderly, making sure not to damage the pages, to wherever he had left off, and made a quick note.

"*Ustaad*, that's a beautiful book. But it's so small. What's it for?"

"No, Baktaash, it's the perfect size. I write poetry in it. If it were any bigger, I couldn't keep it here, where it belongs. Next to my heart."

Turns out Fawad always had two things on him. His comb. And his poetry.

Fawad was the first poet I ever met. Language and all of its beautiful possibilities, as well as its limitations, were everything to him. He knew that the words you use to describe the world around you necessarily shape that world; you can tell someone you love them, "تو را دوست دارم" (literally, *I have you as a friend*), or you can tell them that they are stuck to your heart. I still tell people they're my favorite, content in my secret knowledge that, in my own way, I'm telling them that they're bound to my core.

I don't know if Fawad still teaches at DLI. I've tried to look him up, but transliterations of names are hard, and DLI doesn't have any publicly available list of instructors. Maybe he's still there, carrying his comb around, continuing the fool's errand that is his follicular fight. Or maybe he retired, so he wouldn't have to commute three hours every day from Fremont to teach our ungrateful asses. Whatever he's doing, I'm sure he still has his notebook in his pocket, infusing all of his wondrous words with his vitality.

At the end of my year at DLI, I could debate the merits of divorce and its effects on children in Dari, discuss politics, and attempt to answer the question "What is love?" (This was the last question I was asked in my speaking exam. I would like to think my inability to answer was more due to my being twenty than my lack of language skill.) I could tell jokes, explain the meanings of proverbs, and generally shoot the shit with most any Dari-speaking Afghan. I thought in Dari, dreamt in Dari, and often found it easier to express myself in it. This is true for lots of recently graduated linguists; when we met a newly minted Arabic linguist at survival school and asked him what DLI and learning a language so fast was like, he said it's cool, but it can mess with your thinking a little bit. A couple days later he was telling some story, when he stopped halfway through a sentence, with a dazed look on his face. "Wait, shit. What's the word for that thing you eat cereal with?" "A spoon?" "Yeah, that's it, a fucking spoon. Fucking Arabic."

Like any skill, language can atrophy. After I left DLI, and went to Goodfellow Air Force Base in San Angelo, Texas, for cryptology school, I wasn't expected to speak Dari seven hours a day and I didn't. While we were there, my friends and I still used our Dari, the whole secret language thing feeling like a superpower on occasion, but it wasn't quite the same and so I forgot some words and a few complicated grammatical structures. But after Goodfellow, I wasn't spending time with a group of other Dari linguists. Everyone else in our class had been assigned to Offutt Air Force Base in Omaha, Nebraska, to fly on the Rivet Joint, or RJ, a billion-dollar spy plane with a half dozen plus linguists listening to multiple languages flying on it during any given mission. Back then, if you enlisted as an airborne linguist, this was essentially what you signed up to do; new linguists could only get assigned to Offutt, or so we were told. But something had changed, so I, and just one other student, Taylor, had been assigned to Air Force Special Operations Command (AFSOC) at Hurlburt Field, Florida (affectionately known as Hurby, Hurlburt being annoying to say). This meant that we had to travel separately from our friends, as we had to get different training than them.

Taylor and I did not like each other when we were at DLI. We were both arrogant, confident that we were better at learning languages than our classmates. This confidence was encouraged by our teachers, who weren't paid to teach us how to be good humans, just good linguists. But Taylor's surety had never really been challenged; I doubt anyone had ever told him that he was "the most insecure narcissist I've ever met" (this was said to me by my best friend's mother when I was in high school). If anything, someone had probably told him he was the most *secure* narcissist they ever met, and he had said "Thank you!" with a gleam in his eye and some Cheshire cat in his grin.

Taylor had been speaking the language of confidence his whole life. His dad, Simon, a successful businessman, had given Taylor his first lesson in this language while they were driving through the mountain canyons of Colorado in a Ferrari. Yes, they were going double the speed limit, but Simon was secure in the knowledge that if he did get pulled over, what cop wouldn't let them off the hook, wouldn't understand? After his parents split, Taylor lived with his mother, a nurse who had inherited land in Wyoming, for a time. There, he would become immune to any accusations that he was a prissy city boy, and he could spend the rest of his life referring to "the ranch" whenever he needed evidence of his country and nature bona fides. He'd played sports, done drugs, slept with girls. He didn't even need to enlist, as he'd secured all the letters he needed to attend the Air Force Academy. He had just decided that he didn't want to deal with all the bullshit that goes on there.

When we got assigned to Special Operations, told that we were going to become DSOs, the most elite of airborne cryptologic linguists, Taylor fell for the mythology (a mythology that he knew virtually nothing about) hook, line, and sinker. He managed to keep it to himself when we were at Goodfellow with our RJ-bound classmates, but once he and I went our separate way, on to parachute training before heading back to survival school for Advanced Beatings class, he would tell anyone who would listen what badasses we were, or at least had been chosen to become.

When he would tell some other random airman, "Yeah, we know three languages—Farsi, Dari, and Tajik," I'd supplement this—not complete untruth, but not total truth—with "Well, they're really the same language, but with different accents."

Or when he told one of the other fliers in our interrogation class (the official name for what Advanced Beatings actually is: a week of learning how to deal with enhanced interrogation techniques), "Yeah, we're AFSOC, stationed down at Hurby," I'd elaborate that with "We just got assigned there, it was sort of random. No one knows why they chose us."

He saw my tendency to couch his claims in reality as an undermining of our accomplishments, no matter the fact that as far as anyone knew, nothing the two of us had done had gotten us stationed at Hurby. We literally had no choice in the matter. Orders are orders.

And while I wasn't as confident as Taylor, I was as stubborn, so no matter how many times he told me to stop subverting the sanctity of his stories, I kept bringing him back to earth. The madder he got, the more I felt it necessary to remind him that he wasn't special.

This, it seemed, was an affront to Taylor's self. Whatever he was, or believed himself to be, was predicated on just how very special he was. How unique. If you put it all together—his looks (tall, blond, blue-eyed, not unproud of our nickname for him, Hitler Youth), his intelligence (*technically* he did speak Farsi, Dari, and Tajik, the fact that these are Western colonial names for one language notwithstanding), his background (he might have been the first, and last, airborne linguist in the history of Wyoming)—he was, conceivably, one of a kind. But I wasn't willing to allow that this meant that he, and by association I, was better than anyone else.

Advanced Beatings, no matter how much you try and treat it as a game, inevitably puts you into a heightened emotional state. While you're not always the one getting slapped around, you're watching others take five fingers to the face, or a hand to the gut, and even when it accidentally becomes funny—like when a TACP (tactical air control party), think badass Special Forces type, has to be reminded that, when asked if anyone would like to volunteer for "torture," it's a rhetorical question, and you shouldn't raise your hand—the course is incredibly stressful. It forces you to regulate your emotions so much during class that I think it's inevitable they become dysregulated outside of it.

So I don't blame Taylor for opening my dorm room door and telling me, "Fritz, the next time you pull that shit, I'm gonna punch you in the fucking face."

I had twenty pounds on Taylor (he was skinny, I was skinny-fat), but he was in far better shape: wiry, athletic, and conditioned from fighting with his brothers growing up. He was also very angry.

"What shit?"

I was playing dumb, not completely sure that he was talking about what I thought he was talking about. Given my proclivity for saying dumb shit (I was, and occasionally still am, a habitual line-stepper of the highest order), he could have simply been mad about something particularly annoying I had said earlier that day.

"Stop contradicting me, fuckface. You're being a little bitch."

"I'm not contradicting you. I'm just telling the whole story. You speak Dari, I don't care if you passed the Farsi test, or taught yourself Cyrillic. You're a Dari linguist, that's it. And yes, we're going to be DSOs, so what?"

"What do you mean so what? We're gonna be fucking DSOs. I'm tired of you going behind my back and saying we're no better than those RJ fucks."

"Dude. What? 'Those RJ fucks' are your fucking friends, you fuckface. You could just as easily be going to Offutt, with Ben headed to Hurby. He got the same scores you did."

Taylor and I think similarly, which is to say we often don't, at least not that we're aware of. When I talk, especially when I talk while angry, I don't have plans for the words that are coming out of my mouth. I just plan to have words come out of my mouth. The second the other person is done speaking (or even before) I'll start my rebuttal, and something will piece itself together (I hope).

Which is why when I say that in response to this Taylor opened and closed his mouth, it isn't metaphorical, or a dramatized memory. His mouth opened, ready to say whatever expletive-laden thing his brain was fomenting. And then the rest of his brain, or at least some bit that wasn't hell-bent on proving me wrong, actually heard what I'd said. And his mouth closed.

My memory of Taylor saying everything up until "those RJ fucks" is crystal clear. I think this is because I consider it the turning point in our relationship, the moment we begrudgingly accepted that our lives were entwined, and that if we didn't figure out a way to be okay with that, shit was going to be hard for the next who knew how long. I don't know that he felt the same way, but he listened to me, as I explained that maybe it's not such a good idea to go around talking ourselves up when we don't know what exactly it is we'll be doing (if someone asked us what a DSO did, or how they were different from other linguists, we would hastily retreat under the cover of classification, which, looking back, probably made it painfully obvious that we didn't know shit). And I listened to him, as he explained that we were, at least on paper, better at Dari than most of our classmates, and that even if we didn't know exactly why we were going to Hurby, it seemed pretty reasonable to think that we had been selected.

On arrival at Hurby, it became abundantly clear that we had not been selected. I don't know that we were expecting a hero's welcome (okay, I wasn't, but maybe Taylor was) when we got to the 25th Intelligence Squadron at Hurlburt Field, Florida, home of Air Force Special Operations Command, but maybe at least a "Welcome." We got more of a "What the fuck are we going to do with a couple of dumbfuck Daris?" We didn't just speak languages. We *were* languages, as far as the Air Force was concerned. I didn't notice until it was too late that by succumbing to our normal human desire to have in-groups and out-groups we used this nomenclature too, such that we all too often defined ourselves as these objects. These tools.

Dari is a bit of a useless language to the Air Force. Yes, it's one of the official languages of Afghanistan, but it's primarily used by the government, and yes, we spy on lots of governments, but we didn't really need to spy on Afghanistan's, seeing as how it was little more than a puppet state (in 2009 at least). And yes, there are lots of Afghans who speak Dari in their day-to-day lives, but they're predominantly Northerners, aka not Pashtuns, aka not Talibs, aka not a threat. Even our friends who got assigned to Offutt, to fly on the Rivet Joint, a plane that exists to suck up every bit of electromagnetic information it can, did one deployment on the RJ before getting cross-trained into an entirely different job. Taylor and I couldn't deploy at all, not as DSOs anyway.

And so, what the fuck *were* they going to do with us? There had been a "turbo" Pashto course for the smattering of Farsi linguists who had been assigned to Hurby before us, four or eight or maybe if they were lucky twelve weeks of half days with two instructors having been determined by the Air Force to be equivalent to the yearlong course at DLI. But that was over, and they weren't going to start a new turbo course just for the two Daris. Still, they had to do something with us, in spite of our worthlessness as future DSOs, so we went through our ground training, learning how to operate the equipment that we would never get to use in combat.

But after that we were in limbo. We had to go to work every day, but there was no work to be done. DSOs don't have a mission set when they aren't deployed (other linguists can and do listen to recorded audio for more strategic mission sets, but the tactical nature of DSOing doesn't allow for this), and we were too low ranking to be in any supervisory or otherwise useful role. This, combined with the fact that our squadron was adjusting to having first-term airmen around, meant we spent most of our time doing nothing. At some point, Taylor made the logical leap that doing nothing at the squadron was functionally the same as doing nothing in his bed, so he didn't bother showing up till after lunch.

Which made the morning that I was told our director of operations (one step down from the big boss, our commander) was looking for me and Taylor not a little stressful. This stress was further compounded when I, alone, went into his office.

"Where's your partner in crime?"

"Uh, I'm not sure, sir. I think he might have had an appointment?"

"Uh-huh. Okay. Find out when his appointment's done, and you two come back here this afternoon."

Major Richardson was a shrewd guy. He smiled when I told him about Taylor's "appointment" but also became significantly more serious when he told me to return. I walked out of the SCIF, grabbed my phone, and proceeded to psycho-dial Taylor until he woke up. (SCIFs, secure compartmentalized information facilities, are buildings specially built for housing classified information and computer networks. Cell phones aren't allowed inside them.)

"Dude, where the fuck are you?"

"What? Why?" (Taylor was clever enough not to answer the question, in case someone was making me call him and listen in.)

"Richardson wants to see us. What'd you do? What'd we do?"

If Taylor's mother tongue was confidence, mine was anxiety. Growing up poor, food and home insecure, with a long-gone father and an ill-equipped mother, I was not athletic, not socially skilled, did not get into college, and joined the Air Force as the only way for me to make my way out of Lake City, Florida. While I had been told how "smart" I was most of my life, the Air Force had pretty quickly shown me that this wasn't everything, and even if it was, there were plenty of people far smarter than me.

Even though I went to work on time every day, I figured I was guilty by association, an aider and abettor of Taylor and his efforts to defraud the government (this being the crime I was sure we would be charged with).

"I told you this wouldn't last! Now what's gonna happen?"

"Dude, chill out. You don't know why he wants to see us."

"What do you mean chill out? He said, 'partner in crime'! We're fucked!"

"No, we're not. Keep your mouth shut. I'll do the talking."

When you walk into an officer's office, there's always some level of formality involved. If it's serious, you have to march. Right face, left face, stand at attention, all that dumb shit. If it's unclear how serious the situation is, as it was in this case, you at least stand at parade rest (feet spread, looking straight forward, hands locked into an "X" shape behind your lower back).

"Good afternoon, sir."

Richardson was the rare officer who had been enlisted before he'd gotten his shinies, so he knew that this level of decorum was dumb, but I imagine he also enjoyed it to some extent. He let us stand there for a second, me trying not to sweat quite so much, Taylor probably not sweating at all.

"Relax, guys. Take a seat."

This was unexpected, even by Taylor. I wouldn't say the mood in the room had been tense, maybe more like uncertain, but it definitely wasn't relaxed. As we sat down, Richardson leaned back in his chair, and the sly smile I had seen that morning returned.

"So. How'd you boys like DLI?"

We had moved past unexpected and were firmly into what in the fucking fuck is going on territory.

"Uh, big fans, sir."

"Yeah, sir, really liked it."

"That's good. It's a beautiful place."

"Yes, sir, it is."

"Really nice, sir."

"Great. You're going back in two weeks."

It's worth noting that we were sitting on a relatively small couch, and we are relatively not small men (or, apparently, boys), so when, in response to this question, we turned and looked at each other, it must have looked for all the world like we were about to kiss. Our nicknames of Ginger and Mary Ann, which Major Richardson most likely knew of, without knowing their context, certainly would have contributed to such an interpretation. (I have very red hair, and long ago gave up fighting against this moniker. Hence, Ginger. Taylor and I were close, or at least perceived to be close, the 25th wasn't *not* Gilligan's Island, and the first time someone tested out this new nickname on him he got hilariously mad. Hence, Mary Ann.)

We hadn't turned to look at each other out of romance (it wasn't yet love then, but even if it had been, ours is a platonic attachment), but out of confusion. Going back to DLI is a dream assignment in the military. Monterey is one of the most beautiful places in the country, and when you're there a second time, you're treated like an adult (the first time, not so much). Going back is used as a reward, a way to convince people to re-enlist, four additional years of service not seeming so bad when at least a year of it will be in Northern California. Almost everyone who goes back has been in for a few years, and is a noncommissioned officer, or NCO. At the time, no one had ever heard of a first-term airman, let alone two, let alone two of such dubious quality as Taylor and I, going back for a second language.

"It's an experimental Pashto course, run by the army, but they had two extra seats, and we snuck you in. It's six months, so it's a temporary duty. The other students are all experienced linguists, so the course will be accelerated, but that's the point. Any questions?"

"Two weeks, sir?" Taylor asked.

"Yes. The course starts at the end of the month. You need to get started on the paperwork ASAP."

"Yes, sir. We'll start now, sir."

"Good."

This was our cue to leave, Major Richardson having returned to something on his computer. But when we got to the door, he stopped us.

"Gentlemen. Have fun."

We knew, as Daris, that we were worthless to the 25th despite the fact that the government had allegedly spent a quarter million dollars on training us (The real number is probably closer to 150k). Now they were going to spend another 80k to teach us Pashto? This was the number bandied about, that each of our seats in the class had cost the squadron $40,000. And that was just the course! Normally, when you go back to DLI, it's a PCS, or permanent change of station. Functionally this means you get assigned to the training squadron at DLI and move to California. You rent a house or apartment (buying in Monterey being all but impossible), move (read: drive) all your stuff out, and live there, with the big Air Force, as an organization, paying for all of this. But we were going for less than six months, so we would be on temporary duty, or TDY. We would only be able to take whatever we could fit in our checked bags, would be given a rental car, and would live in a hotel, all of which our squadron had to pay for.

If going back to Monterey is a dream, then being TDY in Monterey for six months is pure fucking fantasy. Being TDY means the training squadron with all of its bullshit has no power over you, you don't have to deal with the hassle of moving, and you get that sweet sweet per diem money, which, in Monterey, was $70 a day (this, on top of all your normal pay). When we told our supervisor about this, his immediate response was a simple "Fuck you." But while he was jealous, this also meant he wouldn't have to keep track of us for the next six months, so he helped us with our paperwork and happily drove us to the airport at the end of the month.

PASHTO, OR EXPERIENCED LINGUISTS

I DON'T KNOW THAT ANYONE told us that everyone else in the class would be Dari or Farsi linguists. I think when Taylor and I heard "experienced linguists" we sort of assumed this, as how else were they supposed to learn Pashto in six months? Yes, once you've learned one language, it becomes easier to learn a second, as you've already figured out how you best learn and study. But it helps if the language you're going back for is at least a little related to the one you already know. This was, in our minds, the justification for such an intense and short course; if you already know Dari, then you know around 30 percent of Pashto, as the languages share an inordinate amount of vocabulary.

Two weeks later, this assumption directly informed my decision to look like a racist on our first day back at DLI. We had returned to speaking a lot of Dari since Major Richardson had told us we were headed back (by we I mean I, with Taylor mostly accepting my nerdery, not always speaking Dari back, but responding in English, which meant he had at least listened to my Dari). Even when we were speaking English, the old habit of throwing in Afghan insults had come back, which, coupled with Taylor's habit of being an ass having never gone away, resulted in my saying "you fucking *koon*" as we were crossing the threshold into our new classroom.

In Dari, *koon* means ass. *Khar* does too (the *kh* sounds a little like when you're clearing your throat), but *khar* means ass as in donkey, not ass as in ass, so I generally went with *koon* (see above re: originality/offensiveness vs. usage). The problem is, this *k* sound is indistinguishable from the sound the letter "c" makes when pronouncing the word *coon* in English. So, to the two black army sergeants who were already sitting in the classroom, one flight suit–wearing white boy had just used a rather strong racial epithet on the other flight suit–wearing white boy.

It isn't really possible for me to turn white as a sheet, or have the color drop out of my face, or some other metaphorical substitution for the sudden appearance of pallidity, as I'm already incredibly pale. That said, I think my freckles might have lost some melanin in that moment.

I was raised to be at the very least a racist, if not to be a "full-blown" racist. My mother is the daughter of missionaries and was born in Mali. As she tells it, she was also raised there, though she spent most of each year in Côte d'Ivoire, at a boarding school for the kids of missionaries (read: other whites). I don't know that she ever understood that this meant that her relationship with black people was necessarily built on the foundation of imperialistic great white saviors coming in to free the natives from their backward, heathen ways. I, however, did have this understanding, and never more so than on the day she attempted to teach me that "there are black people, and there are niggers."

Consequently, when I saw these two people looking at me with disgust on the first of the 180 days I was going to be spending with them, I was deeply worried that they would think I was a racist. Really, I was more worried about their perception of me than I was about the damage my word could have done. My panicked logic was that I hadn't said what they thought I'd said—I was no racist—and once I explained that it was a simple misunderstanding, any harm would disappear in a puff of linguistic levity. The problem was my explanation:

"No, wait, we speak Dari. Don't you speak Dari?"

"No."

"Shit. Okay. Well, *koon* in Dari means ass! Really! Not . . . you know . . . that."

Taylor wasn't helping, as he was too busy laughing at the absurdity of the situation, which only became more farcical when our new teacher walked in and I attempted to hastily explain to him that I had accidentally used a Dari curse word that sounded a lot like a very bad English insult. If he would confirm that *koon* does in fact mean ass, then this whole mess could be cleared up and everything would be great. Except, the instructors aren't supposed to teach us swear words. The man sitting in front of me, our new head professor, Rahimi, definitely wouldn't teach us swear words. But he didn't contradict my story, and I think the combination of my fear and fervor convinced the two sergeants, S. and V., that, while I wasn't necessarily not a racist, I was telling the truth about my word choice.

S. and V. didn't speak Dari, and it turned out neither did anyone else. The course wasn't a turbo course, it was just abbreviated, a way to teach some army sergeants the fundamentals of Pashto before sending them back to their posts to keep learning the rest of the language. For Taylor and me, this meant that after the first two months we were leaps and bounds beyond four of our classmates. But there was a fifth who was a brilliant linguist. Ty too had thought this would be a turbo class, and even though it wasn't, he was still expected to pass the Pashto DLPT by the end of the course. (The Defense Language Proficiency Test is the standardized exam used by the Department of Defense to assess an individual's competency in a language. At the time, roughly 50 percent of people who took the full yearlong Pashto course failed it.) Ty took a monastic approach to language learning and after class would spend two hours reading one news article, looking up every single word. With this effort, while he wasn't quite at our level—we had that whole 30 percent of the vocabulary and an extra year of experience with the vagaries of Afghan language thing going for us—he too was ahead of the rest of our classmates.

Taylor, Ty, and I became fast friends. Ty introduced me to Radiohead (meh), Jonathan Franzen (great), and cappuccinos (life-changing). We talked for hours about Dari and Pashto, Spanish, and English, reveling in our love of languages. One morning, we were bullshitting before class started, and Ty said, "Man, my daughter asked me what *terrorism* means last night."

"What'd you tell her?"

"Some nonsense. She's five. How do I explain terrorism to a five-year-old? I said something about terrorists being bad men, but that's not good enough."

"I mean, I don't have kids, but I like the Dari word a lot better: دهشت افگن."

"Fritz, that doesn't help. I don't speak Dari." (Ty routinely had to remind me of this fact.)

"I was getting there! It means fear-thrower. Someone who throws fear. It makes more sense to me."

This was true then and it's truer now: دهشت افگن (*dahesht aafgan*) (not *afghan*, mind you; different letter, different sound, different meaning) makes far more sense to me than the word *terrorist*. *Terrorist, terrorism, terror*—all these words have become such a part of our everyday language (if you don't agree, I refer you to the five-year-old asking about one of them) that they've lost whatever meaning they once had. Yes, we all know a terrorist is "a person who uses unlawful violence and intimidation, especially against civilians, in the pursuit of political aims." This, like so many of our definitions of war and violence, is so sterile, so clinical, so detached, and so good at discriminating between the actions of an individual as opposed to a state. If we applied this definition to a government, say, the American government during the war in Iraq, then maybe we'd have to stop negotiating with ourselves (outside of Congress, I mean). This definition seeks to define the terrorist from the perspective of the terrorized, thereby making the terrorist automatically successful. It also makes the terrorist sound organized, cool, and calculating, planning that if Bomb X kills Y people then law Z will get passed.

دهشت افگن, on the other hand, *fear-thrower*, for me illustrates the limitations of the English word. A terrorist uses unlawful violence, which would imply that he has considered the law. A fear-thrower doesn't give the laws of man a second thought. A terrorist might try to kill primarily civilians to accomplish his goal. A fear-thrower doesn't target anyone. He just kills. And while a fear-thrower (he is, of course, still a terrorist) does have political aims of some sort, in my conceptualization of this word, those are simply an added benefit. The goal of a fear-thrower isn't political, not really. It's to spread the thing that gives him power as wide and as far as he possibly can, pitching it in every direction, until the fear of fear gives him absolute dominion over his world. I understand that power is often political, but I also think that this is a fundamentally Western view. Sometimes, power is just power. And fear is a heavy thing. If you've trained enough to throw it, you must be pretty strong. Pretty powerful.

I don't know that Ty told his daughter my theories on fear-throwing vs. terrorism, but he was nice enough to let me ramble on. I was spitballing, as I hadn't fully fleshed out these thoughts back then, I just felt that the Dari word made more sense. As the course progressed, this kept happening. I think, in large part, this was due to the shared words between the languages; instead of having to spend hour upon hour learning new words, I was afforded the luxury of really trying to understand how Pashto worked, and often, it was easier to do that in relation to Dari (when English is their third or fourth language, sometimes it's easier to use Dari to ask your professor if the attempt at past progressive you just made in Pashto was correct). Because of this learning of Pashto through both English and Dari, I wasn't only finding the hidden meanings in Dari or Pashto words anymore, I was replacing entire concepts with them. It seemed that Sapir, or Whorf, or both, had been on to something. How I was thinking was changing.

Over the next few months, I spent hours a day talking with our professors. There was Asila, nearly as young and impetuous as I, decidedly younger and more impetuous than my classmates. Najibullah, whose pompadour tried to rival Fawad's but, despite having roughly three times as much hair in it, couldn't hold a candle to The Tornado's coiffure. And there was Dr. Death—whose real name I'm not sure I ever knew—an old crusty Pashtun whose English was very good, but who wouldn't use it to help you out no matter how hard you were struggling. As the course drew on

Rahimi had us talk to the good doctor nearly every day, which we were less than happy about, as he spoke slowly and with a constant emphysematous wheeze, his voice almost whistling as a result, making it painful to listen to him. But then we took the DLPT and discovered that a substantial portion of the audio passages were narrated by the mysterious doctor, who was difficult to understand even when you'd been listening to his voice for weeks, let alone for the first time. Rahimi knew what he was doing, of course, and just laughed his raspy, Muttley-esque laugh when we accused him of preparing us for the test.

We did all this talking in part to prepare for the final test, but mostly because speaking a language that you're learning is by far the hardest thing to do with it; it's much easier to recognize words than it is to pull them whole cloth from your memory. Speaking, putting those words and ideas into (hopefully) the same order as native speakers do, is by far the best way to strengthen your language skills. Taylor and I were both "good" at Pashto, but we had a problem; we couldn't help but speak Dari.

We figured, given the no/minimal English rules, we should just use Dari whenever we didn't know a Pashto word. The result was strange sentences that would be 60 to 70 percent Dari nouns and adjectives, with Pashto pronouns and verbs. Or, instead of asking "to drink څنګه وایئ" ("how do you say" in Pashto plus "to drink" in English) like our classmates, we would inevitably say "څنګه وایئ نوشیدن" say ("how do you say" in Pashto and "to drink" in Dari). The first time we did this with Rahimi he just paused, looked at us both, and said "I understand what you're doing. But I hate this." Us being us, this of course then meant that we kept doing it.

In part because it was fun, his faux exasperation a nice game we could play together, but mostly because we didn't really understand how he could dislike this so much, we kept mixing and matching the two languages. We figured it was super-cool, 'cause like, how many other students could do that? We also figured that while Rahimi's English was great, wasn't his Dari better? Pashtun he may have been, but as far as we knew he was equally fluent in both. But when we finally got around to asking him about it, it turned out that it was harder for him to convert the Dari to Pashto, or vice versa, because he never thought that way. He was perfectly fluent in Dari—the man had been an interpreter all over Afghanistan—but it wasn't one of the two languages he primarily thought in these days, nor did he ever combine it with Pashto. Mixing Pashto and English was common for him; that's what he did all day at work. But if he thought in Pashto, Pashto it was. And if he thought in Dari, same. What we were doing was some weird bastardization of the two that did not sit well with him.

So in addition to whatever was happening in the background of our brains as we were learning, we were actively figuring out how to think in Pashto, which is to say, to think like our professors, as this was how we could talk like them. But we soon realized that we weren't ever going to think quite like Afghans, for more than just the cultural reasons. We would always and forever mix the two languages together, because that was how we could be the most fluent, or at least how we could use the least English. Taylor put more effort into limiting his Dari use when speaking in class, but I didn't want anything to do with such a restraint, no matter how annoyed my classmates got. The goal was to use our language skills, and I was going to do just that.

As the course went on and my Pashto got better, I did, eventually, use only small amounts of Dari. Some of this was a simple increase in vocabulary, some of it my learning to be less of a jerk, and some of it because a number of our professors didn't speak Dari. In hindsight, these were probably the best professors I had (other than Rahimi, that patient saint) because with each hour spent with them, sure I learned more Pashto, but I also learned more about Pashtuns.

Taylor and I had learned about the different ethnic groups in Afghanistan in our Dari course. A major part of the language training at DLI is learning about the history of a given country or area, its people, and its culture. For our class, this ranged from preparing presentations on the government of Afghanistan since 1950, to making traditional Afghan food alongside our professors, to crafting kites for a kite battle (an infamous day, wherein one of the young professors absolutely destroyed one of the older professors' kites, resulting in the older professor yelling the soon to be oft-repeated line "That was not a manly action"). So we already knew that the Tajiks, Uzbeks, Hazaras, and Pashtuns were the major ethnic groups of Afghanistan, and we'd heard a little of some of the smaller ones, like the Baloch and the Pashayi. Some of our Dari teachers had even been trilingual, having grown up speaking both Dari and Pashto before learning English, and had told us about that strange southern tribe and their even stranger language. But they didn't tend to refer to themselves as Pashtuns, just as Afghans.

Our Pashto professors, on the other hand, were Pashtuns before anything else. It's not as if any of them followed the traditional code of honor of the Pashtun people—پښتونولي (*Pashtunwali*)—but they tended to be more conservative, more religious, more accepting of the role that violence plays in the world than our Dari professors had been. Which isn't to say that they were on the side of the Taliban. No, in fact, they were very much on our side, which I came to best understand during a speaking lesson about the merits of nuclear proliferation.

The professor I was talking to was new to me, having subbed in for one of our normal professors who had to leave early that day. We'd seen each other before, nods in the hallways between classrooms and so on, and he had always seemed nice. Very self-assured. I guess he just carried himself well, like you probably shouldn't fuck with him 'cause maybe he'd seen some shit back in the day.

I never learned the specifics, but I did come to wholeheartedly believe that he had seen something(s) or someone(s) pretty awful, because after about twenty minutes of conversation, he told me, in a rather offhanded manner, that he thought we should just nuke Afghanistan.

"Uh, what?"

I thought maybe I'd misunderstood him.

"Oh yeah, absolutely. We should just blow up the whole country."

Nope. Pretty clear, that. I wondered if this was some sort of test. Like, a way to trap me into admitting that I was a racist/bigot and thought we should just kill any and every Afghan. I couldn't really get in trouble for that; I'm sure there were at least a dozen Marines who had said that shit out loud already, but I couldn't figure out a better reason for him to have made such a proclamation, so I asked him if he was serious, and if so, why.

He said something to the effect of, well, there's nothing good there. The people aren't good, the land isn't good, and they're just always going to fight. So we may as well just drop a bunch of nukes, kill everyone there, and get rid of the problem forever. In response to my question of whether he had family there who would be killed by all these bombs, he just said, eh, extended family. That's just how it goes.

Whether it was a good use of my time to be talking about nuking the country I was supposed to go fight a war in is up for debate. I knew, or at least had been told, that this level of understanding would be superfluous, as (1) my job was going to be to listen to the Taliban, who didn't tend to debate much beyond the merits of which weapon to aim at which American or where to place an IED, and (2) I wasn't the talking kind of linguist, just the listening kind. But we were supposed to become as fluent as possible, and because I wanted to succeed (and because it was fun), I kept talking. When I graduated from our Pashto course, I was coined by the commandant of DLI for my performance on the DLPT. This is an informal award tradition in the military wherein a high-ranking person gives you a custom-made coin (think silver dollar, not quarter) that represents an accomplishment. I had gotten higher scores than most graduates of the yearlong Pashto course, in half the time and, I was told, was a credit to the Air Force and to DLI.

But when I left DLI, this didn't really matter, because Pashto changed, and I had to change with it. Pashto was now the language of the enemy. Obviously, I was told, not everyone who speaks Pashto is a Talib, but every Talib does speak Pashto, so if you hear it, expect bad shit, because Afghanistan is a far safer place if you operate from the viewpoint that everyone is out to get you.

BULLSHIT, OR YOU'LL ONLY DIE TIRED

IN THE BEGINNING, there were the words, and the words were with the Taliban, and the words were the Taliban. This then, meant that the words were evil. Because they were coming from the Taliban, who are unequivocally, unrelentingly, and unrepentantly evil.

Oh, and boring. Evil and boring.

This was not a lesson in Arendt; I was not told that the Taliban were Eichmann's heirs. They were banal. And they were evil. But their evil was not banal.

Attacks on helicopters, attacks on planes, attacks on convoys, suicide bombers, vehicle-born IEDs, donkey-borne IEDs (really), roadside bombs, ambushes, mortaring of bases, RPGing of men, attacks on school, acid thrown in young girls' faces, honor killings, subjugation of women, sexual enslavement of boys—these were the evils the Taliban practiced, and these are not things "so lacking in originality as to be obvious and boring."

They, on the other hand, were boring. The Taliban whinged and whined, pissed and moaned, griped and groused. And bullshit (bullshat?). God did they bullshit.

Pashto and Dari naturally lend themselves to puns and insults—there is a lot of rhyming inherent to the languages, and many words share double meanings. A not small part of the Taliban's bullshitting stems from a penchant for repetition. Afghans will repeat a name or statement, or anything really, dozens of times to make a point. But this repetition intensifies when talking over radios. The story of Kalima taught me this. None of us know who Kalima was, though it's generally accepted that he wasn't anyone important. But every Pashto linguist at Hurby knew of Kalima because there was an audio recording of someone—we don't know who—who *really* wanted to talk to him. So he called his name.

"Kalima! Kaliiiiiiiima. Kalimaaaaaaa. Kalima Kalima Kalima Kalima Kalima."

He called his name again and again, at least fifty times, in every possible combination of syllabic emphasis. Kalima never responded. Maybe his radio was off. Maybe he just didn't want to talk to this guy. Maybe he was asleep. All that bullshitting can be tiring.

Bullshitting and evil. Evil bullshitting.

The other DSOs who told me about all this bullshit back at Hurby had listened to the Taliban during the most intense years of the war, 2009 and 2010. The latter was the deadliest year of the war for American forces. This, because of "The Push," Afghanistan's version of Fallujah. The Push was supposed to be this incredible show of force, a way to definitively prove to ourselves and to the Taliban that we meant business and that we could root them out of their traditional stronghold in the city of Marjah in Helmand province. Technically, it worked, in that by blowing up a lot of shit and killing a lot of Afghans we took over the area. But this battle that some were concerned could last "up to a month" would be called a "bleeding ulcer" by General Stanley McChrystal ninety days in. It wouldn't be declared over until the end of the year, just shy of the ten-month mark.

Of course, I didn't pay attention to any of those DSOs. I figured that they were, perhaps, a bit tired, a bit inundated with bullshit, both Pashto and otherwise. Reasonably so, as they had all had to do five-month deployments up at Bagram, freezing their asses off in flight and camp alike. But everyone was still flying, and while maybe there were some grumbles, things were looking up.

Much of my excitement to deploy was admittedly based in a combination of pride, willful naïveté, and religious fervor. I still didn't necessarily think I was the second coming of Christ (unlike a certain someone), but it was hard not to be proud of our accomplishments; we really were the only two DSOs—hell, as far as we knew the only two linguists in the entire Air Force—who had been fully trained in both Dari and Pashto. I was also still a True Believer in the "DSO as Deity" myth and was willing to accept our leadership's claims that they had worked out a number of the kinks in deploying and being deployed. I wouldn't have to do a five-month deployment, just three, and I wouldn't have to deploy as often as the older DSOs had (even though I told our commander that I wanted to go for longer, and as often as possible, so that I could finally kill some Talibs, prove my worth, and so the poor bastards who came before me could finally get some well-deserved rest).

There was also serious pressure on Taylor and me to deploy. Some of this was the general push to get more DSOs into Afghanistan, but some of it was specific to us. The fact that we were now able to listen to and understand virtually any Afghan, anywhere in the country, came with great expectations. We were constantly reminded of how long we had already been in, how much money had been spent on training us, how lucky we were to be first-term airmen doing the DSO mission, and just how much we owed the Air Force and our squadron.

So we were pushed through our flight training, fast, and I got to Afghanistan four months after The Push ended. It was further exciting, if not a little terrifying, that this coincided with the onset of the fighting season in Afghanistan. In the month prior to my arrival, very little had been going on, as a result of the nonstop rain. Every year, this had the strange effect of giving the Taliban time to rest and regroup, and us time to feel pent-up and anxious. This sort of scheduled war, the knowledge that the spring offensive is coming, that though things are quiet now, soon there will be battles, was a strange unease specific to the war in Afghanistan. For us flyers, it mostly just meant that we could expect to be bored for a couple months out of the year. I can't imagine what it felt like for the guys on the ground, knowing that after the boredom would come many, many bullets.

The problem was that in the aftermath of The Push, we weren't sure how many bullets there would be. We'd allegedly taken one of the Taliban's main bomb-making sites, eliminated, or at least diminished, a large portion of their revenue, and weakened their hold on a strategic area (Marjah is very close to Kandahar, so in theory there were now fewer Taliban breathing down the neck of one of our largest bases). Would there be fewer attacks as a result of this, or more? Would the Taliban be cowed or just pissed off? Would The Push be the decisive moment we had been promised?

The year 2011 wound up being the second deadliest of the war in Afghanistan. One hundred and twelve Americans would be killed in action during the three months I was there (this count includes civilians). The Push would in fact come to be seen as a major turning point in the war.

But it was a turn in the wrong direction. Instead of proving to the Taliban (and the world) that we were an unstoppable force who could accomplish anything if we just threw enough money and soldiers at it, The Push only wound up cementing the idea that Afghanistan was unconquerable and that the Taliban would keep fighting even in the face of thousands more coalition troops.

My first mission and the battle in the Barawala Kalay Valley couldn't have been better confirmation of this. The Taliban somehow coordinated a massive surprise attack on a FOB (forward operating base), and while it didn't go well for them, it was pretty strong evidence that they hadn't been cowed. This battle was also validation of the wickedness I had been told to expect. Our men had just been sitting in their FOB, like so many ducks, and the Taliban had tried to overrun them. Those fuckers shot a fucking medevac. And they were so celebratory, so full of pomp and pride. In the middle of this massive battle, this thing straight out of a war movie, they rejoiced about results to come, consistently encouraging each other, secure in their knowledge that they would kill so many more of us.

"Praise God, they are dying!"

"How many have we killed, brother?"

"Hundreds!"

"Keep fighting, keep fighting! They're losing!"

"Yes, yes, we're winning, thank God, we are winning!"

"We'll kill every devil here, all of them!"

This was total bullshit, as their casualties outnumbered ours at least ten to one. And it really was evil bullshit. All that invoking of God's will, his greatness, his power, praise be to him who helps us kill the infidels; it was incomprehensible, this use of Allah for their atrocious ambitions.

The natural consequence of this mission and its verification of what I had already been taught was that I thought and talked about future missions just like everyone else.

"Yeah, we schwacked a few guys."

"Oh man, you should've seen it, there was nothing left of those fuckers."

"Should've kept shooting, but these fucking new ROEs [rules of engagement]. Can't Winchester anymore."

I would like to tell you that this was self-defense, some psychic protectionism, or just me trying to fit in with the men and women I was working with, but it wasn't. To some extent I was trying to conform, as my natural temperament—or maybe nurtured temperament, my childhood having been filled (or I guess emptied?) with abandonment—is one of deep-seated longing for a sense of community. But I didn't have to try all that hard. While I didn't always agree with the specifics—the bragging about "mercing some towelheads" was uncomfortable, and the (thankfully rare) celebrating of the wiping out of some "sand niggers" was outright revolting—I could now pretty readily get behind the excitement of schwacking a bunch of bad dudes or 105-ing a few Talibs. And I could understand the frustration with the changes to the ROEs, such that we had to be far more careful about whom we shot, and how much we shot at them, to reduce civilian casualties. What's more, the Taliban knew about these changes, and used them to become more brazen in their attacks, secure in the knowledge that if they were close enough to some off-limits building, or a collection of civilians, we wouldn't shoot at them, despite the fact that a gunship with a good crew can put a bullet through a basketball hoop from two miles away. We weren't just not Winchestering—to Winchester is to fire every round available on the plane, meaning you have to return to base to reload the plane's entire ammo stores—we were (in our eyes) barely shooting.

There's a lot that informed our desire to kill, and these representations of the act of killing, but each relied on storytellers that were at least one step removed from the actual death we caused. Gunners used their bullets, sensor operators their cameras, pilots and navigators the whole damn plane, to separate themselves from the men on the ground. I used my headphones.

All my fancy language learning meant that my work was predominantly a cerebral process, my metacognition about what I was hearing superseding any feelings I might have had about what the men I was listening to were saying, or who the men I was listening to were. This was my distance, and it meant that I was as excited to kill as my fellow crewmembers were, as we were the good guys, and the Taliban were not just "bad guys," but outright evil.

Furthering this distance was a lifelong exposure to language that axiomatically separated Us from Them. The language I heard growing up in the sheltered, hate-filled communities that pervade the particular portion of the Evangelical American South (these are in fact all equally weighty proper nouns) that I grew up in specialized in this segregation. The language I had heard in history classes throughout my education had its roots in the moral exceptionalism of America, and therefore, of Americans, from the Revolutionary War straight through to today. And, at least in my memory, since 9/11, al Qaeda, the Taliban, Iraq, Afghanistan, these evil things (for what are they if not simple objects?) were spoken of as if they were outside of the human race.

And it wasn't just while flying that we had to put up with the

Taliban and their bullshit. They mortared our base nearly every day. I wasn't necessarily in any serious danger from this; their aim was so comically bad that after a couple weeks of being deployed virtually no one bothered to put on their body armor or take cover in the concrete T-walls set up around our camp when the incoming fire alarm went off. I'm sure they got lucky here and there, but from what I was told they hit the poo pond more than anything else. (The poo pond was a very large, very open, man-made lake consisting primarily of the raw human sewage from the thirty thousand people living on base, though apparently there was also a healthy dose of used cooking oil and kitchen grease dumped in there too.)

All of these thoughts, all of this language that I used to think about and to describe the Taliban and what we were doing to them, it was all gunship language. Real gunship language, AC-130 language. Gunships have been speaking their language, the language of killing people—large numbers of people—since Vietnam. Because I had exclusively been trained on gunships at Hurlburt, their language was the one I knew. The instructors I flew with, regardless of whether they had actually done anything of interest, taught me that while my job was "to provide threat warning," this would often mean that I would be helping to eliminate those threats, and sometimes, if I was lucky, or good, or more likely both, what I heard would be the key piece of information that resulted in us shooting.

I hadn't learned to speak the language of the MC-130s like my friends, didn't understand how to talk about an airdrop, or low-level flying, or evasive maneuvers, all these things done by planes that don't have guns sticking out their sides. I knew how to fly in a NASCAR loop (gunships, like NASCAR drivers, only turn left, at least in orbit), how to shoot, and how to talk about shooting. I knew that we could use the 25 to corral people like they were so many sheep, shooting great lines of bullets to make sure the bad guys ran in the direction we wanted them to. I knew that it was funny when they ran, as if that would help them live, instead of just making sure they died tired when the 40 hit them. And I knew that we could play games with corpses, using a 105 to bounce a body across the earth, assigning points for how far you could make the floppy fuck fly. I knew that we really were modern memitim—angels of death—and that if we so chose, nothing (not no one) underneath us would live to see another sunrise.

The Whiskey crews did not use this same language. They were softer, gentler, still adapting to the newfound role of hunter. They were excited about their new mission set, no doubt about it, but their plane lacked the destructive capability of the U-boats, and so too did their words.

And if language does affect your thoughts, I think this was a major reason the Whiskey crews were so much nicer. Sweet, even. They didn't have to live up to some reputation as stone-cold kill-ers, some need to seem "hard," whatever that means. They could unironically come up with a dance to Miley Cyrus's "Party in the USA" and perform it at least once a mission while blasting that greatest of pop songs over our internal comms. They could buy a football and unsarcastically give it to whichever crewmember had done or said the smartest thing on every mission, with the full intention of sending said football to Miley Cyrus at the end of the deployment. They could also buy a Shake Weight and give it to whichever crewmember had done or said the dumbest thing on every mission (this, in all of its phallic, jizzy glory, would not be sent to the young Miss Cyrus). They were still gross—we all were—but it was a kind, well-intentioned grossness.

There's a brutal simplicity to deployed life. Wake up. Gym. Fly. Eat. Watch TV. Sleep. Wake up. Fly. Gym. Eat. Watch porn. Sleep. Wake up. Gym. Eat. Fly. Sleep. Wake up. Eat. Don't fly. Bullshit with friends. Gym. Sleep.

You can only rearrange that sequence of events so many ways. In Kandahar, at least, there are some ways to add to it, by going to the boardwalk or to a different chow hall on the other side of the base, but essentially each day is the same. And it's fucking wondrous.

When you're deployed, you have no responsibilities. You don't have to worry about all the stupid, annoying obligations that come with real life. Paying bills, cleaning your house, buying groceries— none of that existed in Afghanistan. You don't have to worry about things like social obligations, keeping your friend network happy and healthy, calling your loved ones every so often, remembering birthdays, any of that shit. You get a free pass on all of that non-sense, 'cause hey, you're in Afghanistan.

It is, a little, like a return to childhood, though that's consistent with being in the military in general. (If you want to stay a sixteen-year-old boy, there's no need to go off in search of Never Never Land. It's a lot easier to enlist.) But it isn't as infantilizing as boot camp, or other parts of training, and while it does eventually get old, there's truly nothing to be done about it, so you learn to embrace it for what it is.

More importantly, I was *flying*. I was finally doing the thing

I had spent three years training to do. Taylor and I had spent the majority of our time at Hurby being asked by other linguists when we were finally going to be useful. It was (mostly) good old-fashioned ribbing. Friends who were on their third and fourth deployments hadn't put it that way, as they knew better than anyone just how very "useful" we would wind up being, but they were excited for us to deploy too, as it would mean that their deployments would be shorter, and hopefully less frequent. It felt so fucking good to be able to introduce myself to crews as a DSO, without having to worry about them questioning whether I was a "real" DSO or just another kid in training.

Practically, I was also getting paid, and paid well (you don't pay income tax when you're deployed, they give you some hazard pay for the added danger, and it's pretty hard to spend any serious amount of money when you're out there) to hang out with my new friends on-board $100 million winged death machines. Yes, there was that whole doing my job thing, but it doesn't feel like very much work to be soaring over the countryside, daydreaming with the rest of the crew about how sick the skiing in the Hindu Kush will be when the war is over. And with flying came all the perks of being a flyer: crew rest, wherein, by law, we had to have twelve hours of uninterrupted time, with eight of those hours being available for sleep, before each and every mission. Instead of ABUs (airman battle uniforms) we got to wear our two-piece flight suits, in all of their light, cool, sexy glory. And sure, we were a gunship, but we were also still an MC-130, which meant we could transport cargo, which meant when we flew some guys over to a different base we could take them up on their appreciative offer of a pallet of all the best licky-chewy they had lying around (*licky-chewy* being the admittedly strange term dreamed up for sweets and snacks).

I didn't have to do shift work, I wasn't doing manual labor, and when I did have to do my job, I was doing a Good Thing.

There are also limits to how much a person can fly in certain time frames: 56 hours in a week, 125 hours in thirty days, and 330 hours in ninety days. It's hard to reach 56 in a week, so we didn't usually worry about that one, but 125 in a month was doable. But it could also be waived with relative ease, and it was usually ignored. The 330, though, allegedly took something like an undersecretary of defense to waive, so it was pretty much set in stone. Normal flyers don't have to worry about these limits, as they get what's known as "hard-crewed" when they deploy. For however long they're in country, they're assigned to the same crew, and those are the men and women they always fly with. If a given member of your crew is a jackass, or, gods forbid, your pilot is a douchebag, well, that sucks, but for the most part hard-crewing leads to increased camaraderie, better communication, and smoother flights. Crews also get scheduled days off, such that they don't approach their hour limits.

DSOs are very much not hard-crewed. We could fly with a different crew day after day, shifting our increasingly nonexistent sleep schedules forward and backward to accommodate the needs of the Air Force. All this hopping between crews earned us any number of comparisons to prostitutes, though we were most often referred to as the crews' bicycles (everyone got a ride). With this promiscuity came the challenge of convincing people to like us.

When a DSO flies with a crew for the first time, they're treated with great suspicion; linguists can get pretty fucking nerdy. There's also a lot of ridicule, and you have to balance your response to it. Too much, and you're a fucking pansy who can't take a joke. (I knew a guy who got so upset when someone parroted him—to parrot someone is to put your penis on their shoulder, the idea being that a dick somehow resembles a pirate's bird—that he reported the incident to higher-ups. Even back then it was pretty hard to ignore credible claims of sexual assault, but he had to go up three levels before anyone got in serious trouble, with the end result being that unless it was absolutely required during a flight, no one would speak to him.) Too little, and you're a bitch-ass faggot who's gonna get fucked with from there on out, a naked gunner hug awaiting you around every corner.

The joking I could handle; a lifetime of red hair, glasses, and a freakishly large head meant there was likely nothing they could throw at me that I hadn't heard before. (After the third size was still too small, the person at basic training who was responsible for giving us hats asked me, "What the fuck is wrong with your head?") I also didn't mind the homoeroticism, but the way Whiskeys are set up makes it a lot harder to engage in surreptitious schlong swinging, so I didn't really have to worry about that. The being liked, though, that was a real concern.

I went with the tried-and-true technique of sharing pictures of scantily clad women. While we were not, by any means, roughing it on our camp, with Wi-Fi capable of performing video calls back home, we were in no uncertain terms not allowed to access pornography on any of our devices. Most sites were blocked, but even if they weren't, we had to register our laptops and phones with the intel guys in order to access the network, which meant that our browsing activity was tracked, or at least monitored, and there were serious consequences for going to illicit sites.

But where there's a will, there's a way, and where there's the internet, there's naked women. At some point I had mentioned the dilemma of our restricted access to my younger brother, who told me to check if Tumblr was accessible. Apparently, at the time, hosting questionable material was Tumblr's raison d'être, or so my brother said. Tumblr was also a legitimate microblogging site, and therefore wasn't blocked by most network administrators (or at least it wasn't then). In a great and selfless act of true patriotism, my brother made a post on his account requesting that his followers re-share as many pictures of naked women as possible, to help out me and my fellow deployed service members in Afghanistan. Suffice it to say, his friends supported the troops. So the night or morning before a mission I would visit my brother's Tumblr, make sure the first thirty or so posts loaded, 90 percent of which would be loyal to our cause, and I'd have my DSO Candy ready for the crew. I'm not sure who coined this term, but it stuck, so much so that crews I had never met came to expect said Candy when I flew with them. Whether any of these people actually liked me as a human is up for debate, but they liked me as a DSO, and that's what mattered.

Every flight follows the same pattern. You wake up, go to the camp's command center, get your mission briefing (location, route, weather, support, etc.), head out to the flight line, get to the plane, do your preflight checklist, wait for others to do their much longer preflight checklists, wait for air traffic control to get their shit together, and, finally, anywhere from twenty minutes to two hours after your duty day started, take off.

Within that pattern, though, there's fairly wide variation. An escort mission, wherein you follow and watch a convoy move from bumfuck Afghanistan point A to slightly more bumfuck Afghanistan point B at about five miles an hour, can be eight hours long and mind-numbingly boring. Alternatively, your plane might get called in to do close air support for a firefight that only lasts for an hour, but that hour will be anything but boring. We were occasionally assigned to support infil and exfil missions, aka making sure guys on the ground don't get shot at when they're entering (infiltration) or leaving (exfiltration) an area. But for the most part, on the Whiskeys, we did a lot of armed reconnaissance.

By far the sexiest mission name (though close air support isn't half-bad), armed reconnaissance is defined by the DoD as "a mission with the primary purpose of locating and attacking targets of opportunity, i.e., enemy materiel, personnel, and facilities, in assigned general areas or along assigned ground communications routes, and not for the purpose of attacking specific briefed targets." Or, in English: looking for shit to fuck up.

There are a few problems with doing armed recce during the day in Afghanistan. The primary one being that for the most part, events like my first mission notwithstanding, the Taliban doesn't try and start shit in broad daylight, as that's a pretty good way to get killed. Coming in at a close second is the issue that there just isn't all that much shit to fuck up. Most of the shit has already been fucked up. It also didn't help that while, yes, we were better armed than say, a drone, it was only with a few more silly little missiles.

But there we were, technically armed and doing reconnaissance. The CSOs were the mainstay of these mission sets, what with the incredible cameras stuck to the sides of the Whiskeys. And though we DSOs had nowhere near the capability of those on planes like the Rivet Joints, who were able to pinpoint the origin of whoever they were listening to, the information we provided could be of use.

"By Allah the weather today is good."

"Yes, God willing it will stay that way."

" . . . Salim, are you there? Salim? Salim, are you there? Salim, Salim . . . Salim, brother, are you there?"

"What happened yesterday?"

"No, move the truck."

"Abdullah, are you there? Abdullah? Abdullah, are you there? Hey Abdullah?"

"Is your uncle visiting?"

"Yes, he's here now."

"Mohammed, where are you? Are you there, Mohammed? Mohammed? Mohammed, are you there?"

"The devils were here yesterday."

"Yes, brother, I heard."

"Are they here today?"

"Yes, I heard a monster."

"Stay safe, brother."

"God willing, I will."

The details of how I was hearing all this are, again, not all that interesting. It isn't a completely accurate representation either, because I don't want to type the word "static," or some onomato-poeic version thereof, eighteen or so times. But when we were searching for things of interest to listen to, that's a close synopsis of what it could be like. We could be privy to snatches of eight different conversations in five minutes. This was part of the reason our training was so long; the entire point of our job was to be able to find and translate what the Taliban was saying in near real time, with the only delay (hopefully) being the time it took me to say in English what I'd just heard in Pashto.

The harder part of the job was figuring out which of these conversations to pay attention to. The guy asking "What happened yesterday?" could be just shooting the shit with a friend or he could be a Talib asking about the outcome of a battle. The guy saying "Move the truck" could be a worker on a construction crew or he could be a Talib coordinating an ambush. The guys talking about devils and monsters could be role playing Dungeons & Dragons, or they could be Talibs monitoring the location of various coalition forces.

Except, as far as I know, D&D hadn't made its way to Afghanistan yet (maybe *Stranger Things* has changed that by now). Devils and monsters could only be us, the good guys, but as envisioned by them, the actual fucking demons. You always had to stop and listen if you heard these and similar words, because nine times out of ten, if a couple of guys were talking about military actions, they were Taliban. And generally speaking, the people/teams/units we were doing our reconnaissance for liked to know if there were Taliban nearby and if those Taliban were discussing recent, current, or future fights.

Some missions, I might not hear any discussion of Brobdingnagian behemoths or flying fiends but only questions about visiting relatives, groceries, traffic, the weather, who got to drive the one car used by ten members of some remote village. Other missions I might hear a mix, a couple of minutes of something of interest here, a couple more there, with long periods of the same quotidian fat-chewing in between.

While boring, and not necessarily useful, or actionable, at times these generic conversations were preferable to actually listening to the Taliban, if only because they weren't so fucking repetitive. On every mission where the Taliban was talking, I heard the same bullshitting from them, as no sales meeting, movie set, or locker room has ever seen the level of hyper-enthusiastic preparation that the Taliban demonstrated before, during, and after every battle.

"Are you ready?"

"Of course, we're ready! We'll kill any Devils that come by!"

"Are you prepared for the attack?"

"We're always prepared! This will be a glorious day!"

"The [insert the otherwise innocuous code word that in fact means bomb and which the U.S. government has declared classified, limiting my ability to publish it] is ready for the Americans. God willing, it will reach many of them!"

"Hey, brother, how many did we get yesterday?"

"So many, brother, we killed so many of those infidels!"

"God is great!"

It was maddening, not because they had killed so many of us, but because they in fact hadn't. I wanted to scream back at them, "No you didn't, you fucking liars!" Or "You dumbasses wired the bomb wrong, it barely hurt us." Or "We don't need God to will it, we killed twenty of you dumb fucks yesterday."

As my anger mounted with each mission, the Taliban became more evil. They kept mortaring us, kept ambushing us, kept lying and bullshitting and bragging about how many of us they were going to kill. When they were planning, they were so sure of themselves, so confident they could take out dozens of us, hundreds even, despite all historical evidence to the contrary. On missions where we escorted convoys across the country, I watched massive armored vehicles move three miles an hour as they stopped, time and again, to search for the myriad IEDs planted in the roads. On other missions, these goddamn goat-fuckers routinely attacked our teams that were living in the countryside, trying to build up villages, to provide infrastructure, to win hearts and minds.

Who does that? You're so committed to your hatred that you'll deny those around you improvement in their lives? Your fellow Afghans, the people that you're supposed to be fighting for, supposed to be protecting from the invaders? Hating these men— no, this scum, these cowardly, dumb, backwoods motherfuckers— and believing in their evil, was easy.

This belief was only made stronger by the contrast the Taliban made with the men I was supporting on the ground. Linguists like to brag about how long their training takes, and how high the washout rates are at DLI. They are high, sometimes upward of 50 percent, but that's nothing compared to the 90 percent attrition rate for combat controllers, TACPs (tactical air control party specialists), SEALs, MARSOC (Marine Forces, Special Operations Command), Green Berets, and all the other Special Operations guys actually running around and getting shot at. These are men who get dropped off multiple miles from a village in the mountains of Afghanistan, and after hiking two or three of those miles with seventy pounds of equipment strapped to their bodies, will pause to ask roughly how much farther they have to go. When informed that there's still a couple more clicks to go, they will always, every single time, respond with the tried and true "Too easy." Men who, during a firefight in a village, have asked my plane where exactly the bad guys are, and when told, have started moving in that direction, such that we would repeat ourselves, thinking that they had misheard and were going the wrong way, only to be told that no, they were in fact purposefully making their way *toward* the assholes shooting at them. These men were afraid of nothing and no one, and seeing and hearing their acts of bravery and courage made what we were doing feel that much more righteous.

THREATS, OR IT'S TOO COLD TO JIHAD

ON A WINTER NIGHT in the northern part of Afghanistan, where the average elevation is somewhere above seven thousand feet and the average temperature somewhere below freezing, the following discussion took place:

"Go place the IED down there, at the bend; they won't see it."

"It can wait till morning."

"No, it can't. They could come early, and we need it down there to kill as many as we can."

"I think I'll wait."

"No, you won't! Go place it."

"Do I have to?"

"Yes! Go do it!"

"I don't want to."

"Brother, why not? We must jihad!"

"Brother . . . It's too cold to jihad."

He wasn't wrong. Even in our planes, with our fleeces and hand warmers, it really was too damn cold for war.

Sadly, I didn't hear this particular conversation live. It was a recording that was heard by every Pashto DSO and told to anyone who would listen to the English version of it. I did hear other jokes, though, because it turned out that the Taliban are fucking *funny*.

"Najibullah . . . Najibuuullllaaah . . . Najibullah, are you there, brother? Najibullah! Najibullah! Najibullah!"

"Yes! What is it, brother?"

"Are the things ready?"

"Yes, brother, the things are ready."

"Is the big thing ready? I hear monsters above."

"The big thing is waiting for Baryalai to come back."

"Baryalai is bringing the large vegetables with him? Hahahaha- hahahaha your vegetable is too small to fight the monsters, Najibullah. You always have to wait for Baryalai's big vege- table. Hahahahahahahaha."

"Stay prepared, brother. God willing many demons will die today."

"Najibullah! Najibullah! Najibullah! I am just joking. We will be prepared."

Najibullah didn't laugh, which seemed a bit unfair, as it was a pretty good dick joke, demons or no.

DSOs all traded with each other the stories of what we heard, in part because they were so funny, in part because we could pass off the stories as our own to other crews. Often, the stories were much the same—chatter is chatter no matter what plane you're on—but because they only flew at night, the gunships could offer up prime shenanigans.

Taylor had deployed after me, and he'd gotten qualified on

different planes and been sent up to Bagram. But even Afghanistan couldn't keep us apart, because not long after he got there, a plane he was flying on had a bad enough mechanical failure that they had to make an emergency landing down in Kandahar. While the rest of his crew was enjoying all the amenities of the south, it was decided that the best use of his time would be to fly with Ed to go ahead and get qualified on the Whiskey. No rest for the wicked and all.

But he did have a little free time, and when we hung out, we traded stories from our missions so far. Maybe because it was from him, or maybe because it's simply one of the best physical comedy stories I've ever heard, one of Taylor's stories quickly became DSO legend.

There he was, overhead an op on an H-model, doing his job, listening for anyone talking about doing some bad shit to the Americans on the ground or up above. (It's worth mentioning here that one of the hardest parts of being a DSO is listening to multiple conversations in different languages. Sometimes, when shit was going real sideways, we would only listen to the Taliban, and then relay what we'd heard to someone else, but we also had to be able to listen to all their static-filled radios while simultaneously paying attention to what the other members of our crew, the ground team, and potentially other aircraft were all saying.) Taylor's not hearing much of interest from the Taliban, but he realizes the crew is getting pretty excited, because the sensor operator is tracking a guy moving between buildings.

Sensor Operator: "Hey FCO, I got a guy moving around the compound."

FCO: "Is he carrying anything?"

SO: "No, but he's sticking to the roofs. He just got on top of the southmost building."

FCO: "You think he's a spotter?"

SO: "I'm not sure."

Nav: "Halo 16, be advised, we have suspicious movement in the compound."

Halo 16 (Navy SEAL on the ground): "Hammer [H model callsign], how much movement?"

Nav: "Halo, one MAM [military-aged male], he's now on the roof of the south building."

SO: "Hey, he's doing something, he's squatting down."

FCO: "What the fuck is he doing? Is he putting an IED on a roof?"

SO: "I don't fucking know. It's fucking weird, though."

Nav: "DSO, are you hearing anything?"

Taylor: "No, nothing other than check-ins, the usual bullshit."

SO: "Oh shit, he's done, he's leav—"

FCO: "Did he . . . did he just take a shit?"

SO: "Yeah, I think so. A big one too. Fucking steamy."

Nav: "Halo 16, be advised, MAM took a shit on the roof."

Halo 16: "Well, all right."

People who weren't even in the country at the time wound up telling this story as if they were there. Which like, I don't begrudge them, 'cause who wouldn't want to be a part of the mission where a gunship watched a guy shit on his neighbor's roof?

This, of course, necessitates the story of the best Whiskey mission. It was supposed to have been a pretty generic flight, just doing escort support of some group of mixed Afghan military and coalition forces. But then some Talib on the radio kept asking if any of his comrades were at "the school." This was concerning, as it could have been him checking in on the preparations for an ambush, so "the school" had to be found. While one of the CSOs kept his camera on the convoy, the other scanned the area near the route, and lo and behold, he came across a village with (1) a relatively new building that looked like a lot of the other schools around the country and (2) a shitload of Talibs around said building.

Well-armed Talibs. All around them were Hi-Luxes (Toyota pickup trucks that are seemingly indestructible and therefore the preferred mode of transportation of insurgents worldwide), machine guns, RPGs (rocket-propelled grenades)—you name it, these guys had it.

They also had something no one had ever seen the Taliban with before.

A volleyball net.

There they were, a bunch of Talibs in their man-jammies, surrounded by a metric fuck-ton of serious weapons.

Playing volleyball.

But even with all those weapons, all these obvious Talibs, the Whiskey couldn't shoot, because alongside all the bad guys were a bunch of women and children. Some thought, and some even said, that this was an obvious "fuck you" to us from the Taliban, who were not shy about using human shields. And this may have been the case, but there was the other option, the less villainous one, wherein even a bunch of Talibs have wives and kids. The war wasn't going anywhere, so why shouldn't they sometimes hang out with them, maybe play some games? How many other chances were they gonna have for a nice game of volleyball with the kids?

It wasn't all roof shits and volleyball, though. The Taliban were an industrious group.

"Amir! Amir. Amir. Amir. Are you there, brother?"

[*static*]

"Amir, are you there? Amir. Amir. Amir. Amir."

"Yes, I am here, brother. We are doing the work."

"Where are you, Amir? There are monsters nearby."

"We are on the road, brother. Near the house with the trees.

We are doing the work."

"Stay safe, brother, monsters are near."

"We are ready, brother. God willing, many of our enemies will die."

The only problem was that their industry, their work, was trying to kill us. In this case, they were setting up an IED at an intersection they knew was heavily traveled. But did that necessarily make them evil?

For most service members in Afghanistan, and certainly for the crews I was flying with, this conceptualization held true, as any interaction they had with the Taliban was wrapped up in fighting. Not only were said Taliban bad most, if not all, of the time, they were depraved and degenerate in their badness; they would do anything to kill us in inventive and terrible ways (remember the fucking donkeys carrying IEDs). I had my share of this, but the nature of DSOing meant that my relationship with the Taliban was becoming less and less violent; even if a given mission resulted in actual combat (all my flights in Afghanistan were technically combat missions, but this was only because the entirety of Afghanistan was perpetually combative in our eyes), there were usually multiple hours surrounding the fighting that were peaceful.

And what I had been told by the DSOs that came before me about the complexity of what I would hear held true; the majority of any elaborate speech was centered around active battles. The rest of the time, which was most of the time, what I kept hearing was the lunch plans, neighborhood gossip, shitty road conditions, and how the weather wasn't conforming to someone's exact desires. The name-calling, complaining, and infighting. Yes, it was bullshit, but not all of it was centered around killing us. Turns out you can't spend all of your time talking about fighting, even in a war zone. Maybe especially in a war zone.

How much of my time in Afghanistan was spent talking about fighting versus literally any other topic? Probably a quarter of the hours of every other mission were spent debating whether one (female) celebrity was hotter than another or fantasizing about what we would do with the latest hundred-million-dollar Powerball or whining about annual training requirements. If the Taliban could have listened to us, they wouldn't have heard much complexity either.

So as my flight hours kept adding up, they began to beg the question of whether the Taliban were, in fact, evil, or even plain old bad, most (it was certainly no longer all) of the time. Beyond the bullshit, the Talibs also daydreamed about the future, made plans for when (not if) the Americans finally left, and reveled in the idea of retaking their country. These conversations are somewhat paradoxical in that they were ubiquitous and coalesced into a gestalt, such that trying to write out any individual conversation now would be more or less an act of, if not necessarily fabrication, then a sort of creation on my part. There were specifics, though: Guesstimates, or maybe the better description is informed hopes of when the Americans or Brits or whoever would leave this village or that town. Discussion of how glorious or wonderful or great life would be once those devils were gone. The feeling of how great it would be to be back in control (both literally and figuratively).

This too was supposed to be evil, their desire to remove us and once again be in charge. And it sounded pretty bad, seeing as how it was entirely predicated on their ability to eradicate the world of infidels (aka us) and return the country to the state it had been in back in the 1990s. The only problem was, it was becoming sort of reasonable.

I began to liken it to the notion of a hypothetically very rich, very not white country, let's call it Audi Sarabia, invading a hypothetically very proud, relatively dysfunctional, very white country, let's call it Texasstan. You would have then a country that felt they were morally upright, who, on the premise of rooting out terrorists and extremist ideologues, invaded a formerly independent state with a long and storied history of rejecting invaders and upholding their millennia-old way of life. This formerly independent state would have a working constitution, a (semi-) functioning government, and while maybe not everyone who lived under that government agreed with its policies, well, you can't please everyone.

Now, on invasion, the Audis would say that the government was corrupt (what government isn't), draconian (a little hypocritical, that, but okay), and guilty of harboring and supporting international threats (people, they mean people). The rest of the world would say, "Well, okay, yeah, those are all true statements, so I guess you have a point," and would stand idly by while the Audis went in and subverted an established, legitimate government, in order to stand up a puppet state that would blindly support them in their mission. The Audis would set up shop in the major cities and begin the process of looking for their enemies.

But then, who, exactly, are their enemies? Supporters of the old government, that one's easy. Rebels against the new government, also easy (the Audis prefer *rebel* to *insurgent* in this analogy—has to do with that whole submission to Islam thing). Oh, and anyone that members of the new government say is bad, regardless of any proof supporting these claims, and regardless of the fact that it seems strangely convenient that most of the people being named happen to be political opponents, or guys that the members of the new government feel have wronged them (some of them fellow members).

Over the next five to ten years, the Audis continue to build up their presence, continue to raid homes at night, kidnap people, drop bombs indiscriminately, all the while maintaining that these actions are justifiable and for the greater good. Meanwhile, the Texans, who have had their own culture longer than the Audis have had a nation, replete with their own laws and customs, are told that they should be ashamed of this culture, that it's barbaric and outdated, and that while they don't necessarily need to convert to the Audis' religion (this isn't the Crusades; proselytization is actually illegal under the rules governing the Audis' military members), they should probably think about joining the rest of the world in modernity.

At some point during all this, a number of Texans find themselves wondering whether the old government—which, admittedly, had its problems—wasn't preferable. They were violent, yes, but at least they were predictable in their violence. And they didn't have giant flying bogeymen that went around blowing up weddings or bombing funerals or just generally making violence an everyday part of life. If, then, a number of these Texans begin to feel that they have no choice but to try and fight against the Audis, would that be so unreasonable? And if, once they do start fighting back, their culture and long-standing way of life mean that they fight hard, even fight dirty, wouldn't this too make some sense?

I spent too many hours and too many words developing this brilliant analogy of mine. It was ham-fisted, overly reductive, and failed to extend the grace that was so readily at hand for the Taliban to the American side of things. If I had tried this shit on a U-boat, I probably would have gotten punched, or at the very least told in no uncertain terms to shut the fuck up. The Whiskeys put up with it, for a time. Eventually, though, they'd all heard my little thought piece, and I had enough self-awareness, or at least enough interest in being liked, to not repeat something that no one else found all that thought-provoking.

It didn't help that I never bothered to ask anyone else what they thought about what we were doing. I felt that whatever insight they might think they had would automatically be limited by their not having the same knowledge and education that I did, never mind that half the crewmembers I flew with were college grad-uates, and the other half, while not necessarily diplomates, were also intelligent, thoughtful human beings. But I wasn't interested in debate. I just wanted to lecture. Which I proceeded to try to do to Ed on the occasion of OBL's death.

Though I'd only been in the country for a month, missions and days in Kandahar had come to blur together. Because I have my flight records, I know how many missions I flew in that month, and for how many hours. Without them, the only reason I can separate that first month from the next is because Osama bin Laden finally got schwacked at the beginning of May. Mind you, I/we had nothing to do with it. You'll have to read Mark Owen and Kevin Maurer's book if you want to know more about the actual schwacking.

I may have been closer to the action than (most of) you, but I was also very much asleep in my freight container when bin

Laden got got. I found out when I woke up a few hours after and checked Facebook. Flying life was rarely physically hard. Sure, I was in Afghanistan, but I had just slept eight (mostly) uninterrupted hours and had pretty decent Wi-Fi. Scrolling through my friends' statuses, I remember thinking, *Huh.* It was interesting, the idea that almost ten years after 9/11 we had finally killed our country's biggest bogeyman, and it was *very* interesting that we had invaded Pakistan to do it. But I wasn't, like, happy about it.

It was gauche then, and it's gauche now, to celebrate the deaths of others. It's gauche when the Taliban does it, it's gauche when al Qaeda does it, it's gauche when we do it. It's supposed to be even more gauche when we do it, what with our greater morality and all. It's one thing to say that killing this person or that person will ultimately result in less pain and suffering in the world, and that might be something worth getting excited about. But this isn't what anyone I knew was doing. They were celebrating the death of bin Laden the guy, not bin Laden the idea. As if his murder made up for the murder of all those people lost to the 9/11 attacks he orchestrated.

Maybe I was more tired than I knew, or grumpy, or just acting contrarian in the way that twenty-two-year-olds who feel like they're having deep-and-novel-thoughts-that-others-in-their-small-mindedness-haven't-yet-considered are prone to feel, but I was ready to argue with somebody about the merits of these celebrations. Ed wound up being that somebody. Unfortunately.

I made my way over to the camp's main building. We had our own office space in it, separated from the rest of the various crews on our camp due to our usage of Top Secret networks for which most everyone else didn't have clearance. Passcode-protected door, windowless room that had a feeling of nerdy despair—just a good old-fashioned secure compartmentalized information facility. Ed was already there, which shouldn't have been surprising. I don't think he slept all that much on his good days, and those were plenty rare, so by the time I walked in he had already been up for a few hours, reveling in this now Greatest of Days.

"Man! Did you see! We got that fucker!"

Ed was smiling. Ed has a nice smile. Big, toothy grin—he's got nice teeth, very into his dental hygiene, pretty sure he told me once he'd never had a cavity in all his thirty plus years—that really lights up his face. If you didn't know any better, when Ed smiles, you'd think he was pretty happy. This might be why he's, to some degree, usually smiling. But this morning, his smile was brilliant. It was genuine. He really was happy.

"Yeah, I saw it on Facebook."

The smile faltered, just for a second. Maybe at my lack of exclamation points, maybe at me learning about it on Facebook. I'll admit this is a strange way to learn about something that happened a few hundred miles away from your war zone, but it's not as if I control how information spreads in the world.

"What a day! I've been trying to find pictures but who knows if we'll have access."

"Uh-huh."

The smile definitely slipped, though this didn't register in my brain at the time. An unsmiling Ed was a potentially scary Ed. This is the problem with people whose rage is constantly simmering. If they aren't happy, they're usually not far from something destructive.

"Dude, we should be celebrating!"

I would like to say that at this point I exercised some self-restraint, some critical thought. But I went with the option of the twenty-two-year-old who feels like they're having deep-and-novel-thoughts-that-others-in-their-small-mindedness-haven't-yet-considered. Ten years later, I don't necessarily disagree with twenty-two-year-old Ian's thoughts, but I do disagree with sharing them with someone like Ed.

"Why? What will that get you? He was an incredible human. He changed the world."

No more smile. Some redness though.

"Fritz, shut the fuck up."

"No, but real—"

"Get out of this room."

"Wha—"

"Leave!"

I have a pretty strong memory of there being an additional threat of potential harm, not that Ed said he would hit me, but that he had a strong desire to do so. I will, however, not attribute it as a quote, in case I have misremembered. Suffice it to say that even if it wasn't verbalized, a threat was hanging in the air.

At the risk of sounding like the elitist pricks I so much detested, I didn't expect this response from Ed. From the gunship crews, sure, or at least some of them. Not to say that they weren't capable of the highfalutin' critical thought I was (I told myself) currently engaging in, it was just that they didn't have the background information we did as linguists. To them, bin Laden was the enemy, full stop. To me and, I thought, the royal us, there was more nuance. Which, of course, there is in such a situation. Having an understanding—even appreciation, even respect—for the machinations of a man that unequivocally crippled the last superpower is a necessary part of engaging with the motivation for why that man was hunted, found, and killed. But if we acknowledge that this nuance exists, we must also acknowledge that it doesn't do so in a vacuum. It is inextricably linked to other ideas, other happenings of the universe. Indeed, it is highly dependent on them.

The hunting and killing of OBL was part of his plan. He more or less knew that if 9/11 was successful, the United States in all of its hate-filled hubris would stop at nothing to find him, and to destroy him. By doing just that we made him what he was, and still is. The man Osama bin Laden would have died of old age at some point, but OBL the idea will live on through history, at least our history, because we made him such an intricate part of our story. This didn't have to be the case. Retribution didn't undo 9/11. And if we only felt "better" because we murdered someone else—and let's be clear, Osama bin Laden the man was extrajudicially murdered—then we definitely shouldn't, and probably don't, feel all that good with him gone.

To me, the almost ten years following 9/11, and the however many more since we acknowledged that Osama bin Laden was actively plotting to change the world, offered enough distance to look at him and his plans through a relatively objective lens (objectivity being, as we know, the ultimate goal of the self-styled students of Socrates—emotions and all the other intricacies of the human condition merely the crutches for the intellectually stunted). But while time is, in and of itself, an arrow, capable only of unidirectional flight, the human experience of time is that of a fucking Super Ball launched by a batting machine, zooming about every which way, reversing, forwarding, re-reversing, spinning, back spinning, upending, down ending, side ending, zigging, zagging, insert rather a few more directional gerunds and you get the idea. For all I know, to Ed, 9/11 may have been yesterday. Hell, maybe it was today, the death of OBL having altered the path of Ed's Super Ball such that he was watching the Towers fall in real time, but now, this time,

Osama bin Laden was inside too, hopefully meeting his end with just as much fear as so many of those other 2,958 people.

But then, what would this mean for Ed? He would now have to be celebrating the fall of the Towers. OBL the idea doesn't exist without the Towers. So you can't celebrate the death of our greatest bogeyman without implicitly acknowledging the accomplishment that was taking down those two towers. By daring to offer this, that the life of OBL the man deserved some consideration, not too unlike the other 2,958 lives lost years prior, I was not only committing heresy, but I was also actively interrupting Ed's joy. His celebration. I may as well have kicked him in the balls right before he was about to come.

I sort of sulked, skulked my way out, ambled outside, and dicked around, wandering over to the gunship side of the building to dick around some more. There was little else by way of conversation, and, if nothing else, Ed showed me that I should maybe keep my thoughts on the matter to myself. I didn't bring it up again, at least not to him, figuring that any attempt at justification would be met with more anger, and so I suspect that Ed ultimately felt I was just being a contrarian prick, an edgelord, ever desirous of attention (wouldn't be the first time, or the last). But I wasn't. I wasn't excited that OBL had been merc'd. I wasn't sad either. Mostly, I was confused. Was killing OBL going to end our deployments? Was it going to result in fewer deaths? Was it going to make Afghanistan a better place? Was it going to help the grass to grow, the sun to shine? Was the death or killing or murder or revenge or elimination or neutralization or score-evening of this man going to result in any meaningful, substantial change in the world?

Nope.

Then why be so happy?

Some of this was my contrary nature, some of it my desire to look and feel smart. But much of this—both my lecture to the crews and my attempt to talk to Ed—was the only way I knew how to react to the surprising and unsettling realization that the notion of evil was turning out to be unsustainable. The Taliban had, at first, embodied the traits that I felt were consistent with evil: doing terrible things all of the time (or at least a majority of it) and/or committing such singularly awful acts that it felt logical to assume that their core was bereft of any good. But it had turned out that the Taliban weren't bad all of the time. Which like, okay, had been sort of an unrealistic expectation anyway, but worse than this was the fact that all this boring bullshit I was listening to was serving to humanize those who had before been what.

I never heard another series of "Kaliiiiiiima . . . Kali-maaaaaaaaa . . . Kalima Kalima Kalima Kalima" again. And I never heard Kalima answer the radio. Maybe he hadn't just been tired. Maybe he was dead. It's possible that I had killed him. But I heard countless other men repeating all their friends' names and imploring them to be safe.

"Shpoon Jaan, are you there? Shpoon Jaan?"

"Shpoon Jaan, wake up. Shpoon, there are monsters near. Are you safe, brother? Are you prepared?"

"Yes, brother, we are safe and prepared."

"Stay safe and look for monsters, brother."

"Aziz, are you there? Aziz?"

"Yes, we are here, brother. Are things well?"

"Yes, brother, but there are monsters near. Stay safe and be prepared."

"We will, brother. Stay safe."

"Haji Jaan, are you there? Haji Jaan?"

"Haji Jaan, brother, are you there?"

"Yes, yes, we are here. What is it?"

"Monsters are nearby, Haji Jaan. Stay safe and be prepared."

"God willing, we will be prepared, brother. Stay safe."

"Latif Jaan, are you there, Latif?"

"Latif, brother, are you there?"

"Latif Latif Latif Latif Latif? Are you there, brother?"

"YES! We are here, brother, what is it?"

"Monsters are close, brother, be prepared."

"We are always prepared. Stay safe, brother."

Kalima, or at least the guy who wanted to talk to him, was emblematic of so much of what I was hearing on mission after mission. These men, these Taliban, these guys sitting in the mountains, were bored and tired, but mostly bored. This is difficult to explain in that, while it's easy for me to tell you this, it's difficult for us humans to admit that the malevolent can be filled with the mundane. We want our evil to stay evil, the prosaic to be not just separated from the depraved, but diametrically opposed. But now these two poles were busy converging, and I was feeling less and less sure about my conceptualization of our enemy as somehow less, or at least other, than human.

And then my Mission happened, and none of that mattered anymore.

GRIFFIN, OR YOU
KEEP FLYING

REALLY, MY MISSION WAS a boring one. One of the downsides of flying during the day is that you get tasked to shit like key leader engagements, or KLEs. These don't happen at night, as the military does not count killing or rolling up some high-ranking Talib as a key leader engagement; engagement—like so many other once benign words now adulterated by war—conveniently has myriad definitions spanning the full spectrum of violence. The village where the KLE was to take place was medium-sized, comprised of a few compounds bordering each other, surrounded by mostly flat land, with the exception of a few wadis to the west (wadis are sort of like ravines, or really big ditches). A ground team was going in with the goal of convincing a tribal elder to let them build a well for the village and its surrounding area. The people who lived there had likely done so for decades, and they'd gotten by just fine without a well, but in our infinite American wisdom we had decided that providing them with this modern creature comfort would help us win their hearts and minds.

The funny thing about winning hearts and minds, at least from my vantage point, is that it often involves a number of burly men equipped with guns and somewhat absurd amounts of ammunition being flown in by helicopter, while at least one warplane, along with probably a few drones, looks on overhead. These well-fed and well-armed men talk with some other men, less well-fed though probably just as well-armed, and try to convince them that they are not there to fight, just to help. All the guns and ammo and death from above are purely in case someone else attacks the better fed men first.

KLEs take hours. Hours in which we, up above, fly in a slow, smooth, small orbit; sensors scanning the ground, me scanning the electromagnetic spectrum, the plane burning hundreds of gallons of kerosene an hour. (I did the math once. A C-130 has a fuel capacity of 6,700 gallons. One gallon of JP-8—kerosene renamed jet fuel—is $2.78. Say we flew for seven hours, and, for the sake of easy math, we landed on "empty" with 700 gallons in reserve. Six thousand gallons at $2.78/gal is $2,382 an hour. What a billing rate. And that's just the fuel.)

With that much time, a mission was likely to be mind-numbingly boring. But who's to say? We were flying in the spring, a time known for increased Taliban presence and intense fighting, in a part of the country not known for its fondness of Americans. We were tasked with this mission which, trusting in the wisdom of the Combined Joint Special Operations Task Force, meant that there was a non-trivial chance that some bad shit could happen, so we should be, if not on high alert, then at least paying the fuck attention. On the other hand, this was a daylight mission in bumfuck nowhere that hinged on not even actually building a well but instead *talking about* building a fucking well. This allows for some cognitive dissonance, and perhaps even occasional inattention. But we were professionals, silent or not, and like a Marine major I once worked with said, "complacency kills." So, we sat in our orbit, constantly looking and listening, not expecting much of anything, but ready. Always ready.

And then it was over. The KLE was done. The JTAC, or joint terminal attack controller—the guy on the ground whose job it is to talk to and direct combat aircraft—told us that it was a success and called back for the helo that would pick them up and take them back to their FOB. He and the other couple of guys with him made their way out of the village and regrouped with the rest of the team waiting on the edge of town. The helo was a few minutes out by this point, so they started making their way back to the landing zone where they'd been dropped off. No matter how routine or calm a mission was, when a helicopter was coming in, the sensors/CSOs always looked around to make sure there were no threats, and I always listened more intently to make sure no one was planning to take the helo out. Like the rest of the mission, there was nothing to see, nothing to hear, other than some guy, probably a Talib, noting the movement of the helicopter. This was pretty routine, particularly for that area of Afghanistan. The Taliban has spotters everywhere, and just like us, they try and keep abreast of enemy movements.

There's a decent chance you've seen footage from cameras on gunships or drones. If you haven't, it's always black-and-white, grainy, and while you can definitely tell that you're looking at humans, you can't tell much about those humans. These are the sorts of cameras the old gunships used. It's worth saying again just how much better the cameras on the Whiskeys were, just how much detail we could see. But even with this vision, we didn't see anyone doing anything nefarious, just normal villagers going about their lives.

And after the spotter reported the helo's movement, I didn't hear anything. Well, almost anything. Everyone I know who flew has tinnitus. Most of us don't have it too bad, just a faint ringing in the ears such that the world is never truly quiet. It's better this way, though. When it's quiet, there's nothing happening. When nothing's happening, either everyone is dead or they're about to be.

It was still quiet when the ground team started sprinting for the nearest wadi, ducking and diving into the ditches. We could see the dirt flying up from their boots and the bullets that were hitting the earth around them. What we couldn't see was where the fuck the bullets were coming from. And then I heard them. The men shooting those bullets.

> **Talib 1:** "Move up, they've gone to the western ditch. They're running, move up!"
>
> **Me:** "CSO, I think they're to the east, back in the village."
>
> **JTAC:** "Recoil, what the fuck is going on, where are they?"
>
> **Recoil (callsign for a Whiskey):** "Crimson 12, east of you, shooting from the village. We're searching now."
>
> **JTAC:** "Copy, we're gonna keep moving."

It might be because of action movies and video games, or it might be because thinking about what was happening as something virtual was easier to comprehend, but in that minute of watching these men leapfrog from ditch to ditch, moving just like all the characters I'd seen in media with their crouched bodies, swiveling heads, and constant hand signaling, I felt like I was watching an imagining of what would happen when a group of highly trained men suddenly started getting shot at. It didn't seem possible that this was what actually happened in battle, that I was watching this actually happen.

> Talib 1: "Where's the big gun? Is it ready?"
> Talib 2: "It's coming, we have it, it's coming!"
> Talib 1: "Get it ready! They're moving again."
> Recoil: "Crimson 12, enemy is setting up a big gun."
> JTAC: "Copy. If they get it, our bird can't come in."

The team kept moving and got as close to their LZ as they could. But they had to stay more or less in the wadi or they would have been in the open, completely vulnerable. They talked to the helo pilot, who was willing to come in, big gun or no. But the JTAC had to decide if they were better off having the helo come in and risk it (the helo) possibly getting shot or stay and ensure they (the humans) definitely got shot.

In the next two minutes, nine events take place.

1. Helo lands and team begins loading.

2. We find the guys shooting.

3. JTAC says almost everyone is on and that he'll get on last.

4. JTAC gets shot.

5. JTAC screams.

6. Talibs celebrate because they hit the JTAC.

7. We launch our Griffin.

8. CSO gets the missile just over the edge of a wall
   into the Talib-filled alley.

9. No more Talibs.

> **JTAC:** "Recoil, where are they, what are they doin— Fuck,
> I'm hit."
> **Talib 1:** "Brother, you got one. Keep going! Keep shooting!
> We will kill them all!"
> **Talib 2:** "Yes, we will, the gun is work—"

There are, obviously, many other things that both happened
and were said, and while I recognize those as having occurred,
in my brilliant flashbulb memories, those nine things are What
Happened. I know they Happened in that order because no other
sequence of events makes sense. The Taliban can't celebrate shooting the JTAC unless he gets shot, and we can't exactly have killed
them without launching our missile. But in my mind, in those two
minutes that I have relived hundreds of times—that I'm actively
reliving as I write this—all of those events happened at once, having been compressed into one infinitely expansive instance of time.
Partly, this is because some of them were in fact simultaneous; in
all but one joined breath I heard the JTAC's pained scream and
the Talibs' elated celebration.

There is one other event that could have been the tenth in
that list or shared the spot of number nine. It happened the same
moment the Talibs died/were killed/ceased to exist. We were all
watching the CSO's screen, waiting for the Griffin's impact, worried it might miss. I can't know what my new friend Blackbear
(his last name is Black, and he's big and snuggly, ergo Blackbear)

was thinking in that moment; I don't know what his face looked like before the Griffin hit. I was just as transfixed by the screen as he was. I do know, and will always know, exactly what he looked like when the Griffin reached its targets. Because when the Griffin impacted, one of the kindest, nicest, most soft-spoken people I've had the pleasure of working with leapt into the air, one hand in a fist pump, the other hand ripping off his headset, utterly unable to control his happiness at our kill. That moment is frozen in my head like the end frame of a 1990s sitcom.

This was (1) Blackbear's first kill, and (2) a very good kill—you'd never know that two men had just been in that alley. There was nothing left of them. No pink dust. No legs melted to walls. No pools of blood glittering under IR, like so many modern-age spoils of war. Further contributing to his elation was the fact that this is what he, and we, had been trained to do: protect the ground team. And if that meant killing some Talibs, not just so be it, but hell fucking yeah let's do it.

Except Blackbear was a loadmaster. He'd been trained to load cargo onto planes and make sure all the weights were balanced. The CSOs were glorified navigators, men who'd been trained to calculate bearing and speed, with a little bit of ad hoc camera operation on the side. And I was a linguist, a boy who'd been trained to listen to people talk. We were no killers. And yet . . .

The rest of the crew was, if not quite as exuberant as Blackbear, then pretty happy. I felt bad for the pilots, as they didn't get to revel in the exact moment of death, having been preoccupied with flying the plane, but the video was recorded, so I'm sure they watched it later. We flew back to base, the hour of transit giving everyone time to ride oh so very high on our accomplishment. It had been a long mission, with more excitement than the prior week combined, but when we got off the plane and made our way back to camp there were no complaints about the flight time or worries about tomorrow's mission. There was just this great sense of pride and exhilaration, the bond of bloodshed (well, hypothetical bloodshed; the Griffin had turned even that back into its constituent atoms) having further strengthened the crew's relationship.

I had flown with this crew for dozens of hours by this point. They were far and away my favorite. But I wasn't one of them. I'd flown with a different crew the day before, and when this crew went on to fly the next day, I wouldn't be with them. I may have been "their DSO," but a possession is not the same as a teammate.

Furthering the distance between us was the fact that they didn't fully know what I did. I'm not saying that I fully understood their jobs; I have no idea how to balance a one hundred thousand–pound plane or determine the best route between two bumfuck points in Afghanistan based on weather and air conditions and all sorts of other shit I can't even think of. But I could see what they did, and the results thereof. Most of what I did was a black box to them. And seeing as how nearly all of that "doing" happened in my head, well, that didn't exactly foster camaraderie. This meant that no one else had heard, and no one else ever would hear, the simultaneous screams of the JTAC and the Talibs. Or the sudden quiet when the Talibs died.

I flew the next day. And the day after. The routine helps. It's sort of like being programmed or being on autopilot (using this expression to describe being in the back of a plane has an irony to it that I find difficult to articulate). You have a choice, technically. You can choose not to fly. But that's a little like saying Sisyphus could choose not to roll his boulder up the hill. Technically, he could, but then he'd have to admit that he couldn't make it to the top.

Besides, if you don't fly, then suddenly you have a lot of time to sit around and think. You can hide the thoughts, numb them, avoid them, but there's only so much *Call of Duty*, so much gym time, so much porn out there. At some point the thoughts creep in around the edges. It wasn't that I was upset that we'd killed them; they'd ambushed the team, purely as targets of opportunity. They were trying to kill us (even though the men actually being shot at were ten thousand feet below the Whiskey, it's still a feeling of *us*; you sort of become part of a giant singular organism with enough time). We genuinely had been trying to do something that would have helped the village. So when we killed them, it was primarily an act of self-defense, albeit self-defense that we reveled in.

I was upset that they'd had to be killed. I was upset that as a nation we had decided that this was how we wanted to spend our resources. We'd convinced ourselves that if we gave enough Afghans enough stuff, they'd see the error of the ways of the Taliban, and if not join us, then at least not support them.

But how do you give people enough stuff to make up for all the lives you take in the process? We paid people, sometimes, for wrongful deaths, when their kids got shot during a no-knock night raid or we dropped a missile on the wrong part of town or any of the other myriad ways we "accidentally" killed Afghans. But it isn't clear to me that we actually believed in innocence, at least not in Afghanistan. It seems that we estimated every Afghan as either with us or with the Taliban. And even if they were with us, there was a nagging suspicion that they were just one bad day away from going back to the enemy. We told ourselves that we had this suspicion because of the nature of Afghans, that they're a shifty little brown people with no loyalty, who don't know how to function in the modern world. But they aren't the problem. We are.

For so many Afghans, a bad day consists of their house getting blown up along with the fifteenth family member they've had killed because of this war. It's not hard to understand why they might want to get back at us for that shit. Or maybe their bad day is when, after having been promised a well, a few foolhardy fuckwits decide to shoot at the Americans in broad daylight, and the Americans decide that everyone in that village can get fucked, the well is off. That's if we don't decide to just bomb them, citing "increased Taliban presence."

And then I realized that no, this was the wrong thing to be mad at. Not only was it useless, as my anger could do nothing to stop the U.S. military from carrying out its God-given mission, but it was also just the wrong way of looking at things.

The Taliban had forced our hand. They were responsible for harboring the people who had planned and carried out 9/11. They routinely infringed on human rights, and while maybe we did too, at least we accomplished something when we did it. What were they building? What were they giving the world? Fucking nothing. Killing them, ridding them and their ilk from the face of the Earth was the only way to ensure that no more JTACs got shot, no more girls got acid thrown on their faces, and this war could finally end. The only logical conclusion was that I should, in fact, be mad at the Taliban. Maybe they weren't completely and utterly evil, but that sure as shit didn't mean they didn't need to die.

If I'd been on U-boats, it would have been easier for me to make this a reality, to kill as many Talibs as possible. Hunting humans during the day is very different from hunting humans at night. There's far more chatter all over the electromagnetic spectrum when everyone is awake, and while it's easy enough to differentiate Talib from non-Talib, I still had to sort through all that noise. Visually, a guy slowly making his way from tree to tree with a long stick was probably checking on his orchard. And a group of guys standing around could just be shooting the shit or deciding what non-IED planting work needed to be done.

At two o'clock in the morning, anyone who's talking on a radio is all but guaranteed to be Taliban, or at least Taliban-adjacent. It's also usually a safe bet that the guy trying to slowly make his way from tree to tree, three-foot object in hand, in the pitch-black countryside (not much light pollution in the rural bits of Afghanistan; lack of electricity and all) is up to something less than savory. And if there's a group of guys congregating? Bad, bad dudes, who need to get got before they try and get us.

And so if I'd been flying on U-boats, it would have been so much simpler to make sure more of them died. On the Whiskeys, there was all the daylight activity mucking up our ability to say that guys on the ground were being nefarious, and there was the added complication of the way the seats were set up, such that I couldn't readily look at the camera feeds without everyone knowing that I was looking. On a U-boat, I could sneak a peek over my shoulder and see what the sensor operators were looking at with no one the wiser. Then I could wait a few seconds, act like I was concentrating real hard, take down some notes, and then tell the crew that I had heard something.

"Nav, DSO, I have multiple Taliban coordinating movement south toward a village."

"Nav, IR, I have three MAMs moving south toward the village."

"JTAC, Spooky, we have ICOM and visual on a group of MAMs moving toward your position."

"Spooky, copy . . . Cleared hot."

Or, in English:

"Hey, Navigator, Fritz, the DSO, here. I'm hearing some guys who sound like Taliban coordinating movement south toward our village."

"Hey, Navigator, infrared camera operator here, I'm seeing three shifty-looking dudes moving south toward the village."

"Hey, Special Operator guy on the ground, we're hearing some bad dudes talking on the radio [ICOM] about moving toward you, and we're watching a group of three men move toward you on our disconcertingly old and yet still highly effective cameras."

"Hey, gunship, thanks for letting me know . . . Kill those fuckers."

And my invented intelligence, combined with what the sensors were seeing, would be enough for the JTAC to call in the strike. And then we'd shoot them, and it would be a good, clean kill, and I'd have helped remove some evil from the world, probably saved some future lives, and most importantly, killed some more fucking Talibs. The ethics would be redundant, and uninteresting. We all knew those were bad dudes, there was just dumbass formality shit getting in the way of killing them. Who's to say I wouldn't have heard them coordinating their movements later? Why wait? I was doing them a favor, making sure they didn't die tired.

If I already feel that what I did weakened the tethers of whatever it is, spirit or otherwise, that anchors me to this world and you people in it, shouldn't I regret not sucking it up and taking this to its logical conclusion? Wouldn't I have been worth the erasure of even a little more of their evil? Wouldn't I be a fine price to pay to bring about a sooner end to their regime, to the war, to all this god-forsaken fucking fighting? Wasn't I enough?

I didn't fly on U-boats that deployment. There was a chance I could have, but the way the hours and mission requirements were working out, I didn't switch over. I'm still not sure if that's a good thing. On some abstract level I know that not murdering men—for this is what it would have meant for me to invent whole-cloth things that I was hearing, such that we could, without impunity, shoot those little black-and-white silhouettes moving back and forth across the screen—is better for my humanity, or spirit, or whatever it is that's supposed to keep me attached to this side of the ether. But I also know that in the moment, killing them would have felt good in a way that nothing else ever has or likely will. I know that doing this once would have been a slippery slope into doing it on the next mission, and the one after that, and that I would have been praised for the incredible skill I displayed in finding the enemy and bringing about their demise. I know that some people might have questioned this, but that the machinery of war, the celebration of killing, the fact that the greater the number of enemies killed in action the happier the officers above me would be, as this was one of the ways they could ensure their promotion—that all of this would have protected me from any serious investigation, and that I could have gotten away with night after night of slaughter.

What I don't know, what I still haven't figured out, is whether doing this would have been better for the world. What if after the ecstasy of execution comes the fallout of fratricide? What if I realized that murdering a man, be he Talib or not, is still to murder another human, another person that I'm related to, that I'm supposed to be connected to? So what if by choosing to kill him I forever ensured my removal from the brotherhood of good humans? Knowing what I know, or knew—or I guess I'm not sure I still know but most definitely at the time knew—that there are some people who are akin to things, who can't be reasoned with, or made to see the light, and that sometimes, or maybe even most of the time, the only thing to do with those people-things is to kill them—not remove them, or separate them, or some other humanistic and liberal attempt at saving their useless lives, but kill them—if, when I knew this, I did this, it would have been a Good thing to have done. Now, if I no longer know this, and had done it, what would it have been? And what would it be?

To this day, I don't know how this attack got planned. The village elder must have had notice that the team was coming in, and presumably he told most of the village so that they wouldn't freak out when yet another American helicopter was seen heading toward them. I have to think, or at least hope, that the attack was planned before we showed up. Because if they were planning it that day, coordinating over radios (like they usually do), and I didn't hear it, then I'm at least partially responsible for that JTAC getting shot.

Except, I'm not. I'm really not. I did my job that day exceptionally well. My Pashto was at its peak; I had finished language school recently enough that I still had a large vocabulary fresh in my mind, but I had also had enough missions that I'd heard real conversation in and out of combat and could follow what was being said through all the surrounding chaos. I translated everything the guys attacking said in as near to real time as it was possible for me to get. I relayed the important information and kept the bullshit to myself. It's not unlikely that this mission was the first time I had done my job perfectly right. If there is blame to be had, I don't deserve any of it.

But the JTAC still got shot.

The JTAC got shot because sometimes it doesn't matter if you do everything right. Before my Mission I thought I could save people. I thought that with all my training, with all my brainpower, with all the three years I had spent learning how to do this, I could protect those men on the ground. I couldn't. No one could. You can't save the dead.

A Mission is not defined by its violence or lack thereof. It is not dependent on death, though that is often involved. A Mission is different from the mission that came before it, and every mission that comes after. One Mission might revolve around the death of a bunch of Canadian operators, even though they were told not to go into that canyon full of IEDs. Another might involve watching nine SEALs die because the Pashto was too muddled to be able to tell that they were surrounded. Another might involve realizing that this was the fourth time you were going after the same fucking guy, and the government was just playing catch and release with their so-called enemies. On my Mission, I did my job right, did everything perfectly, and our JTAC still got shot.

A Mission is simply the flight that changes everything. Everyone flies after their Mission. It doesn't matter if every time you walk out onto the runway toward the plane you break into a cold sweat. It doesn't matter if you no longer file your after-action reports, even if you heard actionable intelligence. A Mission is a flight that changes nothing. You keep flying, until the day comes when you have to choose between life and death.

Yours, or yours.

HOME, OR YOU LOOK LIKE
MORE OF A MAN

OF MY THREE AIR MEDALS, two of them deal with flights from my first deployment. The one that chronologically covers the first half of the deployment says that my "superb airmanship and courage were instrumental to the successful execution of twenty combat missions totaling 191.5 flight hours supporting Operation ENDURING FREEDOM. Constantly operating under the threat of man portable air defense systems and anti-aircraft artillery, Airman Fritz provided real time imminent threat warning, situational awareness and non-traditional intelligence, surveillance and reconnaissance to coalition Special Operations Forces executing critical close air support, armed reconnaissance, infiltration and exfiltration missions. Additionally, Airman Fritz passed twelve imminent threat warnings during missions that included short notice launches in support of troops in contact. Additionally, Airman Fritz was able to warn ground forces of possible mine and ambush locations, ensuring the safe return of ground

Special Operations Forces. Airman Fritz and his crew's efforts also contributed to the elimination of twenty insurgents and detention of twelve enemy fighters including two high value targets."

The other medal, which chronologically covers the second half of that deployment, says much of the same boilerplate shit about threat warning and types of missions. But it also says that over the course of "131 flight hours" I "passed eight imminent threat warnings" and that I "was able to provide warning to ground forces of a machine gun ambush and insurgents tracking coalition force movements." Apparently, I further "contributed to the detention of seven enemy fighters including two high value targets."

Together, these air medals state that I flew 322.5 hours on that deployment. The actual number was a little lower, because of the way the dates are set (one of the medals includes a flight or two from my second deployment); I really only flew 316.8 hours in the three months that I was in Kandahar. The first month was the busiest, and I narrowly avoided hitting the 125-hour limit. None of the missions in that month came close to matching the extreme intensity of my first. I don't know for sure why the Taliban had gone through the trouble of such a massive attack in Barawala Kalay, other than this was just what they did in that area. In the rest of the country, they weren't usually too keen on walking into villages full of our waiting bullets. We were at our highest occupation level, desperately trying to prove our power. This meant fewer serious engagements; the Taliban were up against 130,000 members of the ISAF (International Security Assistance Force), 100,000 of whom were the heavily invested, and even more heavily armed, Americans. While the Taliban had proved in Marjah that they weren't just going to sit back and take our shit, that didn't mean they had to be dumb about their fighting.

More often than not, the firefights that happened were small, and they were sudden. The Taliban relied on surprise attacks and attacks of opportunity. The air medals weren't exaggerating; I really did fly multiple missions on short notice launches for troops in contact, or TICs. We were regularly pulled off the mission we had been assigned that day to hightail it over to where some other guys were getting shot at. (Memorably, in response to being told that we would no longer be supporting an Australian team on their admittedly boring mission, one of our CSOs, meaning to make a joke that only his fellow CSO could see, sent the message "Fuck you, Kangaroos, we're out" over the wrong chat channel, such that some colonel flying an A-10 saw this message during a gun run, which he was less than happy about. Said CSO just so happened to answer the phone when this very angry colonel called their unit, resulting in a minutes-long chewing out that I guess did what it was supposed to, insofar as said CSO always double-checked where his messages were going after that.)

My Mission happened somewhere in the latter half of that deployment. Of those 316.8 hours, maybe a hundred or so came after it. By the end of those hours, my anger had receded, my excitement about going home taking precedent over any preoccupation with the Taliban. There was even hope that we would get back in time for the Fourth of July, and what better way to celebrate my joyous return. What's more, the Fourth was on a Monday, so if we got back in time, we'd get a free four days of leave tacked on to the two weeks of vacation we automatically got post-deployment.

Getting to and coming back from Afghanistan is often more stressful than being in Afghanistan. You take a military plane from Afghanistan over to "an unspecified base in southwest Asia," aka Al Udeid Air Base in Qatar, and then you wait for a commercial aircraft to take you back home, with a stop somewhere in Europe along the way. Al Udeid, also known as The Deid, is a massive base with thousands of people and over one hundred different aircraft stationed at it. It counts as a deployed location, but the most dangerous thing in The Deid is probably the access to booze and Ambien. In Afghanistan, there might be mortars, but you can't drink, at least not if you're in the American military. Like all rules, there are ways around this for some people, but as far as I know, none of us ever had access to alcohol while deployed. This was a problem, given how much all of us liked having access to alcohol.

There's a saying in the flying community: "There are two types of aircrew. Those who have puked, and those who will." The more missions you fly, the more likely you'll encounter shitty weather and the constant jostling and bumping and swaying that will result in your vestibular system admitting its weakness and crying uncle as whatever you most recently ate leaves your body in spectacular, half-digested fashion. It is thus recommended that one only eat things that taste the same coming up as they did going down on their first few flights. Bananas, candied ginger, plain bread, these foods are your friend.

I'm not positive that this is as good a truism as those valorous vomiting victims want it to be, as I never puked on any aircraft, even when we were doing evasive maneuvers for an hour, and I know plenty of people with hundreds and thousands of hours of flight time who also never spewed. I have long since decided that this saying was simply a replacement for the less publicly friendly and therefore more honest truism of flying: "There are two types of aircrew. Those who drink too much, and those who drink even more." Because with the exception of people who were prohibited by religion, and so didn't drink at all, every flyer I knew drank too much.

It's built into the community. When you fly your final training flight, you're expected to bring beer for everyone to drink in celebration of your (hopeful) qualification. Sometime after that, in front of the whole squadron, you have to drink a grog, which is a concoction of various (mostly) liquids that are meant to be revolting and difficult to drink: mustard, vinegar, fruit juices, milk, pickle juice, sauerkraut juice, mayonnaise—the list is ever expansive and well nigh all-inclusive, the only limit being formed solids, so that the person chugging the grog doesn't choke. It was said that qualifying either underage or as a Mormon (the two main categories of non-drinkers) made getting grogged much worse, because then you didn't get the "benefit" of the five or six shots of liquor that allegedly covered up some of the more terrible flavor combinations you experienced during the thirty seconds it took to chug a pint of this revolting concoction (the shots did not, in fact, make the grog taste better). The only responsible part of all of this was that it was agreed on ahead of time that the grogee not be allowed to drive home.

The gunship squadron at Hurby has a full, working bar. It leads directly to the flight line. The MC-130s do too. And the CV-22s. And the U-28s. Every flying squadron I know of has a bar. These bars are ostensibly only for after flights, as there are rules about drinking and flying, the so-called bottle-to-throttle rule, wherein all of the aircrew, but most definitely pilots, as they're in charge of the throttle, must stop drinking twelve hours before they fly. But alcohol undergoes zero order elimination by the liver, which means that there is no way to speed up its metabolism; it can only process one drink per hour. You may say to yourself, *Okay, that means they'd have to have more than twelve drinks in the time prior to whenever they stopped consuming alcohol in order for this to matter.* That isn't as hard as you might think. On my twenty-first birthday, I had twenty-one drinks in three hours, or so I'm told, as I don't remember much past number ten (there are a few blurry moments of saying incredibly dumb things around number fourteen or fifteen). I know for a fact that my friend Mike had his twenty-one shots in 2.5 hours, as I'm the one who took him home and cleaned the vomit out of his chest hair. If you're committed, it isn't all that hard to beat the math.

I'm not saying that I ever flew with a drunk pilot, or an actively drunk anyone. But I am saying that I was told many, many times that 100 percent O2, the stuff we had access to on the plane in the event of a decompression or flying at altitude, was the best cure for a hangover known to man.

When you got to The Deid, after however many months of not having any alcohol in Afghanistan, the first place you'd go is the BRA (Base Recreational Area; I guess they couldn't call it the Base Area for Recreation [BAR], 'cause then it would be formally admitted that recreation is in fact synonymous with drinking). The powers that be had set up a system that was supposed to prevent real drunkenness, wherein any one individual was limited to three drinks per day. Every time you bought a drink it got logged on your ID, so if you tried to buy a fourth, the bartender would politely remind you that you had reached your limit. And while it was technically illegal to share your drinks, people developed agreements to forgo a day of drinking and give away their legally purchased three beverages so that their friend could get a proper load on, with the knowledge that said friend would return the favor on a different day.

Alternatively, if you didn't have someone who was willing to help you out, or you didn't feel like having to repay the favor, you could just take an Ambien, stay up a couple of hours till you get a little loopy, then go chug your three Leffes (Leffe Blond has a 6.6 percent ABV, making it much more effective than, say, a Bud Light) and get decently fucked up. Hypothetically.

The Deid isn't all booze and pseudo-barbiturates though. There's a movie theater, a swimming pool, the fabled Dairy Queen—myriad ways to remind yourself of 'Murica in all of its glory. There are giant transient tents, filled with a hundred people on bunkbeds trying to sleep through the 110-degree days, so that they can sweat through only one pair of clothing moving about during the 90-degree nights. The Deid is nice, in its way, but it's also a little purgatoryesque, maybe even Kafkaesque, in that there are large amounts of bureaucracy that somehow attempt to make the "deployment" there seem more dangerous, or of greater importance. When moving about at night, you must, for instance, wear your standard issue neon-yellow reflective belt on top of your camouflage uniform, in case of, well, something. Traffic, I think. So when you get woken up by a full bladder for the third time in a day because you drank fifteen bottles of water last night to try and stay hydrated in spite of the booze and the humidity, and must make your way to the nearest latrine, which is at least a hundred yards away, you must either wear your full flight suit and boots, which like, no way, too fucking hot, or your Air Force–issued physical training gear. Never mind that if you were deployed to Afghanistan you wouldn't have packed PT gear, given that the gyms in Afghanistan allow you to wear normal civilian clothes, so you're required to go to The Deid's Base Exchange (think military TJ Maxx) and hope that they have a size somewhere south of XXXL. And when they don't, you buy it anyway and walk around swimming in too big clothing for however long you're stuck in this silly, silly place.

At some point, you get told that your flight is coming in and that you'll be leaving soon, so you pack up all your shit and congregate at some benches for a few hours, bullshitting with all the different crews from Kandahar, only to then be told that, in fact, said flight is not coming and that you can return to the transient tents. This will happen again the following day. And the day after that. You lose track of how many times this happens, whether it did in fact happen twice in one day, or did time just get all fuzzy courtesy of the beers you downed in anticipation of the flight? But then, finally, the flight really does come, and you make it over to Leipzig, Germany, and someone buys a bottle of absinthe in the duty-free, and as you drink your fourth Dixie cup of it, you note that said Dixie cup is sort of dissolving the longer the absinthe sits in it, and this is an interesting phenomenon given that there is not a small amount of this absinthe inside of you, but eh, the stomach is stronger than a chemically treated Dixie cup, surely, and besides, if you don't drink, the gunners will make fun of you, and isn't this a good time to tell that story about that one chick who said that if you put a dick in front of her mouth she just had to suck it, except I guess you shouldn't have said her name 'cause now this gunship major is pretty mad and is cutting you off from the absinthe, and even through this anise-flavored addlement it's pretty clear that she's pissed, but like, I'm just repeating what Laura said herself, so what's the problem, does she think I'm being sexist, 'cause I'm not; I'd tell this story if a dude had said it too—hell, it might be even funnier then—but oh, okay, she's really serious, fuck, I should go sit over there and be quiet, and I guess I can try and apologize later, and hopefully it will come off as genuine, I mean it is genuine, but there's no way for her to know that; she doesn't know me, and I could just be trying to make sure she doesn't tell anyone in my unit, but really I didn't mean to, like, speak ill of anyone or anything like that, I'm a big fan of anyone who's willing to put a dick in their mouth; it seems pretty unpleasant, so if anything I was celebrating Laura, but maybe trying to explain that won't work as well as I think it will, but like, I can't go find the major on the plane 'cause then everyone would see and that would be awkward for both of us; I know she has to worry about being seen as some sort of shrill ballbuster ruining our fun, but I don't think that, 'cause like, obviously I'm not sexist, but I guess what are the odds I ever fly with her, probably not that high, and worst case, if I do I'll just have to be on my best behavior, which should be a lot easier given that I will hopefully not have just had a lot of absinthe and be trying to impress the guys around me, but then I won't be able to give out DSO candy on that flight, 'cause then she'd for sure know I'm sexist, but maybe I can find pictures of some hot dudes for her, show her that I'm an equal opportunity objectifier, it really isn't a gendered thing, it just so happens that most of the crews are straight men; that isn't on me, I'm just trying to bring some joy into the world, and gods why did I drink all that absinthe, I don't even like the taste of licorice—or is it licquorice?—whatever, it's fucking gross and I'd much rather have had some scotch, why didn't that gunner buy something better—oh, right, he said something about it being "real" absinthe, some shit about hallucinating, but like, would they really just be able to sell that in a normal shop, seems kind of dicey, and how much do you even have to drink before you start tripping, am I gonna be seeing shit on the flight, fuck I hope not, maybe I'll just be able to pass out instead.

And then you pass out, and wake up in Bangor, Maine, for a bit, and then, finally, you're on the last leg and you make your way back to Florida, and now the true celebrating can begin. Between the Fourth and CTO (commander's time off, akin to the Army's more well-known rest and recuperation, or R&R), I don't remember very much of the first half of July 2011. There was a lunch at the Dancin' Iguana, which I got to wear my new white linen pants to. There were a lot of congratulations, people from my squadron excited that I had finally deployed, or even more excited that I had done some shooting on my deployment. But mostly, there was drinking. We did a lot of this drinking at a bar in Destin called the Red Door Saloon. The Red Door was a beloved institution, as they had good bartenders, a decent selection of beer, and no walls, just open access to the water, which meant you could smoke and drink to your heart's delight (or, I guess, dismay, but who asked the heart anyway?). It was crowded, especially in the summer, and more often than not you wound up stuck against one of the side railings separating the bar from the docks, but this was okay, because it was only a couple steps or one drunken lunge back up to the bar to secure yourself another beverage. One of the nights around the Fourth, I think, or maybe the next weekend, not that it matters, really, all of that time being even more interchangeable than the blurred together days back in Kandahar, but one of those nights, I was pressed up against a railing with James and his fiancée, shooting the shit, generally engaged in revelry and merrymaking, relishing my newfound belongingness. An awkward pause came up at the end of some story, when we were all still laughing, but in that half-hearted way one laughs when one isn't sure of where to go from there, or what to say next. Instead of playing along, though, James just stopped laughing and looked at me for what felt like an uncomfortably long time.

I wasn't sure what to do with this moment. James was not a

person who engaged in ridiculous macho shit like stare-downs, and beyond normal joke-making I'd never known him to really fuck with anyone. But then his face softened, and he stopped looking *at* me, and more looked to me, before he said, "You look different."

"I lost some weight. Y'know, no booze, lots of gym time."

"No, that's not it."

"I probably need a haircut, sort of put it off for a while."

"No, you look *different*. You look like more of a man."

He turned to his fiancée and said, "Doesn't he?" To which she replied with a smile, a nod, and a soft, kind "Yeah, he does."

This was a moment I had been craving for years. I was twenty-two, fully grown, but so often treated like a child. Women would be interested in talking to me, until they asked my age, and then would almost universally let the conversation trail off, no longer interested. Other aircrew would talk about me like I knew nothing of use beyond Pashto, like I had no life experience. My buddy Dex had once texted me some random praise while I was at DLI for Pashto, and given that it was a Friday I was fairly drunk and nearly texted him back the opening lyrics to The National song "Baby We'll Be Fine":

All night I lay on my pillow and pray
For my boss to stop me in the hallway
Lay my head on his shoulder and say
"Son, I've been hearing good things"

For James, who was almost ten years older than me—a true elder statesman to my mind—who had deployed who knows how many times, who had lived in Europe, who was overwhelmingly *cool*—for him to say that I looked like a man was exactly the validation I so desperately craved. It was early in the night, though, and because I hadn't yet had enough beer to build up any vulnerability and genuineness, I responded with "It's the dead look behind the eyes, right?"

This was, mostly, a joke. I didn't know whether I did in fact have a dead look to my eyes, and I didn't yet feel like I should have such a look. It just seemed like a good joke to make. But I have this hypothesis that all jokes have some foundation in fact, or at least honesty, even when the joke-teller doesn't know or isn't willing to admit it. Particularly for men, these jokes are a repercussion-free way of expressing at least some of their emotions, but with the safety net of comedy underneath them. In those moments when you feel seen, or heard, or otherwise stripped bare of whatever defenses you thought were protecting you, when it's too painful or embarrassing to confess, but you still want to acknowledge, however dismissively, this recognition of your self, a joke is the only thing that will do.

But James fucked up my attempt to (un)acknowledge my pain by saying, "Yeah. You've got the thousand-yard stare now."

I had started to laugh when he said yeah, assuming that he was going to do the polite thing, or at least the thing everyone else did whenever trauma was brought up, and respond to my joke with another, but when he got to the thousand-yard stare bit, whatever hope I had of moving past this moment of reality faded along with my smile. James was a Buddhist, and not in the way that someone who takes an Eastern philosophy class in college and learns about the Eight-Fold Path and nirvana is a Buddhist, but in the way that someone gives up meat and fifteen years later gets irate when a houseguest cooks chicken in one of his pans, that pan now being permanently sullied such that he'll have to replace it. A true autodidact, James had found Buddhism and fully embraced its teachings. He didn't evangelize, comment on anyone else's beliefs, or get exasperated when someone asked him about his beliefs for the fourth time, said person having not bothered to listen to his explanations the first three.

He also did a job that involved killing a large number of people. His work was different than mine, and to my knowledge he'd never killed people the way I had, in that the planes he flew on didn't shoot the missiles/bullets that did the killing, they just helped direct the ordnance, but to me, he'd been directly involved in or responsible for far more death than I had. But this didn't seem to bother him. He told war stories the way most everyone did, used the same irreverent and dehumanizing language that made it so we weren't killing people, merely enemies, and was otherwise a happy guy who had no qualms with what he did for a living.

Or did he? He didn't say you've got *that* thousand-yard stare now. He said you've got *the* thousand-yard stare. This was not likely an accident; James had once explained to me the difference in pronunciation of merry, marry, and Mary, and was as nerdy about his language skills as I was about mine. Words weren't accidents for him. For him to say *the* thousand-yard stare meant that he wasn't telling me that he was recognizing something that he had seen in so many others. He was telling me that he had looked into the same distance.

I spent the next couple of weeks relaxing, building a bed I'd bought online and had shipped to my house while deployed, playing video games, seeing friends, and drinking. At some point my unit told me that I was due for language training in Dari, which seemed wrong, but then it really had been almost two years since I graduated, and Pashto didn't count toward maintaining my Dari as far as the Air Force was concerned. More specifically, I had to attend a Significant Language Training Event, or SLTE. For this, I would be headed to Offutt Air Force Base, in Omaha, Nebraska. Being told I was going to Omaha in two weeks didn't elicit quite the same feelings I'd had the year before when I was told I was going back to Monterey, but I was excited that I'd get to see a number of my friends from language school who were stationed up there.

I knew from Facebook and texting, and even running into a couple guys out in Kandahar, that my former classmates' lives had become very different from mine. Turns out Dari was just as useless on the aircraft they'd all been assigned to, the Rivet Joint, as it was in AFSOC. The difference was that no one was going to teach them Pashto. They'd all done one deployment on the RJ out at The Deid for a few months, if only so that the Air Force could say they'd finished training them as linguists. But after that, all but one of them got tasked into doing the same job James did: TSO (tactical systems operator, pronounced "tizzo"). Once upon a time, like back when James first started doing it, TSOing was a sexy job. It's highly classified, to the point that even describing what they do could be seen as sharing state secrets. Fortunately, the Air Force has to publish information about most of their career fields. In the official, unclassified document that describes the career of a TSO, it states that they are responsible for the following duties:

Process intelligence information in an airborne environment. Operate assigned intelligence systems and mission equipment. Use operator workstations, graphical displays, recording devices and related equipment. Field and operate sophisticated comput- erized radio receiver suites on various strategic and tactical ISR platforms. Conduct environmental surveys of radio frequency spectrum. Annotate electromagnetic events, measures parameters and compares results to previously catalogued signals to determine likely emitter source. Operate direction finding/precision geolocation equipment. Analyze structure and content of machine-based communications. Digitally archive key events for follow-on processing. Extract essential elements of information for reportable significance. Disseminate threat warning information to affected entities via established channels. Maintain logs to document mission results. Prepare in-flight and post-mission reports.

If your eyes glazed over reading this, I understand. I put it all there, though, because it comes from an unclassified, government-sanctioned publication, and no one can accuse me of sharing state secrets if all I'm doing is copying and pasting the words from an unclassified government document.

There's a brilliance to the language used in this document, in that it genuinely outlines exactly what a TSO does, but these details only make sense if you're already relatively familiar with the career, and/or you know what to look for in all that jargon. The three sentences in the middle are the important bit, and I find them easier to understand if you separate them:

> Annotate electromagnetic events, measures parameters and compares results to previously catalogued signals to determine likely emitter source.
>
> Operate direction finding/precision geolocation equipment.
>
> Analyze structure and content of machine-based communications.

So, a TSO uses a database of information about things that happen in the electromagnetic spectrum, or signals, to figure out what sort of device, or source, is responsible for sending those signals. They can pinpoint where that signal came from by operating their precision geolocation equipment. They can also analyze structure and content—which sounds a lot like a legalese way of saying "read"—of machine-based communications, which could be something like your Internet of Things refrigerator sending a message to your Alexa, or a computer receiving a message from a router, or a cell phone receiving a text message from another cell phone. Who's to say? Machine-based communications encompasses any instance of a machine communicating with another machine, and in the modern age there's a lot of that.

With that breakdown, it makes some sense that this would be considered a cool, or sexy, or interesting job. My understanding is that when it first got started, being selected to do it was a badge of honor, the deployments were to interesting places, and the work was, or at least it felt, important. You may note that this is the same story that was once told about becoming a DSO. Funny, that.

But by the time my friends were doing it, TSOs were a dime a dozen, they most definitely went to places that were not at all interesting, and almost by virtue of how many of them were doing it, the work either wasn't, or at least didn't feel, important at all. For many people, some of my friends included, this was still an upgrade from being a linguist, as doing the TSO mission doesn't require the use of language skills. If you didn't like listening to insert-foreign-language-here in the first place, then you definitely didn't like listening to it in the back of an RJ, so becoming a TSO was a great alternative to being stuck flying twelve- or sixteen-hour missions in the RJ (TSO missions were much shorter).

I knew what my friends did, all the classified details included, as Hurby had many, many TSOs. My friends did not know what

I did, as Offutt didn't have many former DSOs, and the few they did have (1) likely never deployed as a DSO (why would they be back at Offutt if they were actually useful?) and (2) likely had many sticks up their asses that prevented them from describing what DSOs do, under some nonsense guise of "classification." I was stickless, so we excitedly traded stories.

I found that it was easier to talk about missions and battles and firefights when I was back in America than it was when I was in Afghanistan. Retelling war stories, which can often result in reliving them, is a lot more fun, or at least a lot less stressful, when you're not currently in a war zone. If I tell you a war story at home, there's no way for it to become true, as stories are only real in the place where they happened. Anywhere else, they're just memories. This had the strange effect of helping me better understand why the Taliban might not want to spend all of their time talking about battles, because unlike me, when they went home, it would be to the next village over, where the stories were alive, not six thousand miles away, where they faded into phantoms.

My friends mostly talked about all the working out they got to do, which, like, same, but that wasn't the key takeaway from my deployment. I couldn't sort whether they were more detached than I was, or just less invested.

This didn't matter, though; it was just great seeing my friends again, even if we were, perhaps, a little different now. But after my first day of class I was just as excited that I would get to spend an entire month back in a Dari classroom. For the Air Force, an SLTE is significant because it requires 150 hours of language immersion, which conveniently works out to twenty 7.5-hour days. For me, this SLTE was significant because it reminded me that Dari was my first academic love. I hadn't realized how much I had missed my first (well, second, but first non-English) language in all of its nonviolent, organized, logical beauty. And to my pleasant surprise, I still knew it! Pashto and the Taliban hadn't wiped it out of my head; they'd just distracted me from it.

I could still listen to and read the news, get most questions about what I'd heard or read correct, and try to charm my professor with some bullshit about the technicalities and semantics of whatever I got wrong. I still had to be told to slow down, to be patient, and to not talk over others. In a wonderful inversion of my second stint at DLI, I also now had to be told to stop using Pashto words in place of Dari ones. I'd come full circle, and it was magnificent.

And at night I could use my sweet per diem to explore Omaha, a surprisingly great food destination. I could use that money to justify going to the Dundee Dell, aka the bar possessing the world's second largest private scotch collection outside of Scotland, to take part in their biannual mega scotch tasting, during which I would get to taste ten scotches, none of which were younger than me, culminating in a surprisingly large pour of 1964 Black Bowmore that normally went for $200 a dram, making the entire event, really, a steal. And I could go to the Max, Omaha's premier gay bar. I could even volunteer to DD for my friends some of those nights, seeing as how I had just spent the prior month drinking, and I had to take a physical fitness test when I got back to Hurby before I deployed again. Which meant I could dance like an idiot, albeit a sober idiot, secure in the knowledge that this was not a place to get laid, it was simply a place to have fun, except when I stopped caring about being seen as attractive or coordinated it turned out I became more attractive and coordinated. Such that women approached me, demanding to know my sexuality before dragging me off to dance, or in at least one case to have sex in some darkened corner of the club, or in another case to wind up the only male allowed on a bachelorette party bus driving through downtown Omaha, hanging on to a stripper pole with one hand and drinking tequila straight from a bottle with the other, while getting grinded (ground?) on by the woman who had picked me up.

Omaha, despite its reputation of being in Nebraska, was turning out to be a fun time. But then I went out with Ben and his wife one night, and we ate too much and drank too much. Darcy was a Farsi linguist, and she and I spent the first half of the evening talking in Persian, the most memorable part of which was a discussion of bulimia, and at some point we just kept saying استفراغ, because in English it became somewhat onomatopoeic, *estafraagh* sounding, at least to us, very much like the sound someone would make while vomiting. Ben was wondering why we kept saying such a specific word, suspicious of our nonsense, so we just changed the subject—how we went from that to threesomes I'll never remember—and he let it go. (Having spent an entire year in language school with me, Ben knew how much I loved using my Dari, how happy and goofy I was when I got to play with words and sounds in another language.)

Someone had the great idea that we should head across the river to Council Bluffs, Omaha's twin city in Iowa, where Ben had grown up and still had a number of friends, and where you could get a beer for $1.50, because Iowa. Things get a bit hazy from there, but I remember winding up at his friend's house, sitting on the porch, smoking a clove, wondering where I was, and just feeling . . . not nothing, but like nothing? That night is the first I can (sort of) remember wishing I didn't exist, if only because then I wouldn't have to feel anything at all.

But in the morning I was fine; it didn't matter why I'd felt that, I'd had so much to drink that anything I'd been thinking was total nonsense, and everything was fine. In another month I'd be back in Kandahar, and there was no booze there, so really, I'd be fine.

It wasn't until I got back to Hurby, again, that something changed in my thoughts about going back to Kandahar. It was subtle, this shift, in that I didn't not want to go, as that would have been a ridiculous thought to have, for so very many reasons. But I wasn't excited. I figured some of this was the novelty wearing off. I wasn't as stressed about not fucking up on the way out there, now that I'd already figured out The Deid and all its nonsense. And I (technically) had enough hours to be an instructor by now, so the flying itself would be old hat. I wasn't so worried about the Dari course messing up my Pashto; if anything, getting coined again made me feel like I still had the whole language thing down (I had done so well in the class that I was deemed the best student in the schoolhouse that month, which wasn't quite DLI commandant–level praise, but it felt good). And yet, something had me unsettled.

I couldn't articulate it then, but now I wonder how much of this was a result of spending a month focused on and thinking in a language that hadn't been pushed into a constant state of adversariness. We listened to all kinds of news programs about war and fighting and the Taliban, but it was all very objective, and somehow detached. Dari couldn't kill anyone.

There was also, by this point, a pattern in our squadron, such that almost every DSO before me who had gone to Afghanistan had eventually gone a little, or a lot, crazy. Some of the madness seemed to come from the length of their deployments. All those guys had done five months at Bagram for their first deployment, and my understanding was that somewhere around the fifteen-week mark everything got a little weird. The combination of the lack of a sleep schedule, not knowing what day it was, and just the drudgery and physical toll of flying added up. There was also the issue of hours, in that during the last month of the deployment someone might only fly once or twice a week, because they would otherwise exceed their hours limit. At first, this can be nice, in that you're not flying as much, but then you're sitting in Afghanistan, being useless, doing nothing. This is not a good feeling for someone who spent multiple years of their life training to do a job. Then there was the issue of the number of deployments. After their first they only got a few months home before they had to go back out, which, of course, was a violation of the Air Force mandated 1:1 dwell time (the ratio of time between deployments and being home), but, of course, this was (illegally) ignored because of our "mission critical" status.

I say every DSO who had gone to Afghanistan, not every Pashto DSO, because the 25th Intelligence Squadron, our unit, had deployed multiple linguists who had not gone to language school for Pashto, who could not pass the DLPT in Pashto, who would be the first to tell you that they did not speak Pashto. The 25th felt otherwise. They felt that by putting people through a turbo course a few hours a day with one instructor for a few months, they had adequately trained them in the language (Taylor and I got seven hours a day with many instructors for six months at DLI). As far as the 25th was concerned, these Farsis and Daris were now Pashtos. Of the ones who had actually been trained in Pashto at DLI, maybe half of them could pass the DLPT, which is to say, could meet the

Air Force and Department of Defense's definition of proficiency in the language. This is no comment on those men's intelligence. The DLPT pass rate for Pashto at the time hovered around 30 or 40 percent; it's a difficult language that is formally taught in very few places outside of Afghanistan (and maybe Pakistan). DLI likely has, or at least had, the largest repository of Pashto learning material for non-natives in the entire world. And it wasn't a large repository. The instructors may have been native speakers, but that doesn't mean they were formally trained in education, language or otherwise. Hell, one of my Pashto instructors was a twenty-four-year-old freshly arrived from Kandahar whose English was such that she couldn't explain grammar to us without using Pashto. But her husband was related to someone in the department, and she needed out of Afghanistan, so she got the job.

It made sense that the guys who didn't speak the language would go nuts. They were forced to try and do a thing that they were incapable of doing through no fault of their own (they were all, every single one of them, brilliant humans). When they couldn't perform, people died. Sometimes a lot of people. A lot of Americans. It didn't matter that if they hadn't been there those people would likely have died anyway. That's not how it works. They were there, and they couldn't save them.

What was more worrisome was that the guys who were good at Pashto, really good, better than me by far, were also losing it. More slowly than the turbos, and they were still deploying, but they weren't healthy. There was a running joke that Conor was now going through alcohol withdrawal the first few days of his deployments, except maybe it wasn't a joke, because he drank as much as he could every night that he was home, and even with our limited dwell time, that gave him enough nights to regain his dependence. Kasady was the most unsettling. He might have been the only "real" DSO among us, having spent time in Omaha flying those long-ass RJ missions, listening to Pashto for hundreds of hours, but with the ability to stop, pause, rewind, re-listen, ask other linguists if what he thought he was hearing was correct, and overall hone his skills. It was well known that he was the second-best Pashto linguist in the airborne community (he had no qualms with this ranking, and readily admitted how incomprehensibly intelligent the first-best was). He had requested orders to Hurby, had worked hard to become a DSO. But he too was disappearing into his drinks.

None of them proselytized, tried to convince me that I too would lose it. As bitter and unhappy as they were, they weren't so far gone that they tried to bring anyone else down with them. They were honest, unflinchingly so, about what they had seen, the things they had done, or worse, been unable to do. But they never exaggerated, or inflated, or tried to make things sound worse. They didn't have to.

Before my deployment, when they would tell me these things, I was also told how incredible being a DSO would be, how important, how badass, by our instructors and by older DSOs. What I didn't understand then was how little these people knew of what they were talking about. The only ones who stood any chance of ever having been on an aircraft that had killed anyone were the Arabs, and even then, Iraq wasn't Afghanistan, at least not from the air. The rest of them—the fucking Serbs, Koreans, Chinese, Spanish, Russians—the fucking *Farsis* who decided not to go through the turbo course despite years of talking about how incredible it is to be a DSO, these were the people who had been preaching the gospel of the DSO as deity.

What I was coming to see was that it really was just like a religion for them, in that they relied on faith and imagination. None of them had seen God, but they knew he was real. None of them had killed anyone, but they could envision just how good it would feel every time. I didn't blame them for this. Most people want to believe in something, or someone. Belief makes the world that much smaller, that much easier to comprehend. Belief allows for the abstraction of killing, the continued confidence in the *idea* of it, rather than the persistent precarity that comes with the actual event of it; it was very easy to celebrate something you had never done. And it was far, far easier to revel in killing if you had no blood on your hands, and no dead men in your dreams. Before I deployed, I didn't have the ability to tell the difference between what the disciples felt was true and what the apostates knew was true. But if Mark Twain (or whoever) was right and reading the Bible is the best cure for Christianity, then maybe actually killing someone is the best cure for wanting to.

But none of this mattered because the next flight east would be here in a few weeks and I had to get current again: fly a training flight with an instructor because I hadn't flown since I got back from Afghanistan, do all the paperwork and trainings to deploy, find someone who would drive my truck once or twice while I was gone. The one upside of going back out so fast was that most of the paperwork was still valid. Little victories and all. And it would be better this time, not being the new guy, being more comfortable with the planes and the equipment. Maybe I'd split my flights between the U-boats and the Whiskeys. Be nice to be back on a gunship. To be home.

KANDAHAR, OR LISTENING TO AFGHANS

AUGUST AND SEPTEMBER OF 2011 had been a rough couple of months for the guys who were out there. At the beginning of August, a Chinook with the call sign Extortion 17 got shot down, and all thirty-eight of the people on it died. This was the deadliest day for U.S. forces in Afghanistan, and it would make August 2011 the deadliest month of the war. No DSO was on the mission (that I'm aware of), but being out there when something like that happens is still draining. It's not like we forget about death, but we do try and ignore it. It's hard to ignore that much.

So when I got back to Kandahar, the guy I was replacing, Vince, asked if I didn't mind immediately flying that night, as that would mean he didn't have to. I technically had enough time to get my crew rest, and if I got myself on nights now, I might be able to stay on the U-boats for a while. Unfortunately, when I got out to the flight line, there was a SNAFU with my equipment, and I had to take myself off the flight. This was not a good look in the eyes of the gunship guys. It also meant that I had not, in fact, got myself set up on nights, and the next day it was decided that since I had all those Whiskey hours I ought to go ahead and hop back on them for the foreseeable future.

I was less than happy about this, as I wasn't looking forward to doing more fucking recon, and convoy escorts, and glorified babysitting. Silly shit, like the time that an MRAP (Mine-Resistant Ambush Protected, think big-ass armored truck) had been damaged and needed to be towed back to base. It was off in a ditch, and the other MRAPs and trucks that had been with it couldn't pull it out, so they had to call in a wrecker (think big-ass tow truck). It took a while for the wrecker to get out there, so we flew in circles with our thumbs up our asses, shooting the shit. Fortunately, no more attacks happened, the Taliban not being all that interested in a busted truck. Eventually, the wrecker got there, did all its maneuvering, and started to pull the MRAP out of the ditch. I don't know anything about towing, so I'm not sure exactly what happened, but the end result was that the wrecker was now, well, wrecked. It too had flipped into the ditch, alongside the MRAP.

Apparently, a wrecker can't be towed by another normal wrecker, and you need some sort of super-wrecker to unfuck such a situation, all of which felt a little bit like the old "can God make a weight so big that he can't lift it?" joke. It turned out that there aren't very many of these super-wreckers, 'cause like, how often does someone wreck a wrecker, and the nearest one was even farther away than the first wrecker had been. More hours, deeper thumbs. The super-wrecker—which near as any of us could tell was just a crane by another name—did show up, but by then we were out of fuel and had to head back to Kandahar. On the way back we kept listening to the channel we'd been on, and we took bets on how long it would take the super-wrecker to wreck itself, mostly because we wanted to know if there was such a thing as a super-duper-wrecker. By the time we landed, the super-wrecker was still upright, which was probably for the best, as it meant no one got hurt, but damn if that wouldn't have been a perfect metaphor for us being in Afghanistan.

This silliness turned out to be an anomaly, though. While I was back in 'Murica, the Whiskeys had gotten a better reputation. They still weren't a gunship, not in the gunship guys' eyes, or in the eyes of a lot of the guys on the ground, but word had gotten out that there was a daytime pseudo-gunship, and if needed, it could fuck shit up.

It was also now better known that the Whiskeys had DSOs. Daytime DSOs. Guys on the ground love DSOs. When we showed up to missions and radioed down to the JTAC that a DSO was on board, they often got audibly excited. They had access to other versions of us, other linguists in other places who could offer up translation of enemy communications, but those linguists could be thousands of miles away, hearing things on a delay. The JTACs liked having us there, directly overhead, not necessarily in the shit with them, but a hell of a lot closer. Sometimes they had specific requests for things they wanted us to listen out for, and occasionally they would ask if we'd heard anything of interest, either in times of extreme boredom, or in those moments of intense excitement. But for the most part they trusted us to do our thing, to decide for ourselves what information was important, and what needed to be passed on.

On a mission outside of Kandahar, in more or less a suburb of the city proper, the JTAC was more excited than usual to hear that there was a DSO on-board. He'd been in the area for weeks, or months—too long, in my opinion, as he sounded a little on edge—and he had built up a strong knowledge of the network of baddies around him (there were no goodies). He knew, or at least suspected, based on intelligence he'd received, that someone was planning some fuckery in the coming days. What he didn't know was what exactly this fuckery was going to entail, or who precisely would be carrying it out. His hope was that I could help him figure that out.

All right, I thought, *not really my bag, generic intel gathering, but I can give it a go.* Being so near to Kandahar, in the middle of the day, I didn't expect to hear anything of interest, or anything I could really pin down.

"Ay, brother, how are you?"

"Good, brother. You?"

"Praise God, I'm good."

"God is great."

"How's your uncle? Is he better?"

"No, he's still ill."

"God willing, he'll recover."

"God willing."

"How's your cousin Najibullah?"

"Ah, he's good. He—"

I moved on to the next conversation, confident these guys would just keep shooting the shit.

"All this traffic, it's so terrible."

"So terrible. I couldn't get anywhere yesterday."

Yup, yeah, traffic near Kandahar is lame, guess you should get an earlier start.

"Hey, brother, this is good weather today!"

"Thank God, yes, it is."

"What are you doing later?"

"God willing, I'll go see Jaan Mohammed later."

"Good, good."

All right, cool, maybe that's a baddie, I'll come back to that.

"Ay, Asad, where are you?"

"I'm here, where are you?"

This was one of the more frustrating aspects of listening to these snippets of conversation, dropping in and out of them like the auditory version of *Nightcrawler*. Maybe this guy said where "here" was earlier. Maybe he just meant he was "here" like how you're "here" for a roll call, simply acknowledging his presence (this was a common occurrence, this sort of check-in). Or maybe he meant he was exactly where he was supposed to be, given earlier plans.

"Good, good, are you ready for tomorrow?"

"Yes, yes, I'm ready. I'm excited."

Okay. Bad guys. Great.

Anyone planning anything a day in advance was an automatic threat. This was not a particularly nuanced or intelligent assumption to make, but we always made it. Plans were for the Taliban. Everyone else just figured it out on the fly.

I'd been taking my notes, writing down what I wanted to go back to, what I thought was important, who I figured was worth listening to. I could do this for hours before anything useful came up, and often did. But after maybe twenty minutes the JTAC called up, asking what I'd heard so far. I didn't feel that I had anything of interest to relay, but he insisted, so I let him know that a couple of guys were talking about some plans for tomorrow, and that I was monitoring them.

"Who?"

"Uh, two suspicious guys. Possible Talibs."

"No, *who*? What are their names?"

"Motherfucker, what?" I didn't say this to the JTAC, just to some of the crew on my plane, which they laughed at, thinking I was joking. I wasn't. I was annoyed. What the fuck did this dude want names for? Their names didn't matter, not in my work. On nearly every other mission I had flown, names were only important for keeping track of the different guys talking all over each other. I might write down those names in the moment, but they weren't of any use to me once the mission was over, as the next day more often than not I was flying somewhere new a few hundred miles away. The names also weren't of any use to the JTACs; they didn't care what the asshat shooting at them called himself, they just wanted to know where said asshat was shooting from, if said asshat had any friends coming, and whether we could help kill said asshat.

This guy, though, was adamant that I tell him the names. More than that, he didn't want me to editorialize what I was hearing, he wanted strict translation.

"Recoil, I need their names, and exactly what they're saying."

"Who the fuck does he think I am? His personal interpreter?" By now most of the crew were gleefully enjoying my rage. I was always big and loud, prone to complaining, if not outright whining, but always about dumb shit. They'd never seen me so mad about my actual job. I'd never been so mad about my actual job.

"DSO, pilot, can you do what he says?"

"Pilot, I can, it's just ridiculous for him to ask for it."

"Do it."

Normally, I'd be all for arguing with him, or anyone this side of colonel, but there was something in his tone that reminded me that unless they're doing something that's going to get you killed, you can't really argue with pilots. They're in charge.

This was a disorienting thing at times. The military, I'm told, is built on its rank structure. This structure is very important. Lower-ranking enlisted must respect and defer to higher-ranking enlisted, who must respect and defer to all officers, who also have their echelons. It doesn't matter if a brand-new twenty-two-year-old lieutenant tells an E-9 (chief master sergeant) who's been in for twenty-five years to do something that E-9 knows is incredibly stupid; technically, the E-9 has to do it. And if that lieutenant is a real shithead, he (or she, but it's usually a he being a shithead) knows that he has this legal power and will use it. I say I'm told this structure exists, because I almost never saw it in my day-to-day job. In the linguist community, rank is less important. Most of the Pashto DSOs, myself included, were senior airmen on their first deployments. Or their second. Or third. There's no such thing as a commissioned linguist; there were a few officers who were prior enlisted and even a couple who had been linguists, but for the most part, they only had a theoretical understanding of what we did, and so often had to defer to our expertise, resulting in a diminution of distinction. In the flying community, rank is subservient to safety; it doesn't do to have people getting gun-shy about speaking up to the officer who's about to fly the plane into the side of a mountain. In the Special Operations community, rank all but disappears. The JTAC we were talking to could be a lowly E-5 for all we knew, but he sure as shit could tell the major flying the plane what to do. I, in my ankle-high E-4-ness, had been forced to tell officers that they were wrong or that they needed to stop talking so I could listen.

It wasn't that I felt like this was some sort of power I had, and that it had gone to my head, it was just that what I did was so far removed from what most people I flew with understood that I had to assert myself. My instinct had become to argue when someone told me how to do my job. Unfortunately, the pilot was right, in that this was a thing I was (in theory) capable of doing, this detailed translation, and if the JTAC felt that it was important that I do so, well, that was it.

"DSO?"

"I . . . Yes, sir. I'll do it."

Begrudgingly, I started working the way the JTAC wanted me to. Some of my reticence had been due to my dislike of being told what to do or how to do it, but a not small part was a fear of my inability to do what this guy was asking of me. At this point, I had hundreds of hours of translation under my belt, but it was DSO translation, not real linguist translation. Normally, I would hear what an Afghan said in Pashto, write down a near approximation of it in English, and then tell someone else, either the guy on the ground or another crewmember on the plane, my interpretation of it (said crewmember could then relay it to the appropriate interested party). This was its own skill, this ability to compress large amounts of information and turn it into small, easily understood sentences, in near real time. (I can't do actual simultaneous translation, like you see or hear at the UN; that shit blows my mind.) But this skill meant I could leave out extraneous details, like names, which could be annoying to tease out and keep track of in any formal way (I kept track of them in my head, but by no means in any way that could readily be told to someone else). Mr. Super JTAC here didn't just want names, he wanted word-for-word translation.

I gave it to him. Like the child I was, I figured I'd just tell him fucking *everything* and he'd eventually get bored, or overwhelmed, or both, and would back off. And, like the child I was, I figured wrong. He was stoked.

> "Recoil, this is great stuff. I know that guy, he's the local organizer."
> "Recoil, Gul Khan hit us last month. Keep track of him."
> "Recoil, say again, he's going where? Okay, look over there, see if anyone else joins."

The more I told him, the happier he got, and the more I understood why he wanted all these details. Because he had been there so long, this guy had built up a vast knowledge of all the local actors. I don't remember him not knowing a single name I passed down. He knew where these guys lived, who they saw and talked to on a regular basis, what they did for work. He knew their friends, their family members, their daily habits.

This was a whole new world of intelligence to me. I knew, in a sort of technical way, that this was the kind of work that a lot of other linguists did, either in the air on an RJ, or on the ground at some base in Afghanistan, or back in America. They used all this seemingly useless detail to build up these complicated networks of information. I knew that the goal of this was to prevent bad guys from doing bad things. And I knew that sometimes it even worked. But I hadn't ever been a part of this work, hadn't seen how detailed it could get, how much information we had on people who, to me, were little more than random shitheads.

The mission went on for what felt like ten hours. It was maybe half that long in reality. We couldn't fly for ten hours, even if we (or the JTAC) wanted to, but by the end of four or five hours I was exhausted. If this is what it felt like to be on an RJ, thank Zeus I wasn't doing that shit. And like, what the fuck was the point? We didn't shoot anyone; there was no way we were going to accurately get a missile into such a dense area, and even if we could, the collateral damage would be way too high (by this point; if we'd been a year or two earlier it might not have mattered). When we told the JTAC that we had to return to base, he was bummed, but he understood.

"Thanks, Recoil. That was great intel."

In my overly persecuted mind, he was making fun of us, and mostly me, because I couldn't see the point of what we had done. Great, you have some better knowledge of the plans of a bunch of fuckstick wannabe Talibs. La-di-fuckin'-da. You gonna schwack any of 'em? This gonna stop them from shooting at you? Is anything going to change? Great intel, my fuckin' ass.

When I got back to base, back to our office, excited to piss and moan about my terrible fate as this guy's personal Pashto primate, the guy I was complaining to quickly explained to me why I was wrong. He told me how I wasn't thinking strategically, just tactically.

"How many TICs have you been to?"

"I dunno. A lot. Thirty? Forty?"

"That's not that many. But okay, and how many of those were just out-of-nowhere attacks?"

"No idea. We just showed up to most of them."

"All right, well, I'll give you a hint, it's not that many. If you'd been overhead before the shit went down, you probably would have heard something that could've been used to warn them. And even if you hadn't, just knowing who's in the area plotting shit is useful. That JTAC *knew* those guys, man. He has to."

I didn't know what to do with this advice. Maybe there was some sound reasoning behind the old requirement to have a DSO do the normal linguist gig before they found themselves in the middle of actual battles. I knew from Taylor that the gunship folk were more familiar with this sort of intel, as they flew a lot more snatch-and-grab missions (going into a place in the middle of the night and abducting/capturing/obtaining suspected bad guys), which relied on networks of contacts and information. But snatch-and-grabs are very rarely done during the day, and so I had pretty minimal experience with them.

And even though, in theory, I could have contributed to these processes with what I heard during the day, in practice it wasn't that straightforward. Our technologic capabilities as DSOs were too limited for me to provide the complex information that a plane like a Rivet Joint could, and, this JTAC notwithstanding, no one ever asked for it. But it seemed that our missions were changing. More and more, daytime DSOing was becoming some strange, liminal state.

Halfway through my second deployment, the Whiskeys had also, finally, gotten an actual gun. A small one, all of 30mm, but it was an honest-to-god gun, none of this wannabe Predator missile bullshit. Allegedly, it was an improvement over both the 25 and the 40 on the gunships, as it was electronically mounted, instead of hydraulically, which was supposed to mean that it was so accurate that instead of putting a bullet through a basketball hoop from ten thousand feet, it could hammer a nail into the ground from eighteen thousand.

The presence of this gun had a profound effect on the crews of the Whiskeys. It didn't matter that we couldn't yet fire it during a mission. We could use it on the practice range outside of Kandahar, which meant we were that much closer to using it on some bad guys. Just imagine, a gunship shooting an actual gun during the day. I'm pretty sure every time the new guys flew, they had half-chubs at the thought of it.

The Whiskeys were becoming the new hotness. On my first deployment, we were usually just tasked to whichever flight didn't conflict with our crew rest. Now, as more commanders became aware of the Whiskeys, and the presence of DSOs on the Whiskeys, we started being requested for specific missions. But there was no way we could fly on every mission that wanted us; there simply weren't enough DSOs to go around.

As far as we could tell, the people requesting us had no idea that Pashto varies massively depending on where you are in Afghanistan. This was strange, or, really, plain ignorant, as anyone with a cursory knowledge of the language should know that at baseline it has two main dialects that pronounce entire letters differently. Hell, some of the people who speak it don't even call it Pashto. They call it Pakhto. The second letter in the word پښتو, that little collection of three nubs with the one dot above it and one below it, ښ, can be pronounced as either a *sh* sound (though you have to curl your tongue to the top of your mouth to get the *sh* just right) or a *kh* sound (same tongue movement). There's another letter that on one side of the country is pronounced as a *g* and on the other side as a *zh*. The "o" in Pashto isn't always an o, sometimes it's a u, as in Pashtu/Pakhtu.

And those are just the two major divisions, Western and Eastern Pashto/Pakhto/Pashtu/Pakhtu. Realistically there are dozens of dialects, some of which aren't understood all that well even by native Pashto speakers. So, to expect us to be able to fly over bumfuck Khost and have any clue as to what the bad guys were saying was to have no idea of how the language worked. Which, I guess, we shouldn't have been surprised by. Unrealistic expectations being the norm in Afghanistan.

Flying in places where we couldn't understand anything that was being said was both a serious waste of us as a resource and, more importantly, at least to us, boring as fuck. Like anything that you do every day, even flying eventually loses its excitement. After enough missions, all you're doing is sitting in a tiny chair for six or seven hours waiting for something to happen. The fact that you're fifteen or twenty thousand feet in the air traveling at two hundred plus miles an hour falls by the wayside. Those hours are short if you're busy listening to guys planning attacks or actually fighting. They're a little longer if all you're doing is listening to them bullshit. But those six or seven hours feel like an eternity if what you're supposed to be listening to is utterly incomprehensible. What's a DSO to do?

There's the tried-and-true option of doing your own bull-shitting with the crew. But sometimes they're busy, or you aren't feeling social. In which case you can bring a book, either paper or electronic. But then it might look like you aren't taking your work seriously, and that's no good. Fortunately, some enterprising individual had devised a way for us to play old-school Nintendo games. *Tecmo Bowl, Super Mario Bros., Mega Man*, all the classics. I'm not sure how they managed this, and I never cared to know, as it wasn't exactly kosher, but most every DSO knew about it, and it was tacitly approved, or at least accepted. This was probably the safest way to fill the time, as it allowed you to look like you were working, and if you suddenly really did need to work, it was easy to switch back.

Or we could just fly on actually interesting missions.

During my second deployment, I was given the dubious position of NCOIC, or noncommissioned officer in charge, despite the fact that I was in fact not an NCO, or really IC of anything. I was, however, the only DSO in Kandahar that month who already had one deployment under his belt, making me de facto the only one who knew how anything worked. This position meant very, very little, but it did give me the opportunity to bring up the issue of language variation to the Whiskeys' mission commander, Major Stokes. I told him that (1) we didn't want to look like so much dead weight to the crews, and (2) it was super-fucking-boring to go on these missions where we couldn't understand much beyond yes and no. He agreed to let me and the other DSOs see the mission requests each day and, based on geography and known dialects, choose which ones made the most sense for us to go on.

A side effect of this that I hadn't counted on was that now he felt that I should be sent on any mission that went up north, as I had explained to him that only one other guy could speak Dari and Pashto like I did, and he happened to be busy up in Bagram. I had *also* explained that the bad guys don't speak Dari, so it was a bit of a moot point, but he felt that it was better safe than sorry, and that from then on out, assuming I had the hours, I'd go on the Santa Clause-y missions to the fucking North Pole like the good little worker elf I was.

Somehow I had gone from trying to get on the more interesting, shorter missions to basically being singled out for the long-ass boring babysitting shit (it's a lengthy flight from Kandahar to anywhere in the north; Afghanistan isn't that big, but C-130s only fly at around half the speed of commercial jets). The other DSOs thanked me profusely for pointing this out to Major Stokes, by which I mean they pointed and laughed every time I got assigned to yet another mission in the hinterlands.

I got lucky with a few short trips. There was one glorious three-hour "mission" that wound up being 2.5 hours of transit time and only thirty minutes on station, as it didn't matter what elevation we were at, there was too much cloud cover to see the ground. When the CSO asked me if I could hear anything of interest, after thirty minutes of having heard nothing but static peppered with the occasional check-in, I could honestly report no, and back to base we went.

The Whiskey crews didn't mind the long missions. They'd been brought up as transporters, and for years most of them had just moved stuff from Point A to Point B. A seven- or eight-hour flight was nothing to them. Initially, I had a love-hate relationship with these drawn-out flights. On the one hand, they were interminable, and exhausting, and so fucking boring. On the other hand, they got me closer to my hours limit, which meant I would get to sit for a few days. The more long flights I went on, the closer I would get to 125, and maybe 330. The higher my hours climbed, the more I got to sit, aka take a day off.

I had failed to consider that I wasn't going to be deployed for three months, though. On my first deployment, the 330 limit was a real fear, and I regularly had to sit for a day or two. This deployment was only scheduled for two months. At best, I had to worry about 125. Oops. So up I went, in plane and country.

A lot of these missions were in support of the large-scale operation to "win hearts and minds." After ten years and who knows how many dead, it had been determined by those higher up that simply bombing the Taliban into submission wasn't working; not enough bombs, too many Talibs, and the only thing they would submit to was God. This was a good determination.

It was also determined that in lieu of all the bombing, we should send teams of Marines to go live in villages among the natives, er, Afghans. My understanding of the logic behind this was that by having some of "us" live with "them," and assuming that we were on good behavior, the natives, er, Afghans, would see that what they had been told about us by the Taliban and other disgruntled Afghans wasn't true. It would also allow us to engage in more sustained improvement projects in a given area. Instead of just dropping in, building a school, and leaving, we could build said school, put in a well, repave a road, etc. At the same time, we would be able to educate them about the true nature of the Taliban. The hope was that by doing this in enough villages over a long enough period of time we would create a grassroots rebellion against the Taliban, or at least an acceptance of America.

This was not a good determination.

There's a fine line, so fine as to be occasionally invisible, between living in a village and occupying it. When the Marines (or whoever, but it was generally Marines) went into a place, they often simply informed the villagers that they would be taking over a certain compound within the village. Yes, they paid the people who lived there, and paid them handsomely, but they were still forcibly evicting them. And once they were there, even if the Marines were on their best behavior, their very presence meant that there would be increased fighting, as now they were a constant, stationary target for the Taliban, who could dart in, do some damage, and leave, without having to engage in a major battle with a superior force.

This is exactly what happened to some team up in the northwest corner of the country, and that team had then requested that we come in and do reconnaissance for them. When we got overhead, they explained to us how the day before, a number of presumed Taliban had taken a bunch of potshots at them before disappearing into the countryside. The JTAC was convinced that whoever these cowardly fuckers were, official Taliban or no, they lived and worked in the village and its surrounding areas. Our job was to look for anyone engaged in anything that could be construed as "nefarious activity." I don't know how this came to be the go-to term for bad guys doing shifty and shady shit. I suspect someone wanted to sound smart, so they went and found a thesaurus and voilà, *nefarious*.

The word *reconnaissance* has this strange sexiness associated with it. Maybe it's because of the Marines and their Force Recon unit, or maybe it's because of movies and TV where so much of reconnaissance is associated with spies. Maybe it's because it's French. Regardless, the idea of collecting information on the enemies' plans and then using that illicitly obtained information to thwart said plans is exciting. In real life, recon, at least the recon I did, is just the collection bit. Someone else usually got to do the actually interesting part of acting on the collected information. This was still somewhat more interesting than many of our other missions, given the recency of the attack, so we got to work, excited at the prospect of helping this ground team.

I know that the JTAC understood the difference between us and a U-boat, or at least I think he did. It could have been his first deployment, and he could have never been on an operation at night. But with the amount of training he'd been through, and the number of stories he must have heard, he had to have known that there's a difference between the meaning of actions during the day and the meaning of those same actions at night. But for now, for him, anyone could be the bastards who had shot at him and his team.

So we watched everyone. Men, women, kids. There was a hilarious two minutes where a couple of kids were playing, throwing rocks at each other pretty lackadaisically, until one of them just beaned the other, and started laughing when the second kid fell down. The second kid got up, dusted himself off, and walked over to the first kid. He was clearly mad, and we figured there would be a good ole fistfight, right until the second kid kicked the first kid straight in the nuts and shoved him to the ground before walking off like the total badass he was. The comedy was a good omen; this was turning out to be a good mission.

After the kids, though, we mostly watched the guys in the village as they walked from compound to compound. We looked to see if they were carrying guns under their clothes (it isn't illegal to own a gun in Afghanistan, but it's frowned upon by the people who are afraid that those guns are going to be used on them, and it's often an extrajudicial death sentence to be seen with one in their vicinity). We looked for any patterns of movement, whether it seemed like a number of people were slowly headed in one direction, or toward the team's side of town. And I listened. The best I could hope for was hearing someone brag about getting some shots off at the Americans the day before. In lieu of that, I would take discussion of weapons, or plans for further attacks, or plans for meetings. These might not be enough for us to shoot, but it would help confirm the JTAC's suspicion, and if I heard enough call signs, maybe he would be able to figure out who those guys were (assuming they were locals and assuming he had good intel).

All of this is a slow, methodical process. For the CSOs, even with the incredibly powerful cameras the Whiskeys had, it takes time to scan a given area, decide whether something is worth looking at in greater detail, zoom in, and look again. If, during the time it takes to make that decision, the plane's orbit puts a wall or building or some other thing in the way of their view, then they have to wait to come back around, and keep scanning. For me, thanks to all the bullshitting that fills the airwaves of Afghanistan, I had to listen to multiple conversations for extended periods of time, waiting in case in the middle of all the nonsense someone said something potentially incriminating, or at least interesting. Throughout all of this, we updated the JTAC with what we were seeing and hearing. This JTAC was, fortunately, nothing like the one outside of Kandahar, but he was still trying to build up a mental image of what we could see from on high, so we told him everything that seemed remotely interesting.

A little while into this process, one of the CSOs came across three guys working a plot of land. It wasn't a very big piece of land, and since none of us were farmers, it wasn't all that clear what these guys were doing, other than moving the soil around with hoes and other tools. When we relayed this to the JTAC, he immediately perked up.

"Say again, how many?"
"Three."

"Do they have any weapons on them?"

"Uh, no, just what look like farming tools."

"Fuck that, they're up to something."

This did not appear to be the case, to us. It wasn't like this was a road that anyone would drive over, or a path that someone might walk along, so we couldn't imagine the three guys were burying an IED. Plus, doing that in broad daylight would be ballsy, even for the Taliban. If they weren't bomb planting, the field could have been an excuse for these guys to be together in one place so that they could plan something, without needing to discuss it on the radio, where it could be overheard. But seeing as how they didn't have radios, didn't have guns, and we couldn't read their lips from fifteen thousand feet, as far as we were concerned they were three dudes working in a field.

"Recoil, what does the soil look like?"

"Uh, say again?"

"The soil, does it look freshly turned over, or older?"

We were used to thinking about freshly turned dirt when looking for IEDs, as recently agitated soil has a different heat signature to it than the area surrounding it. On a road, or by a culvert, there isn't much of a reason for some random patch of land to have been recently dug up other than for the placement of an IED, so this was an effective technique when doing route recon for convoys. But this was a field that three guys were actively turning over in the middle of the day. There was no difference in the heat signature of any given part, and the dirt looked like all the other dirt.

"Hard to say, Oxblood. Seems like they're working the whole thing."

"Stand by, Recoil."

The CSOs kept watching, and I kept searching for interesting comms. Maybe I had missed something or had deemed something unimportant that was related to this new development.

"Recoil, that field was untouched yesterday."

At this point, we were all a little lost. But you can't just ignore someone over the radio, and the CSO didn't want to sound dumb by asking the JTAC to repeat himself again. So he just said, "Roger."

"They've done this before, they're smart. They know we'll search the houses, so they go and bury the weapons they used. Then no one gets caught."

This was a new tactic to us. It sort of made sense, though. Assuming the team had been there long enough, they would know the houses fairly well, and likely would have found any hidey-holes where a gun would normally be stored. Or maybe the locals really didn't support this nonsense and wouldn't let the bad guys hide their weapons with them. Just because we hadn't seen it before didn't make it impossible, and this guy had been shot at way more than us (which is to say, more than not at all), so who were we to second-guess him?

"Recoil, how many Griffins on board?"
"Oxblood, enough." [Not what we said, but the actual number is probably classified.]
"Roger, stand by."

Nothing had changed. The guys were still working in the field, I wasn't hearing anything of use, but the JTAC was clearly riled up. The crew was starting to get energized, excited by the prospect of shooting. The loadmasters checked everything related to the missiles, and they appeared to be in working order. We were ready.

It was a little strange, maybe, that I hadn't heard anybody on the ground mention us. There wasn't much they could do to us by then, as we'd long ago destroyed all the anti-aircraft guns in the country, and MANPADs were few and far between (Man Portable Air Defense Systems—think classic shoulder-mounted rocket launcher). And even if they had something capable of damaging a plane, those things are limited in their range, and Whiskeys flew much higher than real gunships. I had long wondered if it was this, or the fact that we were flying during the day, or some combo, that explained why I so rarely heard anyone mention our presence. It was almost insulting, compared to the gunships, where anytime you showed up you were paid your due respect by the very, very afraid enemy.

When the JTAC came back on, he told us he'd gotten clearance from the ground commander for us to fire on the men in the field, based on a history of similar, nefarious activity in the area. The crew couldn't believe their luck. This was an ideal Griffin mission. No needing to get the missile over a wall in the middle of some compound. No worry that the guys were gonna run away while it was in transit. Just three easy targets in the middle of an open field.

Firing a Griffin requires fewer moving parts than firing a 105. No one has to load a bullet, close a chamber, or really do much of anything physical. There are some systems that have to be checked, some buttons pressed in the correct order, but it's very digital, this future of warfare. So when the CSO finally "hit fire," it always felt a little anticlimactic to me, with my 105-filled blood. Were you really shooting if the plane didn't buck underneath you, if you couldn't taste the cadmium and lead newly released into the air, if there wasn't a *ka-thunk*? And what's with all this guidance or steering or whatever the fuck it is they're doing with the missile while it's in flight? When you shoot a bullet, once it's out, that's it, you either hit or you miss. No take-backs. That's like, the whole point of aiming. It was far more stressful to watch the CSO oh so carefully direct the Griffin, with everyone worried that it would freak out and fly off in some random direction, miss the target, and, horror of horrors, embarrass us. But the Griffin behaved, and in the split second before it hit, I could see the relief on the CSO's face, his excitement at a job well done.

That relief immediately turned back into anxiety the moment after the Griffin impacted. Instead of exploding, and incinerating the three guys into so much ash, it just sort of smashed into the ground. Bad Guy A, who had been closest to the impact, looked dead, or at least unmoving. Bad Guy B had had his legs blown off. Bad Guy C had been blasted a few meters away, and we figured he was dead too, the shock wave having turned his internal organs into gruel. Okay, so a little messy, but the amputee would bleed out, and the other two were KIA. The Griffin had worked.

"Oh, shit."

The third guy was, in fact, not dead. As evidenced by his sprinting away from the field.

If we'd been a real gunship, we could have killed him in the next ten seconds. He would have been a squirter—a guilty person running away from our weapons, not because it's human instinct to run away from the sudden explosions raining down on you, but so that he could then go get his own weapons and retaliate—not a guy sprinting. And he would have died a Talib, guilty by virtue of his execution. I wouldn't have questioned the tautological nature of all of this, because I never would have heard anything that could insert itself into this perfect loop of logic.

Instead, we watched him keep running back toward the village. While we were telling the now more high-strung JTAC what the fuck exactly had just happened, Bad Guy C had apparently got what he went to find and was racing back to the field with a wheelbarrow. Even in Afghanistan, a wheelbarrow is definitely not a weapon. Which was upsetting, because if he'd done what we'd expected him to, and had something that looked like a weapon, it would have been that much easier to clean up our mess and kill him. Another guy was close behind him, and together, they loaded the newly amputated Bad Guy B into the wheelbarrow.

By this point the JTAC was seriously worried about retaliation. If all three of them had died, there'd be a chance that some locals would be mad, but what would they be able to do about it? And who'd be able to say that the dead men weren't Talib, or at least the guys who had shot at the JTAC and his team the day before? Now the alive guys could call up their friends and swarm the village. So when they loaded up into a station wagon and started hightailing it down the road, the JTAC had us follow them.

It was only once they were in the car that I started hearing anything.

"Go, drive! We're coming."

"Oxblood, targets are coordinating with unknown third party."

"Abdul was hit! We have him in the car! We're coming!"

"Recoil, prepare to re-engage."

"Keep going! Don't let them shoot us!"

"Oxblood, targets are attempting to evade."

"Roger."

"CSO, DSO. I don't think they're going to get weapons."

"What?"

"I think . . . Stand by."

"Yes, yes, we're coming! We will save him!"

"CSO, I think they're just trying to get the legless guy to a
   doctor."

"You sure?"

"I . . . Yes. They aren't talking about weapons. They're just
   trying to get this guy to help."

"Oxblood, targets are not discussing weaponry."

"Recoil, you sure?"

The JTAC wasn't wrong to question me, as the Taliban has a
sort of code for when they talk over the radio. It's not an entirely
different language, but they use what are otherwise innocuous
words when they want to (they think) slyly talk about an impend-
ing attack, or a certain type of weapon, or what have you. The
JTAC was worried that I was taking them at face value, not understanding that, for instance, they might say they're going to get food,
but food would mean bullets (hypothetically). Unfortunately for
the Taliban, we know most of these words, so it doesn't really work.

What the JTAC wasn't considering, and what I hadn't either,
until that point, was that all of those words are in Pashto, aka the
language of the Taliban. The guys I was listening to weren't speaking
Pashto. They were speaking Dari, aka *not* the language of the fucking
Taliban. And while it's possible that there were code words in Dari
that I was unfamiliar with, I simply knew that these guys weren't
interested in retribution. They were interested in trying to get their
friend to a doctor, or at least someone who could try to save his life.

It's this knowledge that made being a DSO difficult. Memo-
rizing all the definitions of words is tedious and time-consuming,
but it's something other people understand. Knowing that a given

word in Pashto, once put into its oblique form, sounds like a completely different word, is maybe less readily understood, but explainable. The fact that words don't exist in a vacuum—that how someone is saying something can be just as important as what they're saying—is difficult to explain in English, let alone in translation. I didn't have to know any code words, or doublespeak, or spy shit to understand that these men knew that their friend was dying, and that in that moment, trying to prevent his death was far more important to them than any payback.

During this, the CSOs were preparing to fire another Griffin, a far trickier prospect given that the target was now highly mobile.

"Oxblood, Griffins are ready."
"Recoil, stand by for orders."

Internally, just on our plane comms, we were debating whether it was legally okay to shoot these guys. Were they retreating? Or were they running away? Those are very different things. If they were running away, then okay, fine, they're not a problem. But if they were retreating, didn't we kill those guys all the time? Retreat isn't surrender, and like the JTAC was worried about, they could come back, with friends (mechanical or meat-based). I felt that not only were they running away, they were trying to treat their wounded, and they were no longer a threat.

We were still trying to figure this out when I heard Guy B die.

Which, of course, I didn't actually hear. What I heard was Guy C say, instead of yell, like he had been for the last however many minutes, "No, brother. He's dead."

And then the car slowed down.

So we didn't shoot.

Contrary to popular belief, it isn't illegal to shoot a retreating enemy. The U.S. Naval Handbook states that "the mere fact that a combatant or enemy force is retreating or fleeing the battlefield, without some other positive indication of intent, does not constitute an attempt to surrender, even if such combatant or force has abandoned his or its arms or equipment." It also, however, states that "offenses against the sick and wounded, including killing, wounding, or mistreating enemy forces disabled by sickness or wounds" can be considered a violation of the 1949 Geneva Conventions. Obviously, none of us had this information readily at hand, making the debate we were having that much more difficult, and that much more human. If these guys were bad—which was the assumption we had to make, given that we had just fired a missile at them, and any equivocation of their guilt would mean that we had bombed three potentially innocent people, which was, of course, out of the question—then by not shooting them we were putting the JTAC and his entire team at risk. If retreating can't be assumed to be an indication of surrender, but the enemy either has no way of signaling their surrender, or just hasn't bothered, given that they're pretty busy with the whole dying friend thing, then the safest assumption is that they're still active combatants.

If we had killed them, none of this would have mattered. We wouldn't have faced any consequences, as it would have been our words, our intelligence, versus nothing and no one. Maybe some other villagers would have defended the dead and proclaimed that they were no Talibs, but we would have ignored them and stuck to our story, our truth.

The mood on our way back to base was about as far removed from the normal sense of celebration as it was possible to get. The air was heavy with denouement, but sans any of the traditional endorphins that normally prevented it from feeling like a comedown after a night of Molly and fucking, all serotonin and dopamine stores depleted, the ability to feel happiness gone with them.

What had we accomplished? I'm not sure the JTAC felt any safer, as now Guy C would be able to tell everyone in the village the horror story that was watching Guy B bleed out in the back of a station wagon, which was not likely to engender further feelings of hospitality, regardless of whether the villagers knew the JTAC had called in the strike. And that was just the immediate response. If those guys were Taliban, then Bad Guy C would be a hero, the badass who had survived a fucking direct-hit air strike, and the other two would be martyrs for the cause. If they weren't Talibs, then they were just more innocent people in the long line of civilian casualties brought on by our fear and faith. Either way, we had basically just made a recruiting video for the Taliban. "Hey, look, they aren't so scary, I survived, we can take them!" or "Hey, look, they're fucking animals, killing our people while we just try to earn our living, grow our food. We have to fight them!" Better yet, "Look how scared they are, not even willing to fight us face-to-face."

For my part, I had saved lives that day. But whose? Yes, they were speaking Dari, which in my hundreds of hours of experience was not something any legit Talib ever did, and yes, it really looked like they had been farming. But then, they were talking on something I could listen in on, which generally wasn't associated with good guys. And who were they taking their injured friend to? Your average Afghan doesn't have a doctor, or medic, or whoever the fuck on call. Should I have saved them? If I'd said nothing—not necessarily lied, just told no one what I was hearing—we would have blasted that car into oblivion. Maybe that would have meant some non-Talibs got killed, but wouldn't the hypothetical end, the killing of Talibs, have justified the real means, the killing of Afghans?

The crew did not feel like they had saved lives, not any lives worth saving anyway. They weren't mad at me, or if they were, they never said anything. I think they were frustrated that the strike had gone wrong, and whatever reputation they had been tenuously holding on to was now that much weaker. If they'd just been able to hit the car, then maybe they could have proved that they weren't fuckups, that the Whiskey was a good idea, that they were deserving heirs to the gunship throne. So, when I put my foot down, and repeatedly said that these guys were harmless, that we shouldn't shoot again, I think they felt that I was actively getting in the way of their mission. Or, at least, I worried that they felt this.

We spent most of the flight back trying to figure out what in the fucking fuck had happened with that goddamn Griffin. Yes, a Griffin is no 105, but it should be more than capable of killing a few humans. No, a Griffin *is* capable of killing a few humans, I'd done it. The CSO hadn't missed, that much was clear. And the missile had in fact detonated, or there wouldn't have been any damage. Did it have a light payload? Can only part of a bomb explode? Was this going to happen again? At some point, someone, one of the CSOs I think, came up with what we all came to see as the most plausible explanation: the soil. Regardless of why they were doing it, the guys in the field really had been working the earth. Most of the soil had been turned over, and the spot where the Griffin landed definitely had been. What if, when it hit, instead of hitting hard ground like normal, the Griffin had managed to bury itself a foot or two into the soft earth before it detonated? That would explain the lack of a normal explosion, the lack of fire and fury, and the lack of more dead dudes. It would also mean that we hadn't fucked up. The bad guys, or guys, had just gotten lucky. Well, the one anyway.

I still don't understand what happened that day, not really. I don't understand who I, or we, killed. I don't understand why we, or I, killed them. I know some of the reasons: The JTAC was scared and angry; he had intelligence that we didn't; killing them was easy. And I know that killing feels good, and righteous, and there is no better way to be sure that you've accomplished your goal. But none of that knowing means I understand.

I do think I understand what happened after, even though I don't know. Because while I don't know whether some men, or better yet (from the Taliban's POV), some boys wound up joining the Taliban because of our choice, I understand that they didn't have to go that far, didn't need to become full-on insurgents. The Taliban didn't need converts, just doubters. Doubters of the American process, America's "good intentions," America's propensity to do the right thing. With enough doubt, we couldn't win hearts and minds. And the Taliban could just take them.

I found myself, again, wishing I'd been on a real gunship, because then we'd have gotten the squirter. If we had, Bad Guy B would have died in the field, alone and afraid. But I wouldn't have to care about that, because there wouldn't be any question of his innocence; it too would have seeped into the soil, mixed with his blood. But when Guy C rescued Guy B, it was a little like watching a saint survive the cauldron of boiling oil. Maybe Guy B was meant to survive, and God was protecting him. I mean, I guess not, 'cause he still died, but even God's best laid plans and all.

I didn't *have* to care about these deaths, or so I was told. But I did. It was too hard to listen to a man die and finish listening to that conversation without caring. It didn't matter that I didn't actually listen to him die, I just heard his last breath come out of his friend's mouth. Somehow, that was harder.

FEAR, OR YOU CAN'T GO HOME AGAIN

BY THIS POINT, the Whiskey crews had developed their own dialect of gunship language. I spoke it with them that day. Sort of. I had to, or I'd become a pariah. You can't fly on a gunship, even a Whiskey, without being excited about killing. And it was still doable, during a mission, to get riled up when shit went down. Adrenaline is pretty good at knocking down moral quandaries; I guess they must be upregulated by the parasympathetic nervous system. But with the post-killgasmic clarity came more and more shame and unease. It was getting harder and harder to care about the missions like the rest of them. But then, there was the problem. Where before, after all my hard work and training, it had been us, now it was them.

I'd had my moments of questioning what we were doing. During my first deployment, after my Mission, back in America, when James told me how well he could see my naked heart, and now, when Kasady lasted all of two weeks on his fifth deployment before getting sent home, his risk of suicide finally deemed too high to keep using him. But I'd always been able to find answers. I saved more people after my Mission, and supposedly this would all add up to counteract that day. James and others had looked into that same distance and were doing fine. Kasady was just overworked, underappreciated, and burned out.

But then, so was Timothy. And Jim. And Conor. And Chris. And Chandler. And Trevor. Ed was nuts, but there was no way he was going to stop giving Big Blue his everything. Schmidt fucking hated it, and his blood pressure showed it. Alexi spent his time reading the Russians; I guess focusing on their despair was good protection from dealing with your own. There were the true believers, like Vince, who had never been on a mission where he didn't feel supremely confident that what he was doing was right. He was tired of deploying, sure, but he wasn't tired of being. And there were others, neither disciples nor apostates, apparent agnostics who were to all appearances fine. They didn't need certainty one way or the other, and without it, they could filter, compartmentalize, and not worry about whether what we were doing was just. The more I thought about it, the more I saw that lined up with what the apostates had told me, the more I worried that I would soon be joining them.

What had been moments of questioning were becoming hours of obsessive circling, both in flight and out. I found myself again and again thinking of my Mission. And of the guy in the wheelbarrow. And another big battle we'd been on out east, way up in the mountains. I'd been concerned on the way over that I wouldn't be able to understand much of the local dialect, but for whatever reason the Taliban were speaking crystal-clear Pashto. Alarming Pashto. These guys were organized, carrying fucking *flags* as they marched down the side of a fifteen-thousand-foot mountain (to the extent that one can march down the side of a fifteen-thousand-foot mountain). It felt like something out of history, a phalanx of men walking into battle, heads held high, ready to confront their enemy face-to-face. I'd never seen anything like it, and neither had anyone else on the plane. What the fuck were these guys thinking?

> "*Walaaaahu akbar.*"
> "Are you in position yet? Make sure the DShK is ready!"
> "We're almost there. It'll be ready!"
> "It will be! God willing, we're going to kill many Communists today."
> "CSO, DSO. Taliban have a DShK and are getting it set up."
> "A what?"
> "Big fucking machine gun. Tell the JTAC, he'll know."
> "Jaguar, Recoil, enemy is preparing a DShK."
> "Copy, Recoil."

A DShK (pronounced dushka) is a .50-caliber machine gun designed by the Russians before World War II. During that war, and in Vietnam, it was primarily used as an anti-aircraft weapon; it, and guns like it, were responsible for most of the destroyed aircraft in Vietnam. DShKs are fucking scary. It wasn't clear that these guys had an honest-to-god DShK, as the Taliban routinely exaggerated the level of weaponry they had (Americans aren't the only ones who are good at propaganda), but they did most likely have some sort of serious machine gun.

I was worried that they might have a real DShK, though, given their labeling of us as Communists. This was one of those rural legends you heard, that there were Afghans who still thought they were at war with the Russians, twenty years after the last Soviet soldier had pulled out of the country. For the most part, this wasn't true, but we made a point to talk about it, as it was yet another way that we could deride those dumb, backward Afghans who didn't even know who they were fighting. I didn't for a second think that these guys really thought we were Russians, but I did know that this meant they were in fact something out of legend; they were fucking muj.

Muj, short for mujahideen, were those "freedom fighters" who fought against the Russians during the Soviet invasion and occupation of the 1980s. They weren't actually "freedom fighters." That's just what we called them, as the American public likely wouldn't have been quite as supportive of their government funding "doers of jihad"—which is what mujahideen actually translates to—as they were of supporting these noble savages who were trying to stop the spread of Communism (though, maybe it would have been fine; I feel like in the eighties we as a country would have fully embraced the concept of fighting a holy war against those God-hating Commies).

The mujahideen are legendary for good reason. They weren't organized in any meaningful way, and they likely couldn't have accomplished what they did without the billions of dollars that we gave them, but they really did drive a goddamn superpower out of their homeland. They'd been driving off Western armies since the days of Alexander the Great (who, in a letter to his mother, was alleged to have called the Afghans a "leonine and brave people," who made "every foot of the ground like a wall of steel." He almost certainly said no such thing, but these quotes still made their way into my language school curriculum). They're the reason we routinely joked that Afghans are immortal (which I thought was a common phrase before I started writing this book, but after many a deep dive into the pages of Google, turns out it isn't).

So it wasn't that these guys were happily marching into a suicide mission, like I'd initially thought. Or that they were stupid and uninformed, still, in their minds, at war with the Russians. (It's also worth noting that they weren't likely to still be "real" mujahideen, that movement having long since been sublimated, in name anyway, by the Taliban.) They simply had decades of experience fighting, and no matter how advanced, or numerous, or really, *who* their enemy was, they knew that one day, like every invader who had come before them, these enemies too would leave.

But until then, the muj would fight.

They were making their way down into the valley, toward the small village where our ground team was. The team had figured there would be resistance, hence we'd been called in, but I don't think they were expecting this level of opposition. No one was. So far, though, we were lucky that they weren't shy with their comms, and I was hopeful that I'd be able to pass more useful intel.

And then someone's jammer went on (I know whose, but classified material and all). We, DSOs that is, fucking *hate* jammers. The logic of jamming, or interfering with the electromagnetic spectrum in such a way that certain devices no longer work—devices like, say, the radios that the Taliban used—was that by preventing communication between fighters you make them less effective. This was a very modern military-centric way of looking at things. If someone jammed our comms, yeah, we'd all be fucked. We wouldn't be able to tell the JTAC what we were seeing or hearing, the JTAC wouldn't be able to tell us to fire, we wouldn't be able to coordinate with all the other aircraft flying in the area—everything would devolve into a total clusterfuck. It was nice for the Taliban to be able to coordinate, sure, but they didn't have planes to direct or intel to pass. All they had to do was shoot at the enemy. Don't need radios for that.

We DSOs hated these jammers because (1) they made us

functionally useless, (2) we knew that the Taliban were still going to fight just as hard, and (3) the tradeoff of us being able to hear what the Taliban was planning was well worth any sort of increased effectiveness they might gain from being able to talk to one another. I don't know that we ever won this argument. To do so would have invalidated the mission of the people doing the jamming, and you could see how they might not want to be told to not do their job, for many of the same reasons we didn't want them to. Everyone wants to feel like they're doing something, which really was the perfect metaphor for us being in Afghanistan.

The next few hours of that mission have blurred together in my memory, given that I personally couldn't do anything, and we as a plane also weren't of much use. The narrowness of the valley, combined with the presence of the drones flying lower than us, meant that we were never going to be cleared to fire any of our missiles. We quickly got relegated to running command and control, which is military-speak for us being turned into a very expensive communications relay. There are highlights, like the few minutes we spent tracking some movement down the side of one of the mountains. We were worried it was a sniper, or a guy with an RPG, basically some sort of lone wolf skirting the edge of the battle, hoping to go unnoticed before he inflicted some serious damage. The mountain was lush, though, and it was difficult to see through all the trees and brush. And it was strange how fast this guy was moving; it was like he was gliding down. Or rolling? The movement was so fluid as to be almost, like, graceful.

"What the fuuuuuuck?"

"What? What is it?"

"It's . . . it's a cat?"

I looked up, and there on the screen, in beautiful high definition, was a snow leopard.

"Dude, no, that's a snow leopard!"

"A what?"

"A snow leopard! They're really rare, Afghanistan is one of the
   last places they live. We learned about them in language
   school."

"Huh. What the fuck is it doing in this shit show?"

"I dunno. Maybe it's trying to get away."

"Wrong direction, buddy."

"Yeah . . ."

We watched it for a couple more minutes, fascinated by how
quickly and easily it flowed down and across the mountainside.
But it wasn't a Talib, so the CSO had to move his camera back
to the action.

Later, I remember a drone firing a missile, and I remember
hearing that it was a good strike, but the details didn't stick out,
didn't seem important. Couple of dead dudes, no big deal. Toward
the end of the mission, after the battle, the JTAC went to assess
the damage of said missile. It turned out that some lucky/skilled
drone operator had managed to get a Hellfire directly into a building with a bad guy in it, seemingly though a window, which was
honestly quite impressive. So when the JTAC came on the radio
and was laughing so hard he could barely talk, we were confused.
Finally, he composed himself, and managed to choke out, "Oh
man, the guy's leg is stuck to the wall!" Apparently, the Hellfire had
blown the guy inside to pieces, and the heat from the explosion
had melted his leg to the side of the building. We were no longer
confused, and so we all laughed too.

* * *

It wasn't that we had done anything wrong on any of these missions—at least, not wrong *per se*—but said missions didn't sit right, if they sat at all. Instead it felt like they were running around in my head like coked-up toddlers who've just realized that they do, in fact, have endless energy. A side effect of this cognitive dissonance was that I found myself hearing things differently. I had by now realized that any conceptualization of "The Taliban" as some cohesive, centrally organized entity was misleading at best. More realistically, this representation of them was an excellent effort by the American government to drum up hatred of the entity that justified our decades-long occupation of yet another country.

Afghanistan is a country roughly the size of Texas, but with a population of 40 million people. (Texas has around 25 million.) Slightly more than 20 percent of Afghanistan's population lives in major cities, with the other 30 million people being spread out through the imposing mountain ranges that cover the country. If the world's most advanced military, using satellites, drones, spy planes, you name it, can't communicate and organize well enough to accomplish anything meaningful in such a place, how the fuck were a bunch of rural, agrarian men using high-powered walkie-talkies supposed to? (The Taliban did manage to get their shit together in 2021, well enough to retake the country, but this was only once America had announced its withdrawal, and when they could mostly walk into a given city and be handed the keys.)

Back in 2011, though, things were more disorganized. There were the occasional big battles, like my first one, or the Battle of Kamdesh, which my buddy Dex flew on (though that was in 2009), but for the most part, the firefights that happened were reactive in nature. When the Taliban did commit acts of terror, or at least horror, it was more a reaction to a threat than some sort of methodical malevolence. If one of our planes got close enough to the ground during an airdrop, they'd take some potshots. If we showed up at a village to talk about some infrastructure project, they'd shoot at the soldiers and Marines as they were leaving. When we did a middle-of-the-night no-knock raid, if their spotters saw the helos coming in early enough, the local Talibs might try and lay an ambush. Whereas before, during my first deployment, I had been able to level my rage solely at the Taliban, now when I listened to them coordinate these sorts of attacks, I wasn't just mad at them. I was mad at us too.

Because while the language the Taliban was using was still simple, it was becoming increasingly less hackneyed. At this point, whenever I listened to them, I didn't have to do much active thinking about what I was hearing. And without that thinking about thinking getting in the way, their stories became a little clearer. Yes, they were shooting at planes dropping supplies. But who and what were those supplies for? Not Afghans. Those supplies kept the enemy forces clothed and fed. The enemy forces who, I was beginning to see, were invaders, overthrowers, and occupiers of a formally independent country—this, despite the fact that not a single Afghan had been involved in the attacks that were supposed to justify the thousands and thousands of deaths in Afghanistan. Maybe those infrastructure projects were designed not only to make the Afghans like us but also to make them dependent on the United States. These no-knock raids, alleged to almost always result in the capture or killing of "high-level Taliban," were increasingly based on "intelligence" from some guy who'd heard this other guy talking about how his friend's cousin told him that his neighbor's daughter's soon-to-be husband said that a guy in the next village over talked to a Talib once. This is a natural consequence of how many raids we were doing, somewhere around six a day. There are only so many actual Talibs. But we were deeply invested in our game of Afghan Pokémon, determined to catch 'em all.

My anger only grew when I was switched over to the U-boats in the second half of my deployment. Whatever excitement I had had about finally being back on the gunship was gone. Some of this was my growing disenchantment, and some of it was the fact that I was now on the back end of the deployment, the light of leaving growing every brighter. I'd also, to my dismay, sort of become a Whiskey guy. I could still keep up with the grossness, the strange combination of homophobia and homoeroticism, and the general distrust of DSOs on the U-boats. (Many gunship guys were still firmly in the "a DSO isn't worth the weight of his equipment" camp; they'd rather have had more fuel and more bullets than some weirdo nerd who didn't appear to be doing anything most of the time, and even though I mastered the art of ingratiating myself to a crew, my presence on any given flight was more of an accepted nuisance, sort of like your friend's younger brother that their mom insists tag along wherever you go, who turns out to be occasionally funny and mostly not annoying.) But the gunship didn't feel like home anymore. I no longer wanted to live among the memitim, to aspire to Azrael. I was tired of killing people.

You can't be a gunship guy and be tired of killing people.

You most definitely cannot be on a gunship and talk about being tired of killing people. I tried. Once. Even in my weird depressive fervor, I very quickly realized that I was not going to get away with the shit I'd been saying on the Whiskeys. The gunship guys wouldn't even tolerate my (I thought) entertaining rant about

Texasstan and Audi Sarabia, let alone any debate of the morality of who we were killing and why. For them, these questions were tantamount to treason. No one ever outright accused me of being traitorous, but a Bowe Bergdahl joke or two let me know what they were thinking.

At that point, the gunships had had forty years to establish their culture of killing. Like any culture, there were rites and rituals, specific ways of thinking and doing, knowledge and lore passed down through generations: The head shaving that comes with your first kill, a celebration of the (hopefully) second time you popped your cherry. The automatic assumption that every movement below you is suspicious. The belief that gunships truly are the memitim, the Angels of Death.

At a minimum, to be a true member of a gunship crew, you must be okay with killing people. Ideally, you don't just accept this task, but embrace it. Some people are born ready to do this. Some are made ready before they even know what a gunship is. I met very few of either of these individuals, and I don't believe that they're common, or representative of gunship crews, but they do exist. For the rest of us, all you have to do is remove doubt.

If you find this hard to understand, the idea that you can take an average person and convince them to enjoy taking lives, I get that. It's unsettling. But teaching men and women how to kill without hesitation is what a not small amount of the military exists to do. And so they remove doubt that the people we are killing are subhuman, and they remove doubt that our mission is ordained by God or gods above, and they remove any and all doubt that if we don't kill them, they will kill us. And then, suddenly, there's a day when it seems not only reasonable, but right, to take great joy in this, your duty.

But without this joy, I was simply mad, and not being able to get these frustrations out was not going well for me. So I did what many of the DSOs who had come before me had done, and started writing. On our equipment, buried deep in some obscure directory that you essentially had to be told about in order to find, was a folder named "DSO poetry." This title was a bit of a joke, the punchline being who the fuck else on a gunship would be writing fucking *poetry*, but the folder did contain a decent number of actual poems. Some were traditional, usually focused on figuring out the maximum number of words you can rhyme "body" with. A couple of haikus were strewn throughout. But most of them were modern, and, to my mind, pure poetry, in that they were clearly thoughts that the men who were writing felt that they absolutely had to get out of their skulls. Trevor was by far the most prolific, and probably the most talented, which was always a little strange, given that he was also the largest and most potentially deadly of us (Trevor was big, strong, and well trained in a number of martial arts; it's not that it's impossible to be large and scary and a good poet, but it is surprising, and maybe even a bit unfair). But then, maybe that's why he had to get his thoughts out. He knew, in theory, how readily he could kill a man, far better than most of us. This then meant that he knew how easy it would be to fail to save a man. But the job had made him know what it was to do both of these things, to be doubly responsible for death.

Becoming another version of yourself—judgment of that version notwithstanding, as it is arguably equally as hard to be as fully good as you are capable of being as it is to be as wholly not—is taxing in the best of cases. If you do it long enough, or are forced to do it long enough, you lose track of the other versions of you that did or could exist. This act of self-reification requires a concomitant act of forgetting. Because once you've forgotten that you were ever something else, ever someone else, once you've committed this fallacy, it is all too easy to believe that you will forever be this new, unyielding thing. It is possible to look at this metamorphosis and say that it is good, and useful. That by becoming a version of yourself that is unchangeable, by losing the belief that you can go back, you have now committed yourself to who you truly are. But a lack of belief and a lack of desire are very different. We wanted to change. We just either never knew how to in the first place (me), or had forgotten that we once could (Trevor, others).

I did not write poetry, as I didn't know how to. I could see that the others had written things that weren't constrained by rhyme schemes or meter, simple stream-of-consciousness wonderings, honest feelings put down without any sort of second thought or revision, but I didn't think that sort of writing was available to me. I was too into/worried about the chance that someone else would read what I'd written (other DSOs could, of course, find this folder). So while I wrote about boredom, daydreams, nascent desires, despair, apathy, fear, confusion, regret, hope, pain—mostly pain—I did so with an audience in mind. I know now that I was essentially trying some version of cognitive behavioral therapy on myself, hopeful that if I got my thoughts down in some sort of coherent, non-circular state, then I would be able to see what exactly it was that I felt. I managed this, I think. But I didn't know where to go from there. I didn't know how to see my thoughts and try to change them. All I knew was that I couldn't stand to look at them.

* * *

As the end of November approached, I was hopeful that I'd be able to finish out my deployment without any more fire missions. The fighting had died down for the season, and at least so far, all of my gunship missions had been uneventful. There'd been a lot of generic chatter, and what seemed like hundreds of check-ins.

On the missions where there was an operation, say a snatch and grab, the ground teams had walked into whatever village or compound their intel told them to go to, searched the area, confiscated shit, rolled up the bad guys, and left. Too easy.

I even had a U-boat crew I really liked flying with. They were also near the end of their deployment and had gotten to the point where their rapport mostly took the form of silliness. The FCO and the Nav (two officers who sit next to each other, literally side by side, in our section of the plane) at some point had realized that not only did they both love Disney musicals, but that they could sing duets from most of them. *The Little Mermaid*, *The Lion King*—they knew 'em all, and what's more, they were both good singers. The memory of the two of them singing *Aladdin*'s "A Whole New World" at two o'clock in the morning as we orbited over the countryside is one of the fondest I have from my time in Afghanistan. I wish it were my last memory of them, but it's not.

Because they weren't singing the last time I helped kill men.

It almost seems, now, like a sort of cosmic bookend, this mission. We killed a good number of guys—it was the most casualties I'd seen in a single flight since my first mission—but it wasn't some big to-do. There was no battle. There were no helicopters or fighter jets or bombs. There were groups of men skulking along a wadi, looking shady as fuck, headed in the direction of the guys on the ground. These crawling men made the mistake of talking about their movements, and the Americans, over their radios. This, coupled with the fact that they were using blankets to hide their heat signatures from our infrared cameras (or to keep warm, but this is not the assumption one makes), meant that they were both bad and threatening, which meant that they had to die.

It took a little longer to kill all of them than we had anticipated. The wadi had a lot of nooks and crannies, so our first rounds only killed about half of them. I'm sure the ones who survived the first barrage didn't feel great, the shock waves from the 105s having pummeled their organs, blasted open their eardrums, and put the fear of us gods into them, but maybe they were hopeful that they could escape.

It was sort of annoying, their attempts to get away. More work for us. At some point someone said what we were all thinking.

"Come on man, don't run. You're just gonna die tired."

A minute or so later, when this prophecy came true, I wondered what kind of tired that man was. Was he only tired because he'd been trying to escape the near certainty that was our bullets? Or was he also tired of the necessity of those bullets, and his bullets, and of all the bullets in Afghanistan?

After we landed, as we were waiting for the SUVs that would take us back to our camp, one of the crewmembers, Scott, asked me when my next deployment was going to be. He knew how often we DSOs got sent out, that I'd been there a few months prior, and that I was likely to be back in two or three. I'd been asked this before, and had said, truthfully, that I wasn't sure; there was some training I had to do, and there were new DSOs getting spun up, so maybe I'd get some extra time back. But this time, I knew exactly when I would come back to Afghanistan.

"Never."

He laughed, along with everyone else standing nearby.

"Yeah, you wish. How many years you got left?"

"Two, two and a half."

"Yeah man, you're coming back."

"I don't think so."

The others laughed again, but Scott could see that I wasn't joking.

"You afraid?"

"Of what?

"Flying. Getting shot. Dying."

"Nah, man. I'm not afraid of them. You know as well as I do that they can't hurt us."

He laughed at this, and I hoped that would be the end of the conversation, but he kept pressing me.

"Hope so. Why then? How come you think you're not coming back?"

"I . . . I just can't, man. I can't do it."

I remember, so clearly, the look on his face throughout our conversation. Part of this vivid recollection is due to his being a strikingly handsome human. He had great bone structure, olive skin, beautiful blue eyes, and was one of those rare guys who doesn't look weird bald, looks natural even, like that's just how he was meant to be. But I've known a fair number of beautiful people, and very few of their faces stick out in my memory like this man's.

I don't think he meant anything by his line of questioning, as he was kind during it, both in content and tone. I think he genuinely wanted to understand why I didn't want to deploy again. And if I had said it was because I was scared of dying, I think he would have understood that. He wouldn't have respected it, or me, but it would have made sense; cowardice may not be a good thing, but it's pretty straightforward. It was when I said "I can't" that his eyes narrowed and went dark, all the luster that had accompanied his curiosity gone in an instant. All his bone structure, only a moment earlier so dazzling and attractive, in the untwinkling of his eye, became sharp and intimidating. It was this transformation, this comingling of confusion and disgust, that etched his face into my memory.

This beautiful, otherwise gentle man couldn't understand, or stomach, or tolerate the notion that I might not want to kill. It wasn't that he was full of bloodlust; guys like him, the ones who'd been around long enough, didn't necessarily feel good about the act of killing (though they usually felt good once the targets they shot were dead). It's just that he was, through and through, a gunship guy. But I wasn't. Which meant I did not feel good once the men I shot were dead.

My slow realization that "the enemy isn't all that different from us" was not novel, or interesting, or even all that intelligent. What made this realization different was who had helped me come to it; I don't know of many other people who underwent their moral reckoning as a result of what their "enemy" was telling them directly.

This is the only way I could understand why Scott, and, as far as I could tell, everyone else I was flying with, showed no signs of the moral erosion that I was undergoing—the blowing away of the, it turns out, incredibly thin layer of topsoil separating white from gray. I knew that some of them understood that those men are not too different from these men, and I knew that this knowledge made war different for them. But it didn't make it that different, and it didn't make it any harder. Because during their missions, my fellow crewmembers still had their distance, all ten or fifteen thousand feet of it. They were still eliminating enemy combatants, or neutralizing insurgents, or taking the fight to the enemy, all different versions of the great and central truth of what we were supposed to be doing in Afghanistan:

Killing the Taliban.

I'd lost my distance. My headphones no longer kept me apart from the men I was listening to, but instead took me that much closer to them. Flying ten thousand feet above someone doesn't allow for detachment if you're hearing them just as well as if you were their intended audience. Knowing about their lives, however mundane and banal, eliminated the sense of remoteness that came with shooting from on high. My missions lacked a "The."

I was just killing Taliban.

There's a great irony in this distinction. It isn't hard to kill a man. He is a soft, weak thing, and we have developed countless ways to destroy him. It's impossible to kill an idea, something that is all but indestructible, only time on a scale we can't comprehend being capable of its extinction. So, in theory, by killing Taliban, these painfully unidealized men, I was doing the easier thing. But it's hard to kill a man whose thoughts you're increasingly beginning to understand. It's much harder to kill a man when you've learned his name, the names of his friends, his goals in life. It's so, so much harder to kill a man when you know him and you know that killing him won't accomplish anything, because you aren't supposed to be killing him as a human, but him as an idea.

I can't say with any certainty why others found this easier, but I think fear has a lot to do with it. The Taliban as an idea was something worth fearing, hence Scott had asked me if I was afraid. But I had come to see that there was no such thing as the Taliban as an idea, and so all I had left to fear was the Taliban as men. And the Taliban as men were no scarier than any other random human. They might have been less scary. Once you hear the bad guys make enough dick jokes, or whine about the cold, or call each other's name over and over and over again because they're bored and probably a little dumb, or any of the other repetitive bullshit that they were so very good at, once you worry that your ears are going to bleed from sheer exposure to their troglodytic tripe, it's sort of hard to be scared of them.

Even if you could still somehow convince yourself to be afraid of them, they were only threatening to us as long as we were in Afghanistan; they have never killed a U.S. citizen who wasn't in their country. Any fear we had of them was utterly self-created. We had convinced ourselves that a bunch of fucking *farmers* (by and large, farming is what our enemy realistically did) were the thing that most threatened our existence, our way of life.

This logic, my attempts to understand the potential inner workings of the minds of my peers, wasn't perfect, and it still isn't. The JTAC from my mission outside of Kandahar—the one who wanted to know every name, every location, every little bit of bullshit said by the men I was listening to—he knew those men, better than I ever would, and he wanted to kill them all the more for this knowing. But his fear of them was legitimate, or at least grounded in the very real probability that they might kill him. Our fear was entirely artificial. Yes, it was possible, in theory, for some random Talib to hurt us in our planes; I have friends who had bullets fly through the fuselage not two feet away from them, and I'd been on a plane that launched flares after the loadmaster thought he saw a missile plume during takeoff. But the longer we were in Afghanistan the less and less probable it became that we were in any danger up in the sky.

And so, when Scott asked me if I was afraid, there's a reason I didn't respond with a simple no.

I was afraid.

Just not of them.

ANGER, OR YOU
CAN'T KILL AN IDEA

I WONDERED IF I SIMPLY wasn't cut out to be a DSO. I still wonder, sometimes. There wouldn't be any shame in this, or at least, not much. It's a difficult job. Flying, just the act of sitting in a cold seat inside a poorly insulated cargo plane that is so loud and so vibratory that it's all but impossible to tell which of these two nuisances is more responsible for your newfound tinnitus (allegedly, it's basically an even split of both), is hard. It's also hard to listen to people talking in another language, while also listening to the men on your plane talking, while also listening to the ground forces talking, while also listening to the sometimes five or six other aircraft in the stack talking, all while continuously deciding whether what you heard in that other language is important enough to translate into English, that is, real English, English that someone else can understand and use, not the weird hybrid of Pashto and English that now exists in your head and can honestly be a little confusing, such that if you're not careful you're going to tell the Nav or the JTAC that "the Taliban weapons have," or "for the attack ready they are," or some other weird adolescent Yoda shit that will, in the best-case scenario, where it's just a casual update that you think someone might find interesting, only get you laughed at, and in the worst-case scenario, where the three seconds it takes you to repeat yourself in normal fucking English are all the time it takes for the Taliban to shoot, or set off their IED, or finish coordinating their ambush, will get someone hurt, or killed.

It's also really fucking hard to learn how to fly on different aircraft, how to communicate on those aircraft, how to properly wear your seatbelt on those aircraft so that when you're doing an airdrop on a plane you've never been on before and the pilot suddenly drops the tail down forty-five degrees to send the pallet of water and food flying out the back and down to the Marines in the middle of bumfuck nowhere, and it turns out the mechanism that locks your seat into place is broken, such that said seat flies backward until it mercifully hits the back of its track and you find yourself sitting with one ass cheek more or less on said seat and the other ass cheek completely off, looking over your shoulder at the ground three hundred feet below you, suddenly acutely aware of the fact that you're not wearing a parachute 'cause like, why would you, there's a seatbelt, except you couldn't figure out how to get the seatbelt around your bulletproof vest, and your survival vest, and your equipment, and they said the bulletproof vest was a lot more important on this plane, 'cause the seat you're sitting in doesn't have any armor around it like the pilots' seats do, and so you listened to them and kept your vest on, thinking, eh, fuck the seatbelt, and besides, you're so used to flying on gunships and Whiskeys that like, why the fuck would you need to wear a seatbelt, what's the worst that could happen, some turbulence? Oh, no, okay, this is definitely the worst that could happen, dying during a fucking daytime airdrop because you're a dumb, fat fuck who should've asked someone to help you with your goddamn seatbelt.

Seatbelt situations notwithstanding, I was a good DSO. I was a *great* linguist. Never the best, but I was up there in terms of pure language capability. And I was good enough at the rest—the technical skills we learned, the situational awareness, the in-flight communication.

I was not a good airman. I wasn't good with authority or discipline or respect. Generally, being a DSO and being an airman were kept separate, so this worked out in my favor. The men I flew with, because they weren't in charge of supervising me or making sure I was adhering to Air Force standards, only cared if I was doing my job well. Those who were in charge of supervising me and making sure I adhered to standards only cared that I did my job at all. Because of this disconnect my worst habits and tendencies were allowed to run rampant. I didn't bother shaving more than once a week, my uniform usually violated four different regulations, and at some point I got so cocky, so sure of my invulnerability (or so uncaring about consequences) that I used the fabled "With all due respect, sir, go fuck yourself" on one of the Whiskey majors. (He did need to go fuck himself, but it wasn't really my place to inform him of this.)

By the end of my second deployment, all this bad airmanship had begun to affect my DSOing. I couldn't see the point of it all anymore. The war, deploying, flying, our missions, any of it. It took every ounce of willpower I had to bother listening to anything the Taliban was saying. What did it matter? They'd kill some of us; we'd kill a bunch of them. My presence had so very little to do with

202 // IAN FRITZ

this, and I no longer believed that my changing those numbers one way or the other was meaningful, or at least meaningful in the way I was being told it was. Even if we did have a fire mission, all I wanted to write when we landed was "nothing significant to report" or NSTR, because what the fuck was significant about us dropping a few 105s on some random Afghans? I was hard pressed to imagine anything less significant.

A few days after Scott asked me if I was afraid, on November 29, 2011, I flew my 100th combat mission (or maybe 101st; I have a couple flights, the seatbelt flight is one, funnily enough, that are missing from my records). The flight was as boring as they came, a true NSTR mission. Utterly uneventful. I didn't hear anything bad, the sensors didn't see anyone bad, and we didn't fire a single round. It was short too. All of 4.7 hours. So I don't really remember it in any great detail. Looking back, this strikes me as strange. Not because I knew November 29, 2011, was my 100th combat mission, but because I knew it was my last mission, combat or otherwise. I knew that I would never fly as a DSO again.

Of course, I didn't actually know this. What I did know, like I have known very few other things in life, was that if I kept doing what I was doing, kept flying, someone, be it me, another crew-member, a good guy on the ground, a neutral guy on the ground, a potentially bad but not for sure bad guy on the ground—it didn't matter who, but *someone* was going to get hurt because of me. It was most likely going to be me, as the times, or maybe the time—I'm not sure how many moments plural have to blend together to create an epoch singular—where I no longer wanted to live had begun at some point during that second deployment.

I don't remember exactly how, or when, or why I first found myself in my freight container with my 9mm in my mouth. I have a feeling of the idea of the event as a memory, but I couldn't tell you anything specific about what pushed me to go ahead and French kiss a pistol. I do remember the fourth time, and the fifth, and all the times after until I left Kandahar. I remember that I was always standing directly next to the door of my room, as I felt that I had to have this gun in my mouth the second I was somewhere no one else could see me, or, conversely, I needed to act out this frustration before I could leave my room. I remember knowing that there was warm, healing sunlight mere inches away, but that I didn't want anything to do with it. I remember how the gun was always empty, and therefore its insertion was probably not much more than some sort of symbolic cry for help, except since no one was around when I did it, I was the only one who could hear my sobs. So who exactly was I supposed to be symbolizing for? And I can't help but remember how I became quieter each time, less histrionic, more genuine, my despair muffling my voice just as well as it had smothered my will.

I don't remember ever having a plan, as the idea of putting a bullet into my own head while in Afghanistan was too pitiful, too clichéd, too giving the Taliban what they wanted. But the haze of depression and morbid ideation that had come to envelop my life was making it harder and harder to think of much else, so while I wasn't sure I could, or would, kill myself, I most certainly wished I were dead. When I did actively contemplate this completion, I always experienced it as just a moment (or moments) of what felt like pure instinct. I say "what felt like" because I'm not able to make out whether this description is wholly accurate, given that the most primal instinct is supposed to be the urge to stay alive. But I don't know a better word for this impulse that didn't feel thought, or unthought, because it didn't seem to come from my mind. The problem was, or is, that I don't believe in souls, even as literary metaphor, and so where was it coming from?

It could have been from others. I'd always been impressionable, in early life because of the suspension of disbelief that the religion I was raised in required, in later life because of the reaction formation against that religion that forced me to be open-minded to everything (except Christianity, of course). This suggestibility was almost pathological in nature, so much so that years later, when I told my friends that I was planning on going to medical school, a number of them asked how I could possibly be a doctor when I would have to ask everyone around me for an opinion on what I was supposed to do. And no matter the stage of my life, there was always my unassuageable desire to be liked, which often forced me to defer to others, my conceptualization of power dynamics and human interaction being that submission prevents anger and a lack of anger is often as close as you can get to love, or even just like, so you'll take it.

So if Ed hadn't told me about the possibility of putting one's gun in one's mouth, maybe I wouldn't have found out what a Beretta tastes like six months later. Or maybe if I'd spent more time with the disciples and their gospel, I wouldn't have developed doubts about what we were doing. And if I hadn't started doubting, and Kasady and Conor and Trevor and Charlie and all the other apostates hadn't been around to spread their heresy to tell me of the futility of their missions, of the power of their nightmares, maybe I wouldn't have felt like such a failure. Maybe, if I'd just lived in the little bubble of jingoistic self-aggrandizing heroism that the few Pashto DSOs who'd managed to maintain their sanity existed in, I would have kept flying, would have gone on four or five or six more deployments like the Air Force had intended, would have given them however much of me they wanted ("three pounds of flesh" is the amount our new squadron commander explicitly said he would take out of Trevor).

But if I had done that, then my fear would have become reality. Because if I had kept flying, without one day finding myself in my freight container with all that cold metal in my mouth again, but this time not having bothered to take the ammo out, and as the steel was warmed by my tongue and breath and therefore began to feel less foreign, and more like a part of me, such that it would only be natural to grip the gun tighter, to feel more of it by resting my finger on the trigger, to test the tension that was somehow a perfect metaphor for so much of my mind, and then, because of fatigue, or love, or fear, or just an accidental slip (no one other than me would ever know, and would I have enough time to know for sure?) to put a bullet through the back of my skull and coat the wall behind me with bone, brain, and blood, if that—which I didn't fear so much as welcome—didn't happen, then as far as I could see, it would mean that, like Dr. Strangelove, I had learned to stop worrying and love the bombs.

Which would mean that it had, in fact, been my destiny to have the anger and fear that I had felt before return, and because there would no longer be a way to escape them, I would embrace these simple, wondrous emotions wholeheartedly (though whether these are in fact separate emotions is unclear, as I have come to believe that most anger stems from a place of fear). This would make me into a monster, an evil thing spreading its corruption throughout the world. In my mind, this was a fate worse than death.

This is what I was afraid of.

* * *

Unfortunately, I didn't know this at the time. I didn't realize that this was the root of my fear until I was in medical school. Alongside all the medicine, medical schools try to teach their students how to talk to people (sort of; patients belong to a separate category of human that isn't quite people). They do this by making use of "standardized patients," actors, professional or otherwise, who play the roles of different patients presenting with all sorts of problems. Sometimes the goal is straightforward: a simple collection of history and the patient helpfully supplies all the information. Other times the goal is the same, but the story is more complicated, and you are supposed to learn how to deal with the patient being purposefully obfuscatory. Other times, the topic at hand is meant to be uncomfortable, or somehow difficult to talk about, like when a young woman goes to a clinic because she's having vaginal discharge after some recent unprotected sex.

A thing you get taught to do in these sessions is to mirror the energy of the patients, so that you're on the same emotional level. This advice can have unintended consequences, like when a classmate of mine was dealing with an irate, screaming patient, and, taking this instruction to heart, leapt out of his chair and began yelling right back at the now confused but still screaming patient (they're good actors). Or, if you're me, and the young woman in front of you is providing simple, straightforward answers to your initial questions, you decide that you should ask similarly direct, straightforward questions about the nature of her discharge, its onset, consistency, color, smell, all of the things that you are taught to inquire about to determine what the causative organism is, and you get to the bottom of it, and politely inform her that it's a simple STI and that a few days of antibiotics should clear it right up, and you go back to your seat and think to yourself, *Well that wasn't nearly as uncomfortable as they wanted it to be, well done, me.*

And at the end of the session, after the instructor debriefs with the standardized patient and it's time for feedback, and the instructor says they want to talk specifically to you and one other student, you think nothing of it because you're good at this, if there's one thing you can do well it's listen to people. But then the instructor says that the standardized patient felt intimidated, indeed, felt *afraid* of you and your direct questions, and you are taken aback, you are fucking shook, because you are not intimidating, why would you try and scare someone in such a setting, that's ridiculous, she misread the situation, and this is the problem with so much of the world, they don't understand that speaking directly is not the same as speaking harshly. That's definitely been the problem since you got out, or maybe since you stopped flying, but that's on them, not me, it was never my intention to intimidate anyone. "I don't want to be threatening, just feared enough to never have to make a fist," though now I'm pretty inclined to show you intimidating, 'cause like, fuck you, you fucking mouse, if that makes you afraid I feel sorry for you and the life of cowering you must live and . . . stop. This isn't helpful.

I spent the rest of that day confused and angry, and angry that I was angry, unable to figure out why I was so torn up by this feedback. I had otherwise received glowing remarks in all of my standardized patient sessions. In far more sensitive scenarios, I had put the patient at ease, earned their trust, and given them the space to speak openly about the things they were struggling with. Clearly this was just a classic case of miscommunication, and not at all representative of me as a person or future physician.

This is what I tried to tell myself, with varying levels of success.

I had, finally, by that time in my life, learned to ask others for help, and so I texted one of my best friends, Jerry, and explained the situation, angrily. It wasn't until I had ranted and raved, sent many messages comprised almost entirely of invective, and just generally whined a lot, that, with Jerry's help, I realized why I was so bothered. Feeling better, and not quite proud, but a little impressed by my newfound emotional maturity, I related this story to the person I was dating at the time. As I got to what I felt was the big reveal, that my being upset was actually disguised worry about being some sort of monster and that this was necessarily tied back to my time in Afghanistan, I expected her to compliment me on my profound insight into my emotions. Instead, she just said something to the effect of "Well, yeah."

To her, it was immediately obvious that I should be worried about being monstrous. Which, I supposed, meant that it was immediately obvious that I wasn't all that far off from being a monster. When I got out, when I had decided that I would no longer be afraid, I did what so many people do, and tried to out-scare the fear. I hadn't considered what this might make of me, what it would require of me and my presentation to the world.

I know that this worry is childish and reductive. I know men and women who continued to kill people, or Talibs, without undergoing any sort of transmogrification. I do think that they probably lost some "good" part of themselves, but that doesn't mean that they then became moral vacuums. And I know that monsters aren't real, but if they were, Jerry had pointed out the obvious, that "monsters aren't interested in repenting. They aren't interested in atonement or forgiveness or anything else. They're monsters." So, by virtue of questioning being part of that category, I excluded myself from it.

But back then, back in Afghanistan, I didn't know how to ask for help. Even if I had, I could only hold so much cognitive dissonance in mind, and I was already overextended from having considered the Taliban's side of things and the ethical grayness of our role in Afghanistan. This, coupled with my willingness to believe the worst of myself, meant that I was committed to this binary conceptualization of myself as good or evil, which meant that by having done anything remotely monstrous, I had necessarily become a monster.

I said that it's unfortunate that I didn't know any of this at the time, because this lack of self-awareness resulted in months of my anguish being compounded by a very real fear of prosecution. I'm not blameless in this, as I made a lot of mistakes when I stopped flying. I told anyone who would listen, and lots of people who wouldn't, that I was done. I skipped about four levels of the chain of command and in a strangely offhand but very matter-of-fact way told our commander that I wouldn't be deploying anymore. To his credit, he let me do this and just walked away, perhaps if only because he was more confused than angry in the moment. My biggest mistake was how often I seemed happy about it, a big smile on my face when I told even complete strangers that I wasn't going back. My second biggest mistake was trusting that the Air Force would give two shits about my emotional instability.

In AFSOC, after any deployment, you get up to four allegedly off-the-books sessions with a mental health professional (psychiatrist, licensed clinical social worker, psychologist). These sessions are supposed to allow you to decompress, to at least get off your chest (if not out of your head) whatever things are bothering you, without having to commit to (or be committed to) ongoing therapy or treatment. Given the size of AFSOC, these sessions are not at all off-the-books, as there's a good chance you have to walk into the appointment wearing a uniform with your name on it, and if you manage to get the appointment scheduled in your off time, as soon as you tell someone your job, or something as simple as the plane(s) you fly on, they know exactly what squadron on base owns the people who do that job or fly on that plane, so it would take all of two phone calls for them to know exactly who you are.

The major contribution to the façade of anonymity is the appearance of no records of the conversations one has with whichever shrink (they're all shrinks, doesn't matter what degree they have) one gets assigned to for these four sessions. They inform you that they don't take notes, and that unless you violate the sacrosanct by telling them that you intend to hurt yourself or others, nothing you say will leave the room. (I understand this disclaimer, it's a rule of medicine and mental health, but it's sort of laughable when your job involves killing people. If you don't intend to hurt others, it gets a little hard to fight a war.) Maybe this promise holds true if you see someone other than the person I saw, or maybe it's true if you really do only need the four sessions. But if you actually need help, then four 30- to 45-minute sessions aren't likely to accomplish much, particularly if that time is spent with someone who (a) doesn't understand what a linguist is and therefore (b) needs a primer on what exactly a DSO does but (c) doesn't have the requisite clearance to be legally told what exactly it is that said DSO does, such that (d) you spend too much time trying to talk around what you did instead of just telling them why you're there. So when my four free sessions were up, and this patient person in a Navy uniform with an officer's rank insignia on it told me that they thought I should continue with real, on-the-books care, and that there was a waiver that would allow them to share their notes with my commander, and that signing said waiver would be for the best, just to make sure everyone's on the same page, I said "Sure, Doc, I can do that."

What this person didn't tell me was that (1) they weren't in the military, but part of the United States Public Health Service Commissioned Corps (PHSCC), and so entitled to wear their fancy Navy-looking uniform with their shiny laden lapels, (2) members of the PHSCC are legally noncombatants, and so even if this person had deployed, there was fuck-all they could possibly understand about my job, and (3) they were a slimy piece of shit for suggesting, let alone encouraging, and then, after my hesitation, eventually cajoling me into, sharing my mental health records with my squadron. I have tried to extend grace to this person, to assume that they had good intentions. I know, on some cognitive level, that they didn't have it in for me specifically, no matter how annoying or confrontational I was. But I also know, on an emotional level, that they did have it out for me, generally. Me as an idea.

I know this because not long after my sessions became official, my supervisor called me and told me that this person had recommended to my commander that I be charged with malingering and cowardice, for both of which I could (and in their mind should) be court-martialed. When I first wrote that sentence, the one you just read, I included this person's name, gender, and rank, because of the amount of anger I feel every time I think of them. The indignation is such that I have hopes that publishing all of this information about them will somehow damage them and their career, and make them feel as violated as I did when I heard what they thought of me and what they wanted to do to me. But I went back and took out their rank and name. I switched the language to gender-nonspecific pronouns. An enterprising individual might be able to figure out who they are based on their "branch" of service and the timeline I've established, but that would take some serious effort, and I find it hard to imagine that anyone else would bother to do this much work.

This person didn't decide that I should be charged with these heinous crimes without, in their mind, serious evidence that I was faking mental illness to get out of doing my job because I was too afraid to do my job. At the beginning of every session, I was given a depression inventory that I was told to fill out completely honestly. The answers I provided created a picture of an individual who should show signs of serious depression and extreme mental anguish. When I then met and spoke with this person, I appeared sarcastic, blithe, and perhaps even chipper at the prospect of no longer DSOing. My understanding is that this contradiction between my answers and my affect led this person to believe that I was malingering, and that I was a coward.

I can only manage the requisite level of objectivity for a few minutes at a time before my rage returns, but in that short time I can force myself to imagine what this person was seeing: a young, brash, obnoxious man-child who was so sure of himself as to be wholly confident that he could up and quit whenever he wanted, despite his having signed a six-year contract committing him to as many deployments as the Air Force saw fit, and that this young man-child had a smile on his face every time he asserted—as if it were a foregone conclusion, as if it were a fact—that he was never going back out. When I carry out this thought experiment, I can see how one might think that this young man is smart enough to know that high scores on the inventory can earn him a diagnosis of depression, which at the very least will get him out of his next deployment, if not all of them, and I can then see the logic behind leveling the above charges.

What I can't see is how someone who had been practicing for as long as this person had wouldn't bother to ask the stupid young man why his affect was so inconsistent with his inventories. Why he got that dumbass grin on his face whenever he proclaimed his status as a non-deployer. Why he seemed so happy to be talking to Mental Health, an act that, at that time, was associated with weakness, with faggotry, with being a pussy-ass little bitch.

Because this person didn't ask these questions, I didn't tell them that yes, I appeared happy, and, yes, I was afraid. And if we assess cowardice as simple fear, then I suppose it's possible that I was, in fact, a coward. But if we understand that cowardice is a fear of doing dangerous or difficult things, then I was no coward, as I wasn't afraid of doing such things. I was afraid of wanting to do them. And so the sarcasm, and the blitheness, and the general holier-than-thou, smug-as-fuck looks on my face weren't because I was malingering. They were because for perhaps the first time in my life, I was standing up for something I actually believed in, and because I was sure that by doing so I was saving myself, and that this decision did, in fact, make me quite righteous—likely more righteous than anyone who was willing to become the monster—I was, paradoxically, pleased with my decision. I wasn't happy, but I was also unwilling to break down and show this person my fear, my sadness, and my pain. This bravado is what accounted for the discrepancy between paper and person and was cited as the main evidence against me.

When I found out what this person had told my commander,

214 // IAN FRITZ

I refused to see them again. But by now I was in the awkward spot of being forced to go to Mental Health, so I had to see someone. Because of the limited number of appointments available with the handful of other providers, I was told I would be seeing the officer who was in charge of Mental Health. This sounded like a threat and continued to feel like one when I met the Mental Health Clinic chief, who was, let's say, suspicious of me and my intentions.

The Air Force kindly gave me a copy of my mental health records, in all of their unfiltered glory, when I got out. I was not liked by most of the providers I saw. I both remember this—one of them called me an asshole to my face during a session (he later got a DUI, so it seems his judgment is questionable)—and have the documentation to show it.

Reading their notes, I am presented with the image of a person who is claiming to be suicidal on paper, but then denies intent in person, a person who claims that they are mentally unstable, but refuses to accept medication or therapy to treat this instability, and a person who is committed to no longer doing their sworn duty, no matter the cost.

Which was all true. Saying out loud that I wanted to die, or no longer exist, was shameful. I was too proud to tell them about how often I locked myself in my room at home, because I knew that the kitchen had the knives that would get the job done, and as long as I kept drinking, eventually I would pass out, and while I'd feel pretty shitty the next morning, I would have survived. I was also too afraid of being committed, certain that any sort of inpatient treatment was akin to imprisonment (being from Florida and being raised in a family rife with mental illness, I was all too familiar with the power of the Baker Act). I was, moreover, being threatened with prosecution for having even broached the idea that

I might be afraid, and then chastised, and threatened with more punishment, for not talking about my feelings, aka the possibility that I might be afraid.

I was similarly suspicious of therapy, or at least my conceptualization of it, and convinced that it was a cure worse than the disease. I couldn't bear to think about my missions, or being a DSO, or even Pashto, without breaking out into a cold sweat and becoming nauseated, so how the fuck was I supposed to talk about all the shit that had gotten me to that point? Couldn't they just give me what I wanted and let me never hear any of it again? Seemed like an equally effective "treatment" to me. Between all the side-effect horror stories I'd heard and my certainty that I was unfixable, I wasn't willing to consider taking the meds they were proposing, because I just knew that I too would wind up initially being prescribed two antidepressants to keep the suicidal ideations at bay, and then when those (and the fear of nightmares) kept me up at night, I'd be given some low-dose benzodiazepines to take the edge off, and then when those, combined with my preexisting and severe alcohol consumption, led me to be groggy to the point of falling asleep at work, they'd add on some methylphenidate so that I wouldn't be a completely useless zombie. Just a mostly useless one. This isn't a hypothetical regimen; it's exactly what Kasady was prescribed.

As for doing my job, I was fine with that, as long as my job didn't require killing people. I was then reminded, repeatedly, as if I'd somehow forgotten, that I had in fact joined the military of my own volition, and that the military tends to go about killing people, and therefore this is what I signed up to do. Never mind that at the age of eighteen I enlisted to perform a different job on a different plane, assured that the closest I'd be to combat was, literally, thirty thousand feet above any potential battlefield.

Never mind that if I'd asked my recruiter, or my instructor at basic training, or an instructor at language school, or an instructor at intelligence school, or an instructor at survival school, or a linguist who worked aboard RC-135s, if I had asked fucking *anyone* if I'd be responsible for killing people as a linguist, I would have been called an idiot and laughed out of the room.

So while Captain B., said Mental Health Clinic chief, had a reputation for being a ballbuster (if she hadn't been a she, and hadn't been blond and attractive, she most likely would have just been seen as serious, or straightforward, but, y'know, sexism), I can't help but think that her demeanor at the outset of our meeting was in large part due to having been warned about me. Thankfully, she was still professional, if not exceedingly direct. She outlined for me all of the above problems with my story, and while she didn't call me a liar, she made it very clear that it wasn't hard for others to think of me as one.

"Do you want help?"

"Yes, ma'am."

"Then you have to see the psychiatrist, you have to do therapy, and you have to cooperate with both."

"I . . . Okay. I will."

I think she expected me to argue with her, like she'd been told I had with everyone else, because her face sort of dropped for a second when I said this. She reset it, but her posture and presence softened. More gently, she said, "Good. Why the change of heart?"

"I can't keep feeling like this."

"Like what?"

"Like I want to die."

"Do you want to hurt yourself?"

"Fuck! Sorry. No, that isn't it. I just don't want to be alive."

"Do I need to send you to the hospital?"

"No. I'm not going to kill myself. I don't want to. No, like. I don't want to want to."

"Okay. If that changes, do you have someone to call?"

"Yes. I have friends. My roommate helps, too."

"All right. You're going to do therapy with one of our social workers, and you'll see Dr. S. next week about medications."

"Yes, ma'am."

I would like to think that I would have come to this decision eventually, regardless of who was recommending, or even dictating it, but I suspect that this might not have been the case. I'm hopeful that someone else would have understood that not having a plan to commit suicide doesn't mean you're not suicidal, just that you're impulsive, but no one else had up until that point, so I'm not sure. Whether in prison, or dead, or just mired in my miasma of melancholy, I don't know that I'd be here without Captain B. So, thanks, ma'am.

While the person who recommended the charges didn't have it in for me personally, they did for me as an idea. I was not the first DSO threatened with prosecution for malingering and cowardice, and I wouldn't be the last. None of us wound up being charged with these heinous crimes, because the crimes were nonexistent. The only heinous thing lying about was the accusation that any of us, who had seen more combat and killed more people than any of those trying to accuse us, were cowards. We were just tired and angry. Maybe tired of being angry. Those in charge, however, were well-rested, and they were fucking furious.

By the time they were considering levying these charges against me, I was the seventh DSO who'd been to Afghanistan to quit for mental health reasons (there were others who left through more official channels, and so it's unclear what, if any, issues they were dealing with). We came from varying socioeconomic classes, separate parts of the country, different religions, politics, upbringings, marital statuses, age groups. The only common thread between us (other than the usual maleness and whiteness) was our experiences in Afghanistan. It seemed pretty self-fucking-evident that we were not the problem, the mission was.

But at almost every level, our concerns were ignored. When Kasady talked to our leadership about the suffering he was seeing, about the fellow DSO who had told him "I got a dog just to make sure I have a reason to come home," they did nothing. Well, that's not true. In what appeared to be some misguided attempt to bolster his career, our leadership sent the most bumbling dumbfuck captain they could to Afghanistan, where he attempted to swing his nonexistent dick around (the man tried to write formal letters of reprimand for other grown men refusing to go to bed when he told them to), only to be laughed at as others outside of our leadership quickly realized how much of a fucking moron he was.

Upon being told that most of the DSOs in Afghanistan were operating at around a 30 percent capacity, that they had only received enough training to be capable of understanding 30 percent of what they were hearing, the commander of the 1st Special Operations Wing, a man who is now a three-star general and the head of all of AFSOC, responded with "I'd rather have 30 percent of a DSO than no DSO."

The context here is important, in that these weren't individual asshats carrying out some vendetta against us or the people of

Afghanistan. All of these poor decisions—sending out undertrained people, sending them out with a less than 1:1 dwell time (despite the fact that this requires the signed approval of the secretary of defense, which our squadron leaders most certainly did not have), threatening people who were claiming mental health problems with punishment unless they went back to the place and job that they were claiming was the root cause of their mental health problems—were symptoms of the greater disease that was the "war" in Afghanistan.

Those quotes are there because despite what you may have heard, what we did in Afghanistan wasn't a war. Not according to a senior NATO commander in 2009, who upon being asked about the type of fighting that was going on, replied with "We checked with the legal team and they agree it's not a war." Not according to General Stanley McChrystal, the (oh so very supreme) commander of Afghan operations, who wrote in an official report that what we were doing was "not a war in the conventional sense." Not according to U.S. law, as we hadn't declared war against anyone, and even if we'd bothered with this ludicrous formality, that really seems like such a waste of time when the only people affected aren't the ones doing the declaring, and who would it have been against? The Taliban? They gave up way back in 2002. *Afghanistan?* (Dear reader, please read that italicized word with as much snark and contempt as you can muster. For the world's last superpower to think about declaring war against a "country" that only exists because of arbitrary colonial lines drawn one hundred years ago after the British finally admitted defeat is laughable in the extreme. But then, I guess, Grenada happened. And bananas. So maybe not.) No, we were at war with an idea.

Not terrorism, by the by. We knew that was unkillable. (In 2011, the undersecretary of defense for intelligence, Michael G. Vickers, said about the idea of al Qaeda, "You're never going to eradicate that.") We were at war with the idea that we weren't all-powerful, untouchable, and fully willing to do whatever it takes to show the world just how true these things were. This mindset had metastasized to every part of the military, including my leadership. They weren't mad at us for the act of quitting. They were mad at us for why we were quitting: because we knew that what we were doing was pointless.

When you deal with people who are infatuated with the idea of something but have never had a tangible interaction with it, there's always going to be major conflict. Some of our leadership had, at some point, killed some folk. So, for them, we were doing what they had done, or at least what they told themselves they had done: killing evil men. This is one of the easiest things anyone can do, as it requires no justification, no second thoughts. Killing evil men is righteous, both ethically and morally. But we knew that these evil men weren't evil all of the time, or maybe any of the time. Either way, this meant that sometimes we were just killing men. This was not something they were familiar with.

Even the other DSOs, the non-Pashto, non-Arab ones, took it for granted that we should have felt all the same things they did—pride, excitement, joy, even. But then, I guess that's just a natural consequence of people who have to imagine an experience they've never had.

There were members of our squadron who tried to do their best by us. Regardless of their feelings for us personally, they knew that we weren't being treated fairly. Even Ed, in all of his Big Blueness, had to admit that the squadron had not taken good care of its people. One of the senior Arab DSOs supported us as best he could, albeit while still serving the needs of the Air Force. Another Arab, not a DSO, but an incredibly gifted linguist, understood what it meant to do things that in the moment you knew were necessary, like shooting and killing the armed teenagers driving a jeep at full speed directly toward you somewhere in the sands of North Africa, but that later, when you were home again, playing with your own children, might fuck you up pretty good. But there was only so much they could do, and it wouldn't make sense for them to jeopardize their careers when the outcome would be the same.

They knew that there was no arguing with the idea that was this "war." Because it was a war against an idea, I think that for so many people, the killing too was just an idea. They bragged about how they "hear dead people" and "kill people and break their shit" and all the other euphemisms for war, but because they hadn't done, well, any of that, any dead people that they associated themselves with weren't actual persons. They were monsters. But then, monsters aren't real. So they were ideas, effigies. And while it might be satisfying, the burning of effigies only accomplishes two things: the propagation of violence, and the preservation of the idea you're supposed to be destroying.

This might be why the only name I find appropriate for what we did in Afghanistan is "The Forever War." The point wasn't to rid the world, or even Afghanistan, of al Qaeda, or the Taliban. The point was to make sure that we could always, for fucking ever, be trying to rid the world of al Qaeda or the Taliban. If that meant we made new versions of each of these groups, well that was no problem, as we would just get more enemies. More effigies. More ideas. More war.

INFINITY, OR WHAT I WISH I HADN'T HEARD

ACCORDING TO MY OFFICIAL Air Force records, I do not have, and in fact have never had, PTSD. Formally receiving this diagnosis would have required an official admission that what I did and saw and heard was in fact traumatic and that it wasn't normal, which would only have served to justify my reasons for not wanting to go back. You can see why the powers that be wouldn't want to admit this. And while this diagnosis wasn't true when the Air Force made it, it might be now. Time doesn't heal all wounds—some simply can't be treated—but eventually your mind can bring the edges together, and while the scar is ugly and imprecise, the gaping hole has, finally, closed. These days I can listen to Pashto without breaking out in a cold sweat, get on a plane without thinking about the guns that ought to be attached to it, and talk about war without wanting to curl up in a ball and die. This, then, is understood as meaning that my PTSD has been cured (never mind that curing something that was never supposed to have existed creates some mild metaphysical stickiness).

In the time since I wasn't diagnosed, the military has embraced a different terminology to attempt to describe the turmoil that I and so many others experienced: moral injury. The idea of moral injury has been around since at least the 1980s, though the explicit term was coined by Jonathan Shay in the nineties, when his work with Vietnam veterans led to his writing *Achilles in Vietnam*. Today, Syracuse University's Moral Injury Project not only defines moral injury but attempts to explain why and when it happens:

> Moral injury is the damage done to one's conscience or moral compass when that person perpetrates, witnesses, or fails to prevent acts that transgress one's own moral beliefs, values, or ethical codes of conduct.

This is a good definition; it is thorough while simultaneously casting a wide enough net to embrace the myriad reasons any warfighter could suffer such an injury. Being a DSO allowed for perpetration, witnessing, and failure. Certainly, my moral code was violated. But I don't think moral injury fully encompasses just what happened. It's not that I, along with almost every other Pashto DSO, wasn't morally injured. We were. But it's not entirely accurate to say that there was "damage done to [my] conscience or moral compass." It's more like, along with the many men I killed, my consciousness was blown the fuck up.

With the exception of spies mythical and real, most warfighters throughout history have not been tasked with killing people they know. Even in our modern wars, in Iraq and Afghanistan, the majority of killing is done by complete strangers. There is, I assume, a feeling of knowing associated with killing someone in close combat, even though you may have no knowledge of anything that defines that person as a unique human. But this is different from understanding what makes that person a person, from killing someone you know. With modernity came the ability to have this knowledge.

The most famous of these warriors are drone operators. These men and women face issues that I can't begin to understand, as the cognitive dissonance that they experience is so strange as to be something out of science fiction. If anything, it seems that their injury is arguably worsened by the moral contradiction of being so far away from the "threat." These are people who wake up every morning and drive to work like any other commuter. Except, their work is hunting people. They do this work for twelve hours (or more), and at the end of their shift they head home. Just like any other commuter. Maybe their significant other calls them and asks them to stop and pick up some milk on the way, which they obligingly do, maybe grabbing a candy bar or a six-pack at the same time. And then they sit down to dinner with their loved ones, the memory of the missile they fired five hours earlier destroying a man still playing in their head.

Often, the man that was destroyed by that missile was a target that this drone operator had been following for days or weeks. This work is done to establish what is known as a pattern of life (POL), aka the shit someone does on a regular basis. POL is supposed to help determine whether the things someone is doing or the people someone is meeting are happenstance or more purposeful. Did that guy go talk to a known bomb-maker who also happens to be a tailor just once, like someone who was trying out different tailors might do? Or did that guy go see his "tailor" two or three times a week for a month, all while wearing the same ill-fitting clothing? In the course of this work—sometimes as a side effect, sometimes completely on purpose—one begins to develop an idea of who that target is.

In a *New York Times* article exploring the effects of this work, of the damage done to the men and women who perform this function, an unnamed drone operator says that his injuries resulted from "cognitive combat intimacy," a term so apt that I wish his name were published, if only so he could get the credit he deserves for such an accurate neologism. The day in, day out watching of targets, learning about their lives, their habits, their likes and dislikes, results in a strong sense of familiarity, and sometimes, even closeness (a friend of mine who did this sort of work once told me that he and his team could always identify one particular target based on the highly specific porn searches said target made on various devices that he used, which while comical, is indeed also quite intimate). And then, after you've come to know so much about this person, in fact *because* you've come to know so much about this person, you kill them.

The work I did was not this in-depth, and nowhere near as detailed (I didn't hear of any porn searches, though I did learn about a few sexual preferences), and so it could be said, in relation to others like these drone operators, that I didn't know much about the men I was listening to, not really. The sense of closeness I had with the men I listened to was not a cognitive process, but an emotional one (whether and how these two processes are actually different is a matter of debate, but in my usage here I mean to have *cognitive* equate to an objective, fact-finding affair, and *emotional* to mean a subjective, desire-discovering activity).

I spent a long time fighting this realization. I had been okay with intellectualizing the Taliban as a movement, analyzing their motivations, trying to understand why they might do all these terrible things. This was okay to do, as knowing your enemy is part of being a good warrior. Loving them, not so much. This might be a me-specific problem. I'm not certain, as articulating it is hard. But I find it impossible to feel another human without simultaneously loving them to some extent.

So when I say that my consciousness was blown up, while I'm being a little melodramatic, for the most part I mean it. If we define consciousness as "the normal state of being awake and able to understand what is happening around you," then I sure as shit stopped being conscious at some point, somewhere in Afghanistan, sometime around the impact of a missile or a bullet. I couldn't understand why I felt this love for these men, and I couldn't understand how I was supposed to kill them once I knew that love existed.

What I now think is that this love hinged on a simple grammatical conceit. That of the collective, proper noun, e.g. the Taliban, vs. that of the singular, common noun. Because the whole of the Taliban did, in the end, tell me of their evil. I have no love for them. Any given talib just told me who they were. I couldn't help but love them.

When the Taliban told me of their plans to kill the men on the ground I was working for, I hated them, and longed for their death. When a talib told me of these plans, were they any different from me or the people I was working with who were actively plotting that same talib's death? When the Taliban fantasized about the glorious day when the invaders would be gone, they reeked of despotism and tyranny. When a talib dreamed of that future, were they any different from an American patriot who wouldn't stand the trespasses of another? When the Taliban lamented their losses, I scoffed at them, and laughed at their pain. When a talib lost his friend, was that any different from the ache I felt when my JTAC got shot?

Wouldn't I, and virtually everyone I knew, do the same thing if we were in their position? Of course I would defend my country, my *homeland*, and my way of life. Of course I would readily fight and happily kill those who I felt were threatening the people I loved. Hell, wasn't that why we were fighting this war? Wasn't that exactly what I was trained to do?

Because I could hear it all, both sides of this strange and eternal war, the boundary that was supposed to separate them from us no longer existed. Even if I only spent six hundred hours listening to the Taliban, or even just a portion of that, I spent thousands of hours hearing them in my head, building their camaraderie, telling me it was too cold to jihad, or breathing their friend's last breath.

And so, at some point, were we not all brothers in arms?

This love that I had, or have, was a one-sided affair. They knew I was listening (if not me, specifically, then at least me, conceptually). Whether it was a good or bad thing (from their perspective) that I was hearing them was irrelevant, as there was nothing they, or I, could do to stop me. I was their captive audience, held at gunpoints. Sometime during my second deployment I suddenly appreciated how this explained much of their bullshitting; it's a good idea to let your enemy hear that not only are you indefatigable, even after ten years of war, but that you're also excited to continue fighting, day after day. The enemy (aka me) hears this and becomes frustrated, disheartened, and confused, which are more or less the three things you want the target of your psychological warfare to be.

Their knowledge of my presence explained their ridiculous

projections, their claims that they had somehow killed hundreds of us, even when their attack had only targeted a few dozen guys out at some FOB. With time, my anger, my desire to confront them with their falsehoods, was replaced by exhaustion (as, I suspect, all anger eventually is). Once I was too tired and too sad to be angry at hearing them repeat these lies, I could hear them differently. I could hear them like a talib heard them. To a talib, these outrageous claims weren't lies. When they killed a few of us, say in a firefight, where they could be more certain of the deaths, they knew the real count; they had watched three, or four, or ten of us die (as opposed to a random mortar attack, or even an IED, where they couldn't be sure of the number dead). But it wasn't how many of us they killed that mattered, it was the fact that they were killing us at all.

U.S. (and many European) fighters are so well equipped, so technologically advanced, so well armored as to be mythical. SEALs, Green Berets, and other special operators are trained to continue moving after they've been shot. (I've helped them with this training. The rules were that when we, the "bad guys," got shot, we went down. If they, the "good guys," got shot, they were supposed to keep advancing until they neutralized us and completed their mission. All of this was done with simulation rounds, but there's still impact, and the guns we were using were real; they really were getting shot.) The purpose of this training is to impart a psychology of undefeatability. It is singularly terrifying to shoot multiple bullets into what is supposed to be a human and then watch that (alleged) human continue to push forward as if nothing happened to them. Yes, somewhere in the back of your mind you know that they are wearing a bulletproof vest and other pieces of body armor and that these are the things keeping them alive, but that knowledge doesn't make the six-foot-tall, two-hundred-and-fifty-pound creature coming at you any less intimidating. To kill such a being is to kill a god. I could now see why a Talib might feel entitled to inflate his kill count.

In addition to this sort of allegorical accounting, I wondered if, in a way, they weren't actually right about how many of us they were successfully killing. At the very least, a lot of us were dying. And I couldn't help but think, if a warfighter dies because of a war, does it matter if they died on the battlefield? Does it matter if their death is "self-inflicted"? All those men and women who made it out of Afghanistan, only to commit suicide once they were home, are they not casualties of war? Didn't the Taliban kill them?

Equally disheartening was my newfound understanding of why the Taliban seemed to ignore, somehow discount, our kills. On the missions where I knew we had killed dozens of them, they routinely refused to acknowledge all of the deaths. Some of this was attributable to their haphazard organization; they didn't exactly have rosters of who was fighting in a given battle, or dog tags to identify unrecognizable corpses. Our jokes about them being immortal had stopped being funny, because now I couldn't help but wonder if they actually were. They were suffering thousands of casualties per year, which I always heard about, but not once had I been told that the Taliban was growing weaker, getting smaller. It was like we were playing whack-an-Afghan, and every time we managed to hit one, another popped up one wadi over. How many times had we rolled up the same guy, interrogated him, probably tortured him, eventually released him, only to wind up hunting him down again weeks or months or years later? They were constantly replacing themselves, either literally or figuratively, and we had fallen for the trap of thinking of them as interchangeable, thereby placing them beyond the constraints of ordinary humanity, allowing them to become the superhumans they claimed they were. So, while I knew they were dying, I no longer believed they were dead.

You may have noticed, or maybe not, how slippery I have been with the verb *to kill*:

"I killed."

"We killed."

"I helped kill."

This is no grammatical slip, an inability to keep track of who did what. These variations are there because there was, and is, an argument to be made about my role in any killing, as that's not how gunships, or Whiskeys, or DSOs work. No single individual is held responsible for the people that our planes kill. It's a crew effort. There is no ammunition without a loadmaster to balance the plane; a FCO can't fire that ammunition without gunners loading the weapons; the gunners won't ready the weapons till the sensor operators find a bad guy; the sensor operators couldn't find that bad guy without pilots flying the plane; the pilots couldn't have flown the plane to the location where the sensors found that bad guy without a navigator guiding them across the country; the navigator couldn't have safely gotten across that country without an EWO making sure no one hit the plane with a rocket; the EWO couldn't have used his equipment without a flight engineer making sure everything was in working order.

I didn't mention the role of DSOs because DSOs, while nice to have around, are not remotely necessary for a C-130 to carry out its mission. And so, if I heard something that proved to be the key piece of information that resulted in us shooting, a piece of information, that, if lacking, would have prevented us from shooting, then didn't I kill someone on my own? Conversely, if I didn't hear anything that was related to why we shot, then did I kill anyone at all?

The problem with this argument is that according to my official records I have in fact killed 123 people. The actual wording is "123 insurgents EKIA" (EKIA = enemy killed in action, so not quite people, but definitely killed). These records don't say that I was part of a crew that killed these people, or that I supported other people who did the killing, just that I killed those 123 humans. I can't know, and will never know, if all of these kills belong to me. I do know, and will always know, that I belong to all of them.

To have felt these men, and to have consequently loved them, was an exercise in radical empathy, long before I knew that such a concept existed. For a long time, I struggled with how to explain this to people. Some of this was a problem with who I was telling the story to. Americans have been well trained to respect, and even idolize, those who go off to "fight for their freedom." They have not been taught how to listen to those men and women tell their stories when they contradict the greater narrative, when they conflict with their conception of their nation's infallible moral excellence. But most of it was a problem with my storytelling; I wasn't able to describe my thoughts without my emotions confusing the message. So when I told people there were things I wished I hadn't heard, their natural assumption was that those things were all of the violence, and the killing, and the dying. In response to this, I would get upset that they were missing the point and then fail to explain myself properly. I didn't know how to say, instead of scream, "No, that's not it! That's the job! That's just what you hear."

I was talking to a friend about this, probably the best Pashto DSO of any of us, and he too spent years struggling with his telling. Maybe we've softened with age, or maybe it's because now he's a physicist and thinks about things at scales most of us can't comprehend, but he finds it easier to explain now. What he told me was that while any given person can be infinitely different from another, you can only be so different within the human experience, because "that infinity is still confined between zero and one": human or not. What we listened to made this infinity that much smaller. Not the killing, not the dying, but the everything else.

The run-of-the-mill, everyday this is my life and it's full of just as much petty bullshit as yours, so I'm gonna make a decent number of dick jokes to try and brighten it up a little bit (dick jokes, it would seem, are universal).

Or the well, yeah, I'm trying to kill, I mean, not you in particular, but the men like you, but hey, aren't you trying to kill me and my brothers too? All's fair, man. Besides, I never did anything to you. Look what you've done to us.

And the I can't wait till this shit is over and we can get back to our lives.

These are the things I wish I hadn't heard.

If I hadn't heard those things, infinity would have remained, well, infinite. I would have been able to tell myself that the Taliban were not men, were not even human, that they were in fact Enemies, whose only purpose was to be Killed in Action. If I hadn't heard those things, I wouldn't have loved the men I was listening to. If I hadn't loved them, killing them would have been easy. If killing them had been easy, my consciousness would have remained intact.

To say that I loved the Taliban is surely anathema to most anyone who reads this. It doesn't feel good, or right, for me to say it. But I checked, and of the many definitions that exist for the word *love*, one of them is the following: "strong affection for another arising out of kinship or personal ties." I most certainly had personal ties to the men I was listening to; they told me shit they wouldn't tell their best (non-Talib) friends, their wives, their fathers. And at some point, not because they were Talibs, in fact in spite of that, because they were human, I came to have the strong affection for them that I firmly believe it is impossible not to develop for virtually any other person if you can get past your own bullshit and just accept that they're people too.

Let me be clear about something here: I in no way support the Taliban, their stated goals, their practices, or really anything about them. Nor do I support the individual men who comprise the greater Taliban. Their movement and many of their beliefs are an affront to modernity in all of its complicated, messy, but ultimately better than the shit that actively and gleefully removes myriad human rights from everyone who isn't a God-fearing man, splendor. They are not the good guys.

None of these things detract from the fact that they're still human. They're still people. I have no desire for you to identify with them or wish for their lives to be spared. What I do ask is that you understand that I did identify with them. I had to. My job required it. All that talking with my teachers in language school, so I could figure out how they think? That's what made me a good linguist. The translation we did isn't something that can be done by a computer or a robot, it isn't the simple transformation of the sounds of one language into another. You have to understand the intent, the tone, the playfulness, the fear, the anger, the confusion, all of the nuances that attach themselves to spoken words and drastically change their meanings. It was impossible for me to do this without internalizing the speakers' logic (it's possible for others, but I don't understand that process).

It was also impossible, despite all this knowing and feeling, for me to wish for their lives to have been spared. To have spared their lives would have been to guarantee that many others would have been taken. And if Camus was right, and "There is but one truly serious philosophical problem," it isn't as simple as suicide or not. Whether I think my life is worth living is unimportant, or at least less important than the lives of those who know that their existence has merit. And if it's in my power to not only help them keep living, but ensure that they can, am I not obligated to carry out that duty? If, in this act of protecting life, which, at least in my case, often required the taking of other lives, my life becomes threatened (but only by me), when do I stop? Can I? If I can physically keep flying, keep listening, and by doing so save ten, or twenty, or maybe hundreds of other lives, but with the knowledge that at some point, I will kill myself, which is more moral? Sparing their lives? Or ending mine? This was the only truly serious philosophical problem. Not if I kill myself, but when.

I've managed to piece it back together, mostly. Said consciousness. I have an idea of what's right and wrong in this world, whom I (truly) love and don't. But like anything else that has been shattered, once I, or at least my I, was rebuilt, there were pieces missing, structures weakened. The part of my mind that could hear Pashto without having a panic attack was gone. The bit of brain that understood that violence isn't always the answer was strained, at best, bearing a larger load than it had been built for. And, for a long, long time, I couldn't find the section for empathy. I thought, in that time, that it was gone forever.

Because I couldn't feel anything for anyone. Not the Taliban, not you, not me. Initially, this felt like your average disdain;

anything anyone tried to tell me about DSOing, or the war, or how to feel, I simply dismissed as irrelevant. In the words of Trevor, "No concern that any human has is worse than any mission I've been on." At some point though, this dismissal metastasized. It was too much work to feel that the things people were telling me were irrelevant. It was far easier to just know that the people telling me were.

The way I figured it, if I'd already been forced to kill those I loved, then how was I supposed to attach meaning to anyone else's life? To do so would have only served to set me up for further trauma. This is a known side effect of combat, described by Shay in *Achilles in Vietnam*. He felt that it was a survival skill, a thing we naturally did during war just to make it from one day to the next. We stopped feeling bothered when we referred to dead civilians as collateral damage, so as to eliminate their humanity, as this meant we didn't have to worry about killing civilians. We stopped caring when they extended our deployments or gave us half the people to carry out twice as many missions. We stopped hoping for a day when the war(s) would end. We stopped wanting anything, stopped willing *anything*.

But for me, apathy wasn't sufficient. Not caring wasn't good enough, wasn't powerful enough. Not caring is only one step removed from yes caring. I needed to be further away from whatever it was that was allowing me to see and understand the Taliban as human. I needed negation. To say that someone's life was meaningless wasn't enough; I had to know, and had to let them know, that their life removed meaning from the world, such that, if I could invalidate them, or even just kill them, we would all be better off.

This antipathy, or maybe even dyspathy, is still around in some ways. I'm cold and calloused about death. When I was applying to medical school, I had prepared an answer for a question I was told I might get during interviews: "How do you plan on dealing with death?" The first thing I had to do was learn to stifle my laughter, it being comical that these people would be asking me that question. Then I had to learn how to not respond with "What the fuck do you know about death?" Finally, I learned how to tell them what they wanted to hear. "Well, when people die, it matters. But you still have to fly the next day. Or, I guess, operate, or you know, go to work." I found the question a little silly, for, as Erich Maria Remarque wrote, "when a man has seen so many dead he cannot understand any longer why there should be so much anguish over a single individual." Besides, I wasn't interested in watching people die—been there, done that, pretty over it—I was interested in saving their lives. Everyone has to die some time, what's that got to do with me?

When I was in medical school, this skill served me well. There was no trauma, or illness, or story that could unsettle me, as I knew that watching people die was easy. All you have to do is sit there. I could absorb pain, heartache, rage, sadness, insanity, despair, this-can't-be-happening's, no-God-no's, that-can't-be-right's. I could soak up joy, relief, acceptance, surprise, happiness, thank-God's, we'll-fight's, I'm-gonna-do-this's. There was no emotion that I couldn't drink in without a benevolent look on my unreacting face.

Even now, when my partner tells me about the people she sees with cancer or some other terminal illness in the emergency room, my first question is always "How old?" and if the answer is greater than sixty, I scoff and say, "Eh." Sixty years is about twice as long as the lives of most of the men I killed, so like, shit sucks for sure, but fuck 'em, that's a good run. I don't consider the other lives that will be affected by this person's illness and subsequent death, because they too are irrelevant.

I could do this, can do this, continue to do this, because I am not interested in your suffering. It is gauche and weak and self-absorbed. But most of all, it's unbearable.

I cannot fucking bear to see, to acknowledge, to speak into reality any of the suffering that exists in this world. If I do, if I feel any of these humans, alive and dead, then I will feel all of them again, and I will cease to exist. Because it turns out that the part of my consciousness responsible for empathy wasn't gone. It had just gotten so big that I couldn't see the forest for the stumps.

I won't presume to speak for anyone else who has, or had, or "doesn't have" PTSD, as it isn't some singular, identical bogeyman that haunts everyone the exact same way. I just know that for me, and I believe for many others, the thing that became most disordered was what and how we feel. The boundaries of what can or should be felt were erased, leaving us lost, somewhere in infinity.

TINNITUS, OR YOU
SEEM FINE NOW

YOU DO GET WARNED about some of the, let's call them side effects of flying. The perforated eardrums that come with flying with a sinus infection. The hazards of inhaling all the various heavy metals that waft around the plane after every 105 round is fired. Eventually, the squadron's best efforts notwithstanding, some of the newer DSOs even got warned about the risk of morbid and/or suicidal ideation. But I don't know that anyone ever warned me about tinnitus. I don't think it's because they didn't have it, as I'm pretty sure that almost everyone who flew does, albeit to varying extents. I've wondered if it's because it's so hard to explain, the tried and true "ringing in the ears" not really doing the reality of tinnitus justice. I guess the warning was implicit, as I was told to wear "ear-pro," hearing protection, in the form of soft earplugs underneath my headphones. But only other languages recommended this. No one who had actually listened to the Taliban did that dumb shit. Pashto is hard enough to understand without foam blocking your ears.

My tinnitus is mild. Occasionally it worsens, makes its way up the volume dial to medium-bad. I got lucky. Other guys didn't. Taylor is one of these guys. Six deployments and a couple thousand flight hours made his tinnitus terrible, up there at eight or nine, occasionally blasting its way to eleven. Hell, I don't know that he even remembers what it's like for the world to be quiet.

Unfortunately for Taylor, there is no cure for tinnitus. There are some pills and other treatment options out there that are supposed to make the ringing more akin to a distant alarm clock instead of the cathedral bells going off in his head at all times, but he doesn't bother with those things, as he's already found the treatment that works for him: more noise.

This makes tinnitus an interesting disease, one wherein the treatment is remarkably similar to the symptom. Part of the reason that there's no known cure is because the disease itself is very poorly understood. We don't know why some people develop it and some don't (plenty of people have had their eardrums burst, theoretically an excellent inciting process, and then not developed tinnitus); we don't know how it works (there's decent evidence that whatever the mechanism is, it involves areas of the brain that don't have anything to do with "hearing"); and we don't have a good way to model it (it's easy enough to make a mouse hear a ringing noise and determine whether said noise interferes with the mouse's ability to hear other things; it's an awful lot harder to ask that mouse how said noise affects their mental health). If the problem is the constancy of sound, then a logical treatment is the reduction, or removal, of that sound. But it's difficult, if not impossible, to stop your brain from hearing one specific frequency, particularly when it's not actually "hearing" that frequency, simply experiencing it. It's far easier to mask the sound with other noise.

This is a common remedy, used by metalheads, construction workers, and linguists alike.

So Taylor's life is perpetually even more unquiet. Alongside the tinnitus, he falls asleep to the sounds of a fan (every night) and an audiobook (most nights). Even then, the hum is still there (it's more like a buzzing than a ringing, but it's very high-pitched). The only time it truly goes away is when he's back where he belongs, back where it began, sitting next to a plane's engine roaring to life.

If Taylor and I talk about Afghanistan, we note many of the same things. The number of rounds fired, missions flown, Taliban heard, men killed. We talk about sleeping during transit, or how boring so many missions were. But it's never the same story. There's a difference in his voice when he talks about the "real" missions. He's proud of that one where his crew had to go back to base for more ammo *twice*. His eyes gleam a little when he mentions the time he heard, found, and pushed the button that killed the enemy hiding in the night.

So when he told me that it doesn't really bother him, this ever-present sound, that it's just a physical remnant of a life long ago left behind, for a while, I believed him. Of all of us, he was, perhaps, the most resilient. He's killed as many people as me, probably a lot more. He spent twice as long in Afghanistan, at a worse base, with far fewer "amenities" to distract him from his missions. He's never wanted to kill himself, never gotten taken off flight status for his craziness, and he didn't try and drink himself into oblivion for a few years.

But then I was visiting him after we'd both been out for a bit, after he'd had time to rest his ears. We'd gone down to Pacific Grove to pick up some pizza, and as we were driving back up the hill to his house a car door slammed, or someone dropped something heavy, or who knows maybe a 105 really did get fired into that California neighborhood, aimed directly into our brains, and he swerved so hard away from the sound that our guts were left three feet east. After he put the car back in the correct lane, he asked me, "Do you think normal people would have done that?" and I wondered if he wasn't stretching the truth about his tinnitus. When I looked over at him, I knew he was.

It was like looking at my heart projected on his face. The fear, anguish, and uncountable memories of that sound. That wondrous sound, all forty-five pounds of bullet being fired, that gave us the gift of tinnitus in the first place. That incredible sound that is forever linked to the voices of the men who roamed the mountains below us. That beautiful and terrifying sound that simultaneously eliminates and creates so much more noise, the voices gone, replaced by the crackle in the radios that has nightmared us for so long. In that moment, we felt each other's pain. And their pain. And your pain. I'm not sure we didn't feel all the pain the world had to offer.

The more I think about it, the more I realize, of course we never were telling the same story. Not really. How could we?

This is the paradox of tinnitus. It is a disease, a pathology, and having it means that the world is always noisy. But this disease, this permanent rain of sound, protects you from a far worse din: the quiet. When it's quiet, no one is talking or joking or saying what needs to happen next. There is no next. Because when it's quiet, nothing's happening. When nothing's happening, either lots of people are dead or they're about to be.

But when there's noise, everything's okay. You're moving, talking, figuring out where the enemy is hiding. And then you're reloading, and repositioning, and then, finally, shooting, and everything is magnificently loud. But then you're watching them atomize, knowing there's the initial boom of impact, the whoosh as the air itself is broken and scattered, and the instant stillness and fucking *quiet* like no other that lies in the hole where there were once men.

The quiet is why it has taken me so long to tell this story, and why you've likely never heard it. Because when we tell this story, people always get quiet. Sometimes it's for a second before they offer their thoughts, condolences, or advice.

> "At least you did something."
> "There are happy stories too, right?"
> "Why not just stop thinking about it?"

With others, the pause is longer, full of discomfort, while they try and think it through, and find the words that won't be cliché or judging or otherwise out of place.

> "I'm sorry."
> "That sounds awful."
> "Have you talked to someone about it?"

If you think that the latter set of responses is preferred, that I want you to think before you speak, before you give me the chance to realize that you're a fucking idiot, the chance to want to make you permanently quiet, you'd be right in a way. It is nicer when you don't immediately react, or when you try to sympathize, hell, even, in your mind, *empathize*. It lets us know that there are still people who are good, kind, and thoughtful.

But these responses are bittersweet, as they remind us that, maybe, we aren't those people, not anymore. My buddy Chris used to be so affectionate, so full of glee every time he was around those he loves. But then he lost his empathy in some battle, on some deployment, doing to other families that thing he most feared happening to his own. If he hears you talk about your child, he pictures the children he saw playing in a street with IEDs on either side of it, and he wonders who's the happier parent: you or one of those kids' mothers? If your relative dies, he thinks about how this is an occasion for you. A rarity. Whereas there, a young girl woke up every day knowing one of us might kill another member of her family. How could he be a good man, a good father, when he had killed so many other fathers (and probably children)? How could he feel anything for anyone after that?

There are others out there, who think that they're like us, those who decided what our stories meant long before they ever heard them. Their responses vary in content, but not in tone.

"You got to hunt the best prey."

"Well, I voted against the war."

"Should've glassed the whole place."

"Isn't that what you signed up for?"

And while I have little faith in humankind, we who together are incapable of nothing, I can't help but believe in humans, who alone are capable of everything. So I maintain that most of you are good and that most of you will try to listen. I used to think that this was a bad thing, that if you listened, I might somehow give you my pain. Admittedly, there was an attraction to the idea, to being rid of this weight. But I knew the heft, and I knew that even if I could somehow give it to you, in the end I wouldn't. Because if I did, you might understand how I felt the first time I decided men I'd never met would die. How I felt all-powerful and utterly impotent in that moment. How I felt while I listened to them talk, and laugh, and celebrate. If you could feel that, then what was to stop you from feeling the incandescent rage that has licked at my soul ever since the day I realized I did everything right, everything *perfectly* right, and good people died anyway? What would stop you from feeling that rage melt through another mental support beam every time you watched a celebration of death? How could I want you to feel that? What would the benefit be? I feel a little bit better, a little bit lighter, but now you have to shoulder that burden too? The math doesn't add up. Two people suffering isn't better than one.

So, I lied. I told you it's okay. It's a job. People die. It doesn't matter. It was a long time ago. That was a different world. I laughed, and told you about the good times, the great friends, the it's too cold to jihad story. And I told you a very old and terrible lie until you said those magic words:

"You seem fine now."

The truth wouldn't have let you say those words, because "the truth does not instruct, nor encourage virtue, nor suggest models of proper human behavior, nor restrain men from doing the things men have always done." The truth would have made those words, in that order, impossible.

But now, ten years after my last deployment, I wonder. What if it's precisely *because* I lied that this suffering continues to exist? If you could see it, help carry it, just for a day, what might happen? I'm not sure that this is possible. I can't give you my memories. I don't think making you watch or listen to war will help (violence as media meaning less than nothing to us anymore). I don't believe in compulsory military service; no one should be forced to be a part of an entity whose true purpose is killing.

The problem that I've come to see is that if we lie, war will always be there, at the backs of our minds, preventing us from feeling as if we can share this world. We will try and forget. Pretend it never happened. But the lies perpetuate the trauma. The truth may not set us free, but at least it won't contain us. If we don't share our thoughts and memories, we will be trapped in the never-ending cycle of consumption that is war. And so we must tell our stories, for ourselves, and for you.

There's already a day set aside for this. November 11. This is not what it was established for, nor what it is currently used for, but it has evolved with time, and I think it could be changed again.

It used to be called Armistice Day. The holiday was established for the celebration of World War I veterans, with the date corresponding to the armistice with Germany that formally ended combat on November 11, 1918 (note, formally; fighting continued for a few days after that, as it always has, informally). In 1945, Raymond Weeks, a World War II veteran, proposed that the day be renamed to Veterans Day. For Weeks, it was important that all veterans be honored on this day, not just those who died in the first Great War. In 1954, Congress enacted this change, and we have celebrated Veterans Day since.

The VA asserts that Veterans Day be spelled exactly that way, in the attributive case, with no apostrophe. They feel that this spelling is important, as Veterans Day is meant to honor all veterans. If you use the possessive case, that is, with the apostrophe, then Veterans' Day belongs to veterans. This spelling choice made sense in the wake of World War II. In 1950, 12 percent of Americans actively served, and virtually everyone in the country was involved in or affected by the war effort, be it via rations, or rotary clubs, or relatives.

This is no longer the case. The number of Americans who join the military, and subsequently, the number of veterans, has been steadily decreasing over the last forty years (roughly since the end of Vietnam). Today, less than 1 percent of the U.S. population actively serves in the military. Veterans are only 7 percent of the population, down from nearly 20 percent in 1980. Outside of the South and Mountain West, the majority of Americans are not likely to know someone who is or was in. No civilian American without a relative who joined has had to contribute to the wars in Iraq or Afghanistan. À la Toby Keith, they don't even have to know the difference between Iraq and Iran, and à la almost everyone, they don't have to be able to find Afghanistan on a map.

There's an implication in the fact that the question of the apostrophe exists, grammar somehow necessarily raising the issue of who the wars belong to. As it stands, without the apostrophe, the wars we fought are American wars, and they were fought by Veterans. But this isn't true anymore. Our recent wars aren't Americans' wars. They're Veterans'.

So, the way I see it, we have two options. The first is simple: we add the apostrophe, make it Veterans' Day. This would better represent the reality of the last twenty years of war. And it would remind other veterans, and me, that these wars do in fact belong to us, and us alone.

You aren't wholly to blame here. So much of your ability to care or be involved is dependent on sifting through the noise of what the military-industrial-news complex tells you, and it would be a gross understatement to say that they have been less than honest. But you also didn't want to hear the truth. You were too busy thanking us for our service, calling us heroes, tying yellow ribbons around your trees, hoping that we could come home safely.

It would be dishonest at best to say that this worship of warriors can't be beneficial; I got to go to Columbia and medical school because of it. I have free healthcare for the rest of my life, in a country where a sudden illness can bankrupt you. Your adoration has given me the advantage of the apotheosed.

And this is an improvement over the treatment of Vietnam veterans, those poor men (literally, look at who the draft selected) who didn't have the choice to go to war, facing atrocities beyond comprehension, only to come back and be spat on, called baby killers, denied jobs. You'll note, though, that this too was an extreme. As in so much of American life, we've lost the ability to have a middle ground, to recognize the wide and varied reasons someone might join a war machine. Or why they might leave it.

But there is a second option. If every year, for a single day, you are reminded that, as Helen Oyeyemi says, "What Is Not Yours Is Not Yours," then maybe you'll be able to see the extent of what is ours. And if you catch sight of it, if you look upon our works, ye Mighty, you must not despair. There is no story, as there is no storyteller, that can turn this wanton destruction into something parsable. No matter how hard they try, how much they glorify it, how much they lament it, how much excruciating detail they go into—war is something that must be done if you are to know it. This doesn't mean you can't know of it.

And so you must ask yourselves.

Do you want to know?

If you do, you have to wipe out all preconceived notions you may have of what this knowledge is, what our works are. Not all of us fought. Most of us didn't; only 10 percent of active-duty military personnel technically see combat. So when you meet someone who was in, consider *not* immediately asking them if they "were overseas" or "went anywhere." Maybe don't try to establish their bona fides by trying to suss out if they had enough "tours" to meet your preconceived notion of what exactly it means to have served. Don't stop listening when they tell you that they were a cook or a dental assistant or in finance or logistics. All of these people were in, all of them were a part of this thing that made them separate from 99 percent of the rest of Americans.

If you do meet the ones who fought, the ones who killed, listen carefully. Take in every detail, whether it's the bloodcurdling way their face lights up as they remember how good it felt to take a life, or the way their eyes go dull as they try to stop knowing how bad it feels to lose one. You may not know their specific pain, but they don't know yours either. Remember, infinity isn't so big. We're not that different.

It's also not all on you, this burden. We must make our efforts too. It's all too easy to imagine ourselves as completely separate, to discount any and all experiences you've had as trivial. Or irrelevant.

Because they aren't. The entire purpose, allegedly, of what we did was to ensure that everyone can have those banal and boring experiences. To safeguard the right to have the most stressful part of the week be sitting behind some fool checking their phone at the newly changed light, or the overly talkative person in front of you in line. Or your kid refusing to listen to you. Or losing your job. Or watching your loved one die in a hospital bed. These are not experiences I understand, and that is equally as problematic as someone else not understanding what it means to be in the military, or to go to war.

When you're done listening, be it on Veterans(') day or any other, you're not obligated to honor us. But if to honor someone is to regard them with respect, you can't do that unless you know what exactly it is you're trying to respect. What you do once you figure that out, that's entirely up to you. But at least let your decision be yours. Don't let the noise make it for you.

Maybe no one warned me about tinnitus because they didn't find it that annoying. You can learn to live with most anything, I've been told. Or maybe it was because they knew there was nothing to be done about it. You can learn to accept everything, I've come to know. Or maybe it was because there's a lot to be said for something so reliable. Something that you know is like your memories. Permanent.

I've learned to tolerate my tinnitus, and sometimes it's even interesting, almost likable. Some of this tolerance is simply due to distraction, as while somewhere in my mind I know that the sound will always be there, in our modern world there's usually something around to mask it. Except when I'm reading, and when I'm writing. Then, because everything else is quiet, it's there, inescapable and immutable. In those moments the hum is almost like a physical thing, a sort of pressure against my ears. It's not uncomfortable, this pressure, but it's very present. It's this sense of nearly corporeal company that I find interesting.

But sometimes it changes, or maybe a better word is transforms, stops being a sound, and becomes The Sound. The Sound is this great swell, a rise of volume and associated feeling that I've come to like. I don't know what brings on this transformation, though I haven't tried particularly hard to establish a pattern. I can always feel it coming, though. There's a sudden change in the tone of my normal tinnitus; it becomes brighter, almost phosphorescent, or whatever the auditory version of phosphorescent is. Pure, I think. Other sounds become muffled, and for an instant the ringing collapses to a single, brilliant point of pure resonance. And then it explodes, like I know all sounds eventually do, and it expands rapidly outward in a great wave of sensation and noise until, eventually, everything goes back to normal.

Above is my attempt at a visual representation of this. If you've watched a movie or TV show where a grenade, or bomb, or any general explosion goes off near a character, and the volume of all the sound around them is lowered, overwhelmed by a single high-pitched tone, you've got an idea of what I'm trying to describe.

I came to accept The Sound in part due to its random nature. It was never problematic, but I didn't like the suddenness, the way it took me out of whatever moment I was in. But once I recognized that it was unpredictable, it stopped surprising me; I guess I came to expect the unexpected.

If you were to watch me when this happens, when my normal sound becomes The Sound, you would see someone acting out a scene wherein he is lost in thought, ignoring those around him, addressing the invisible audience via voice-over. Not quite *Fleabag*, not quite *Scrubs*, somewhere in between. I actually tilt my head; the sound is often louder on one side, so my head turns in that direction as I try to focus on it, try to listen carefully, try to make out what I think it wants me to hear.

But, capitalized or not, it's still a sound, a trick of physics, or in this case, neurons (still physics, really; it's turtles all the way down). It doesn't want anything, least of all me. But then, why does it happen when it does? It happens in myriad times and places, making it unlikely that it's influenced by setting. Which begs the question: Is it dependent on me? Does it somehow correlate to my state of mind, or is it truly stochastic, such that even if I did bother to track it I'd never be able to predict it? Am I responsible for it?

Is it a memory?

I don't know the answers to these questions. I doubt I ever will. But I don't know that the answers matter, as it seems that the simple act of asking them served to change The Sound, or at least my relationship with it. So now, while it may look like I'm lost in my mind, The Sound actually returns me to the world. Because the problem with hearing the *ka-thunk* of the 105 every time a car backfires is that it means you don't hear other things instead. The Sound has helped me remember that not all things worth listening to have to be associated with fighting. It has helped me remember that what you have to say, and who you are to say it, are relevant.

And because of the difference in magnitude, when The Sound calms back down, my normal tinnitus seems so soft as to be gone, such that for a moment, the world is quiet like it hasn't been since 2011. This used to terrify me, but I'm learning to sit with it. The quiet doesn't have to be bad. It doesn't have to be an omen. It doesn't have to keep me from being fine now.

Sometimes, the world is just quiet.

May as well use that time to listen.

REAPING,
OR FUCK 'EM

THE ONLY PROBLEM with taking that time to listen is that sometimes I don't want to hear what's being said. Like when someone asks, "Was it worth it?"

This is probably the most common question I get asked by those who think they're interested in my story. This is the number one request, over war stories (being friends with mostly liberals means no admission of bloodlust, desire for violence, or relishing in power), over mental health (being friends with mostly Americans means no acknowledgment of the ramifications of war, imperialism, and removal of life), and over "what it was like" (being friends with mostly humans means little attempted acknowledgment or seeking out of another's soul).

It comes in a number of forms, this question, each version carrying a separate tone that allows the speaker to keep the question open, to carry an unsaid parenthetical. It could mean:

"Was it worth it (for you)?"

Or

"Was it worth it (for us)?"

Or

"Was it worth it (for them)?"

Or

"Was it worth it (for anyone)?"

The first version, wherein the tone implies a "for you," I have an answer for, an honest one. It was. Joining the Air Force is the best decision I ever made. Unforeseeable, or at least unseen, downstream effects included. Getting out was the second-best. My decision to get out was a personal one, and while I may have complicated feelings about what I did in the military, I don't begrudge anyone who stayed in, is in, or wants to be in. I would only say to the latter group, be careful. It might not be worth it for you.

The second version and third versions of this question are, in my experience, the more common ones. These are the questions that undergirded much of the news and commentary that surrounded the "fall" of Afghanistan. They aren't unreasonable questions, on their face. How much time, how much money, how many lives did we as a country devote to fighting in a country completely devoid of any strategic importance? No matter what the policy wonks want you to believe, as they will tell you that Afghanistan is bordered by Iran and Pakistan and China and once upon a time the USSR, thereby making it important for global security and affairs, except Afghanistan as a country is little more than a fairy tale, simply a place we (the West) decided to name and impose these borders on so that we could have a location that was (a) conveniently surrounded by our enemies, and (b) ours for the taking. Any importance it has had on the global stage in recent history was purely invented by those who conceived of it in the first place. And how much suffering did Afghans have to go through in that time? Constantly living under the fear of the Taliban's return, their reversion to the dark ages, their loss of, gasp, democracy.

These verbal isotopes are convenient, as they protect the speaker from asking what they actually want to know:

"What do we get out of it?"

Or

"What will Afghanistan look like thanks to us?"

Often, the person asking one of these questions is hoping for an answer to both; it's more of an "and" than an "or."

I have answers for these questions too, though they aren't honest. They're not as ready, not as pithy as my first answer, as they largely depend on the context of the conversation. But as a rule, said answers usually involve deferring, demurring, de-something-ing, instead of saying what I usually want to: "Fuck you."

Fuck you and your newfound, if not completely artificial then at least conveniently timed anxiety for a country of 40 million people, except oh wait, for you they aren't people, they're "those poor people" or "all those Afghanis" (an Afghani is a currency, not a person, by the by), or, best of all, "those *women*," said with every bit of emphasis you can muster on the plight of those poor creatures who will return to being if not beasts of burden then at least subhuman under the Taliban's rule, a predestination that you have a Calvinist fervor for because you already consider these women so much Lesser Than. You aren't asking "What will the women in Afghanistan do?" You are asking "What will happen to the women in Afghanistan?" Your conceptualization of these vibrant, exceptional humans who are part of a culture millennia older than almost any you could claim completely denies them agency. They are not women, they are Other, and you are a sanctimonious fuckwit for deigning to think of them in your moments of outrage that only come into being when directly confronted with the consequences of your particular brand of American exceptionalism.

If you want to care about women's rights, buy a bicycle. Or at least an electric car. Stop buying oil and supporting the world's most fervent exporter of regressive, subjugating, militant, violent Islam. (Hint: It's a place that, unlike Afghanistan, is actually mostly desert.) At least stop to consider the number of things you purchase that were made in a country that is currently, actively, sterilizing women of a certain ethnic minority. (Hint: It's a place where most things are made.) Or, maybe, I don't know, fucking vote, and not just when it's a convenient way to virtue signal once you finally realize that oh, women's rights in this country are at risk too.

If you want to know what Afghanistan will look like, it isn't that hard. Look at any picture of it from the last ten years. Look at all the blown-up buildings, the walls that are more bullet hole than concrete, the miles and miles of burned poppy fields. Watch a video of the aftermath of the suicide bomb that killed at least 170 people when we withdrew from Afghanistan, dozens of their bodies floating in a blood-tinged canal. Note how the person filming's hand doesn't shake, their voice doesn't crack, there are no screams of surprise or fear. They've seen worse, and they've seen it more times than you can, quite literally, imagine. (You could also look at pictures from Iraq. Or Syria. Or Libya. Or Yemen. Or any of the other places we like to drop bombs on. Dealer's choice.)

Once I'm done screaming at you in all of my inarticulate rage, you may say, "Whoa, whoa, but like, what about what the Taliban will do now that they're back in power?"

Fuck you. What about it?

Less than a week after our nation's ill-fated flight, Anand Gopal published a piece in the *New Yorker* entitled "The Other Afghan Women." In it, he detailed the state of affairs in the countryside of Afghanistan, where more than 70 percent of the population lives. He was there in the early summer of 2021, before all of Afghanistan had been officially reclaimed by the Taliban. But most of it was under their rule, including the areas he was traveling through. The people he talked to, more specifically the women he talked to, were significantly more at ease now that the Taliban was back in control. Without Americans fighting them, and without the monstrously corrupt Afghan National Army being backed by American forces, violence was at its lowest point in years.

A week and a half after that the *New York Times* published a separate piece that further detailed the new quiet that pervaded the countryside. There were no air strikes. Firefights, once a daily occurrence, were few and far between. There were fewer check-points, Talib or otherwise. Afghanistan was, in fact, safer with the Taliban in charge.

What is it that you're so afraid of the Taliban doing? Enforcing their own moral code on those who don't wish to live by that code? Drive to Texas. Or California. Same thing's happening there. It's called government.

Enacting retribution without courts? I refer you to the time we used a drone to kill a sixteen-year-old American citizen because his dad—another American citizen who we killed without due process—had been deemed a terrorist.

Killing people for no reason other than their ancestry? We got lynchings aplenty here.

The argument implicit in this question of what the Taliban will do is that we were somehow doing better. I suspect this argument is unavoidable; most people or institutions are the hero in their own story. Or at the very least what they're doing is "worth it." Ends and means, etc. But the United States isn't interested in being in the story. They want to write it. Because if they don't, it gets a lot harder to see their actions as valorous.

There aren't too many people who would say the guys blowing up a hospital in one of the poorest parts of the world—a hospital staffed by international volunteers, all civilians—are particularly good. The guys who shoot up weddings because someone fired a gun in the air at one, maybe aren't so upright. The guys who invade a country with the pretext of rooting out a movement, who, when that very movement offers to surrender, say no, sorry, not unless we get to kill most, if not all of you and remove any of the power you once had; guess we'll just have to stick around and make sure you don't come back, but oh, shit, you mean to say bombing the random citizens of this country will encourage them to join, or at least accept you? You don't say.

Afghanistan is, by no means, better off with the Taliban in charge. Sharia, as interpreted by the Taliban and their Wahabbist ilk, is a stain on humanity. The subjugation of women, ethnic minorities, and, in short, anyone who disagrees with them, relies on a combination of cruelty, ignorance, and violence that has no place in the modern world. Unless they really do change, which seems unlikely, human rights will continue to be violated under their rule. The Taliban are, in fact, fear-throwers.

But there will probably be fewer casualties of war. Definitely less collateral damage. Fewer blown apart—literally—families. This isn't because the Taliban will be kind or good or just. It's because we weren't any of those things either.

All of that said, many, many people are likely going to die as a result of the Taliban's incompetency. They do not know how to govern. They don't care about helping the people, just ensuring that their worldview is fulfilled, their pockets lined. But for those in the gallery ready to comment on how corrupt this is, how inhumane, before you open your fucking yap, let me remind you of specks and planks.

As for what we get out of it, it depends on which "we" you feel a part of. We the hawks made a hefty profit. We the blood-thirsty got some delicious retribution against all those brown, Allah-loving heathens. We the politicians got our re-elections. We America got yet another hysterically funny loss added to our war record. We the people got an extra trillion dollars added to our deficit. (I'm no economist, and I don't care if one of them tries to explain to me that the production of bombs and planes and tanks and all the other apparatuses of war contribute to our GDP or some other ridiculous metric of growth, none of these things added any benefit, any surplus, to any American citizen's life. If you are inclined to argue that they keep American soldiers alive, then I'm inclined to remind you that you're just a tautology-loving moron who can't see that these weapons wouldn't be necessary to keep said soldiers alive if we didn't create and use them in the first place.) We the fighters got prosthetics. And lifelong meds. And coffins.

Doesn't really matter which "we" you belong to. My answer is the same.

Fuck you.

Because the thing is, you don't care. Everyone wanted to talk about "Afghanistan" when we were withdrawing, but that was only because it was an excuse to talk about ourselves. Now that we're out, and millions of Afghans are starving, unable to afford food because we, in all of our pride, refuse to give aid to the country that we helped demolish over multiple decades, there's a lot less chatter. All because we lost. This is the actual reason, no matter what anyone says. It isn't because the Taliban are "bad." We give Pakistan billions of dollars every year. The ISI (Inter-Services Intelligence) doesn't exist in the same universe as good. Israel, Mossad? Same. Am I cherry-picking and just choosing the worst arms of these governments? Yes. Are the worst parts of a government representative of what that government stands for on the whole? Also, yes.

So, you see, fuck you.

Fuck me too.

More than anyone or anything, fuck me for not just moving on. For not finding new stories to tell. Fuck me for not being able to hear the other stories.

And fuck me for not screaming this shit from the rooftops a decade ago. It's not like it wasn't just as evident then. We all knew. I don't know a single Pashto linguist who didn't call the Taliban's return to power. It was so obvious that it became unspoken; only idiots point out what everyone else should already be able to see.

Fuck me for worrying about the potential social consequences that come with considering the Taliban's side of things. Fuck me for giving a single flying fuck about what anyone else thought, or thinks, about my trying to understand why the Taliban, or really anyone, might find it worthwhile to shoot at the people who came into their country, subverted their constitution, and installed a new government, despite the fact that not a single Afghan was involved in the attack that was supposed to justify these actions.

If these thoughts sound repetitive, just a different rehashing of what I was thinking and saying when I pissed off Ed with my validation of OBL, it's because they're related, though not the same. Thinking about bin Laden had been academic more than anything else, his mythical status allowing comparisons to all the other villains of days gone by. But these men, the ones I killed, were so many pawns (this is not derogatory, for what was I other than a slightly better trained tool), only allowing comparison to other humans, real and painfully unimagined.

And if, at this point, you're still on the side of the Taliban being evil, or at least cowardly, I get it. Ambushing people is some chicken-shit nonsense. Killing men when they're just trying to do their job, trying to make the world a better place, trying to make sure that the right ideals are spread throughout the land, while maybe not fundamentally wrong, is at the very least base, and ignoble. Blowing somebody up when they're standing in the middle of a field, because you are certain that they're going to try and kill you later, is unjustifiable. I should know. I've done it.

The difference between what I did, launching a missile from a plane flying many thousands of feet above Afghanistan—so high, in fact, that an average observer on the ground might not even take notice of it until they heard the sound of the air above them breaking—and placing an IED in the culvert of a well-traveled road is a matter of degree, not kind. They are both forms of guerilla, or at least atypical, warfare. They are both simply attempts at a surprise attack that are meant to give the attacker some sense of advantage and control, while also creating distance, both physical and metaphorical, between the attacker and the enemy. They both intend to target certain people, but often wind up hurting myriad others. They both malfunction, sometimes with almost comic results (the suicide bomber gets a spam text and blows himself up, the drone operator loses the satellite connection and the drone nearly flies into a nearby plane).

To hear us tell it, IEDs are used only by spineless, sneaky, yellow-bellied cowards. Weaklings who aren't willing to fight head-on, like men. Drone strikes, though, those are just good, superior technology. We only think IEDs are cowardly because they're so good at killing us. And maybe they really are just the paraphernalia of the pusillanimous. But they're also efficient. And they're no more evil than any other method of killing.

And lest you think I am a traitor or peacenik hippie, FUCK the Taliban. Fuck those stone-aged, misogynistic, pederastic, tyrannical, extremist, violent, ignorant fucks. Fuck them for their dedication to living in the past, for using religion to justify their bullshit, for being utterly unwilling to approach living in this century, or fuck, this fucking millennium. Fuck them for not listening.

Because even if I tried to tell it to them, the Taliban could never hear this story. I could broadcast it to them for hours and days and weeks and months and years, and no matter how long and how clearly I spoke, the Taliban could not, and would not, ever hear my story. Or your story. Or any story that doesn't involve them winning, taking back their country, and remaking the world in their image. The Taliban cannot feel anything other than what they have always felt. This is a broad, sweeping, overgeneralized statement about a group comprised of many individual persons with their own life stories, thoughts, and feelings about the future, thereby making it reductive and likely untrue, or at least lacking insight into all of the various truths that could exist for each person that is part of the greater Taliban.

I stand by it.

Ten years after my last deployment, and after twenty years of combat with the world's richest, most advanced military, the Taliban reclaimed Afghanistan. Whatever delusions existed about whether this would happen or how long it might take were dispatched as efficiently as the Afghan security forces were by the Taliban over a single week. What little gains had been achieved in women's rights, education, and poverty were systematically eradicated. Any semblance of democracy was lost. And while there might be "peace," it will come only after any remaining forces of opposition are overwhelmed or dead. The Taliban told us this would happen. Or at least they told me.

They told me about their plans, their hopes and dreams. They told me exactly how they would accomplish these goals, and how nothing could stop them. They told me that even if they died, they were confident that these goals would be achieved by their brothers in arms. And I'm sure, because they fucking told me, that they would have kept doing this forever.

I stand by my simplistic assessment of all these men precisely because of what they told me. Because they told me how they planned to keep killing Americans. They told me the details of these plans: what weapons they would use, where they would do it, how many they hoped to murder. Often, they told me these things while doing the killing. They told me that, God willing, the world would be made in their image. And they told me what so many others refused to hear, but what I finally understood: *Afghanistan is ours.*

AFTER, OR YOU
CAN'T UNKILL THEM

IF I THINK OF MYSELF NOW, with my desire to experience things and understand my experience of those things, with the strange penchant for nostalgia that showed up sometime around my thirty-first birthday, I can envision myself taking one last walk around a gunship before I got out. Going out to the flight line, walking around inside the plane, taking stock of this wondrous machine. But I didn't do that. Not for the gunship, not for the Whiskeys. Since November 29, 2011, I haven't set foot in a C-130. For a long time, I simply didn't have it in me. And then, after that time had passed, I no longer belonged in them. I spent many years unthinking about them, not trying to forget, but not trying to remember either. So when I began writing this, I was worried that I wouldn't be able to visualize them anymore. I thought I would need to watch videos, or look at blueprints, something to remind me of what it was like inside them. But I didn't. I can see the insides of these planes as vividly as I can see the double-wide trailer I grew up in.

On the U-boats, I can instantly see the 105 in all its splendor, the gunners standing all around it, worshipping. The ammo, so organized, so exactingly stacked, ready to be used as quickly and efficiently as possible. The 40, and the 25, all scrunched up next to each other. Here's the booth, my seat and my equipment, the EWO's seat with all of his weird-ass sensors. Here's the FCO and Nav, the TV and IR. Here are the stairs to the cockpit, narrow and steep, almost like moving up some sort of crevasse, the distance of those steps always feeling so much greater than the three feet they actually traversed. And here's the cockpit, which somehow always surprised me with how small and cramped it was, and how much of the world it let me see.

The Whiskeys aren't all that different in size, though the lack of a booth makes the layout so much more open. With that openness came the glorious urinals, no piddle-packs on a Whiskey, they'll always have that over the U-boats (and with the urinals the memory of the time I almost passed out in one, thinking that I'd be fine walking the thirty feet over to take a leak without using any supplemental oxygen when we were flying unpressurized at around twenty thousand feet, which, of course, I wasn't. Thankfully it wasn't a long piss, or I definitely would have wound up flat on my back covered in my own urine). I can feel the cargo ramp below me, cool and vibratory, as I catnapped during transit, the loadmasters watching, waiting till I was unconscious so they could hog my hat (read: draw a dick on the inside lining). I can see my strange middle seat, so much closer to the action of the sensors than on a U-boat. I can feel how close to me the two CSOs were, one at each hand, but off in their universe of sight, so far from mine of sound. And there's the new 30mm, almost sparkling in its newness, so modern, somehow so different from the U-boat guns.

This seems like an incredible amount of detail, given that, on the high end, I spent maybe a thousand hours split between the Whiskeys and the gunships (there's time spent onboard an aircraft pre- and post-mission that doesn't count as flight hours, and during my training in Florida I spent a good amount of time just walking around the U-boats, getting familiarized with them). Generously, I spent a total of 41.666667 days in these planes, or .3 percent of my life to date.

I thought about making that the title, or at least subtitle of this book: 42 days, or 1,000 hours, or .3 percent, or something like that. They're interesting numbers; 42 with its fun Adamsonian coincidence, 1,000 with its sense of nice, even largeness, .003 with its feeling of rarity or specialness. They're hooky and intriguing, these numbers, which is useful for me, an author, wanting to grab the attention (and money) of you, the reader.

But, you'll have noticed, none of those are the title, because it felt wrong to try and summarize my life with something so clichéd, so Gladwellian (this is no insult to Gladwell, I'm just not him). Those numbers, or even just one of them, let's say 1,000 hours, it being the hookiest and most aesthetically pleasing, have defined, continue to define, and near as I can tell, 87,660 hours (or 10 years) later, will always define my life. They defined my dreams, motivating me to go to medical school so that I could one day help people without having to kill others in order to carry out that helping. They defined my nightmares, forcing me to go on the antidepressants that I still take, and will continue to take, as I now know that no matter how healthy I become, if I go off them the desire to cease existing always returns and overwhelms the fortifications that I thought I'd made. Those numbers, along with the other one, 123, the number of people I have allegedly killed, or helped kill or been in the vicinity of when they were killed, made me, and make me, who I am.

I tried to make myself into someone else.

After I quit flying, and once I got the appropriate help, I became a (slightly) better airman. Taking certain antidepressants automatically disqualifies you from flying (or did then anyway) for an extended period of time, and eventually my "story," aka my mental health, was reviewed, and it was decided that it wasn't in the best interest of the Air Force to have me flying again. But I had also signed a contract and had a duty to fulfill for a couple more years. So I helped teach future DSOs, in the ways that I could, ways that didn't involve listening to Pashto. I was put to work in our tactics office, helped develop some of the training material for Dari linguists, and volunteered to become a certified crew resource management instructor; if nothing else, I could help others learn more about communication. And I thought a lot about what I could do to fix myself and my place in the world.

I genuinely don't remember when or how, but at some point in that thinking I decided that becoming a physician would Solve All My Problems. I went to the community college near my base to take some pre-reqs, transferred to a university soon thereafter, got my degree, and applied to medical school. This is what I wrote in my application:

> *There was a time when I could see everything. I could hear almost everything too; that's the whole point of being an Airborne Linguist. The desert was miles below me, but I could hear the insurgents tracking an American convoy, and could tell the Special Forces captain on the ground to adjust his team's route. Being 10,000 feet above the Earth allowed me to do this. I always enjoyed the*

altitude—with it came perspective, and with the perspective came clarity. But sometimes, the sky fills with clouds, and suddenly all the world's a blur.

Blurriness wasn't something I wanted when I was the only translator working on Special Forces missions in Afghanistan. I couldn't be hazy when I was translating Taliban communications in real time. So I had to be careful. I had to look, listen, and think. Eventually, I could see and hear everything through the clouds. Now though, my senses were better honed, and I began to notice more details.

Many of these details were associated with my job, but some of them were about myself and what I wanted out of life. I had already come so far, from a childhood where even the most basic things like food and shelter weren't always assured. I'd left behind the poverty that kept me from pursuing higher education, and joined the Air Force so I could learn languages and see the world. I excelled at this, and became fluent in two new languages in less than a year. Based on my test scores, I was selected to join Special Operations, where I learned from and worked beside some of the most exceptional individuals I have ever known.

Most importantly, I was doing something that was meaningful—I was protecting human lives. Though this was my primary role, sometimes protecting certain people meant harming others, and that detail wasn't something I could reconcile, or find a solution to. All of the clarity that I'd worked so hard to achieve started to blur around the edges.

Toward the end of my first deployment, and throughout my second one, I searched for an answer to this apparent contradiction. I knew I wanted to serve, help, and protect other people, but not at the expense of others. This reflection culminated in a fascination with medicine. When I made the decision to pursue becoming a physician, I still had over a year left in the Air Force. Telling my coworkers about my newfound goal was ill-advised; after all I hadn't even been to college, let alone taken the demanding courses required to attend medical school. But with the support and advice I received from friends and mentors, I was fortunate enough to end up attending Columbia University. Just as I had enjoyed the intense challenge of language school and special operations training, I relished the academic rigor I encountered at Columbia.

At the same time, I sought out new volunteer opportunities that allowed me to give back to communities that were similar to the ones I grew up in. I shadowed physicians and saw that many of the skills I gained in the military were applicable to medicine. I saw the same teamwork, honesty, and work ethic that I loved in the military being used in new and exciting ways. I even learned that aspects of aviation like checklists and Crew Resource Management are now being incorporated into many parts of the medical field.

Eventually, I became a Research Assistant at the Veteran's Affairs hospitals in Manhattan and Brooklyn, where I enrolled patients in a nationwide genetic study, and conducted research on mental health populations. Although I was nervous about communicating in the medical profession, I quickly realized that my old skills were just as applicable in this new environment. The professionalism and calmness I used on the radio naturally extended to patient interactions. I found that because my former career was a solitary position with no one around to offer backup, I was prepared for almost any situation. I didn't always have the right answer to difficult questions—no one ever does—but I was eager to tackle any new challenge with the support of the people around me.

Sometimes I miss the physical clarity that being 10,000 feet in *the air offered, but the intellectual and moral clarity that medicine offers more than make up for that. It also offers me a career that feels familiar. My experience with stressful situations and accelerated learning will give me the strength to excel during the rigors of medical training. I know how to think quickly and calmly, and how to remain focused under pressure, and I believe that the communication, leadership, and teamwork skills I have will allow me to become a good physician. And everything I've done so far in pursuit of this goal has only reinforced my original reasons for starting along this path. No longer is there any contradiction, or concern that I should be doing anything else. And that's not blurry at all.*

There are some, let's say, extensions of the facts in there. Some technicalities. I passed the final exam for Dari at the six-month mark of my yearlong course, and because my Pashto course was just shy of six months long, I can honestly say that "I became fluent in two new languages in less than a year." I was just careful not to note the chronicity of that year. I received good feedback on this essay, and I was told by a few schools that it played a large part in my being offered an interview.

I wrote something similar when I applied to residency. It had some more details that were specific to the career field I applied to, anesthesiology, but was otherwise largely the same. I received similar feedback on this essay; multiple interviewers told me how upon reading it they knew "they had to interview me." I am proud of my education, of the fact that I graduated from medical school, that even if I didn't go to residency I will always be a physician. But I'm not sharing any of this to show off or prove my accomplishments. I worked hard for them, but they're also in large part due to luck and the graciousness of others.

None of what I wrote in my personal statements, either for medical school or residency, was untrue. But neither of them featured the whole truth. I originally wrote an essay with that truth in it, and my advisor told me that if I used it, I likely wouldn't get accepted to medical school. Here is some of it:

"Because I'm tired of killing people." When I first decided I want to be a doctor and people asked me why, that was my answer. It was and is the truth, but this didn't mean that people were any more comfortable with it. It's surprising, and not a little unsettling, but the truth is the truth and I saw no reason not to speak it. Today, if you were to ask me the same question, my response would be a lot less bothersome, but also a good bit cliché. "I just want to help people." Which is also the truth, albeit a different version thereof. I do JUST want to help people. It's all I can imagine doing with my life. But, as a lot of people have pointed out, there are easier ways to help people. There are even better, more impactful ways. I could be a teacher, and help young people learn, and love to learn, and maybe even decide what they want to be. I could do cancer research and maybe help develop a treatment option that will help tens, if not hundreds, of thousands of people. Hell, I could be a nurse and help people in a clinical setting in three years instead of eight.

And I've actually thought about all of those options. I love teaching, have experience doing it both in the military and as a civilian, and I'm not half bad at it. Cancer and many other diseases are fascinating, and though I've only had a small taste of it, I find research interesting, and despite the occasional tedium, ultimately rewarding. Nursing would become a reality much sooner, and is largely about directly helping people, which is what I crave. But when I think about these or anything else as my future, there's this feeling of emptiness. It's not fear of missing out, or the thought of twenty years down the road wondering if I could have made it as a doctor. It isn't the status, or the compensation that comes with being a physician, though those are nice.

It's that to this day, the most important thing in my life is the lives I took in Afghanistan. Those lives define my life, almost every part of it. They dictated my education, where I live, who I interact with and how. What I believe, my political leanings, what I'm willing to accept as true, all of this and more is governed by 123 people that no longer exist.

"But they weren't people." That's the argument countless fellow airmen and civilians alike gave me. They were militants, or Taliban, or terrorists, or otherwise enemies. These too are a truth. But they aren't the truth. The truth is that they were people, no matter what terrible things they'd done, no matter what their motivations were, no matter how many of us they had killed. And while there are those who can kill others, I am not one of those people.

Now, I firmly believe it is my duty to heal people, or at least that I should do everything in my power to make it my duty. I need to do it as a doctor, because I need to make those decisions again. But they can't be life or death. They can only be life. I know that I won't be able to cure every patient, or even treat some of them. I know that many will die, despite the best efforts of me and my future "crews." That won't necessarily be okay, as I hope I'm never perfectly at ease when someone dies under my watch. At least I'll have tried though. At least I'll have attempted to give life, or ease pain and suffering. At least, at the very least, I won't be tired of killing people.

As you can see, I dutifully changed it. Took out the rawness and the defensiveness. Added some nice, palatable, cinematic visuals.

Obviously, we'll never know if I would have been accepted to any schools if I had used that essay, but I suspect my advisor was right and that I wouldn't have received any interviews, let alone acceptances. There's a part of me that finds this irksome, the idea that others would prevent me from pursuing my goals because they believe they know what are and aren't the "right" reasons to become a physician. As long as it isn't because they want the power to harm others, I don't think it matters why anyone wants to be a physician.

The other part of me, the one who, in the end, decided not to go to residency, not to practice medicine, knows that they're right. Being a physician was never going to unkill those 123 men. Nothing will.

There is no atonement, because I did nothing wrong; I am no sinner.

And there is no absolution, because I did nothing right; I am the worst sinner.

While writing this book I spent a lot of time thinking about the people I used to work with. Some of this was selfish, wondering who would be most interesting to include, then weighing those thoughts against whether they would want to be included and wanting to verify that some of the things I remembered weren't completely wrong. Some people I just sort of stalked on Facebook, unsure if they would want to hear from me, unsure if I actually wanted to talk to them. Some I found, and sent vaguely platitudinous messages to, getting varying levels of well-worn responses. Some I couldn't find, and I suspect didn't want to be found.

There were those I still knew and routinely saw: Dex, Trevor,

Taylor. And while we hadn't kept in close contact, I still counted Kasady and Chris as friends, guys I could readily call up and talk to about these things. But as I thought about other people I'd worked with, I wondered if any of them would want to hear from me. None of us were going to be lifelong friends the way Taylor and I are (how many of those do you get?) or even just good buddies like I am with Dex and Trevor, who text on birthdays or other big life events and make plans to see each other if we happen to be in the same city. I figured that things like age, faith (in God and/or country), or just personalities made it so that once we no longer worked together there would be no reason for us to communicate. It wasn't that I didn't consider these people my friends, or, despite my cynicism, because of any suspicion of hatred or even just dislike on their end. (I don't believe that most humans can have enemies, as very few people think about you as much as you think they do. And even if they do in fact give you that much consideration, who are you to be so important that said person is going to be actively opposed or hostile to you, seeking to injure or harm you all of the time?) I just thought that when you don't talk to someone for two, or five, or ten years, why would you? What would there be to say?

But then I got Vince's phone number and sent him a text asking if he had some time to talk. Vince and I had not exchanged so much as a single hello since 2012. But a couple hours later he said sure, how about Tuesday, after the kids are in bed. *The kids*, I thought. Plural. Wow. The first few minutes of the call were a little awkward, each of us unsure of the role to be played, how much of our lives we needed to share to be polite, how many questions to ask. But after about six minutes or so, everything clicked back into place. It hadn't been ten years since we talked, it was just yesterday.

The same thing happened with Paul (kids and all), a former

TSO. And Jack, another DSO. And Sue. As I kept talking to people who I thought were more or less gone from, or no longer a part of, my life—even people who I wouldn't have necessarily felt comfortable saying were ever a part of my life, more just connected to it—the same sequence of events took place:

1. Awkward reintroduction

2. Commentary on awkwardness of said reintroduction

3. Mention of others we knew in an attempt to ease the aforementioned awkwardness

4. Pause

5. Beginning of a lovely, warming, kind, long, and generous conversation between two people who know that they will always know each other in a way that very few other people can

I was surprised by this, but after the second time it happened, it started to make sense. It didn't matter that we both knew there was a good chance it might be another ten years before we spoke, if we ever did again. The nature of our work, of having done something so rare, so incredible, meant that we would always be able to talk like we'd just seen each other yesterday; our Super Balls, conservation of energy be damned, are still flying around even now, in orbit somewhere over Afghanistan.

In the course of all these conversations I also found out that, of course, war doesn't give with both hands. While we might never forget each other, almost none of us speak Pashto anymore, no matter how good we were or weren't in the first place. Certainly, some of this loss is due to lack of use, but then, I don't use Dari anymore and can still put together a fair number of sentences in it. I think the thing about Pashto is, or was, or will be, that to think it is to be fighting again. Turns out trauma can make you forget all sorts of things. Even an entire language.

And then I called up another friend, someone who was also a DSO once upon a time, but a non-Pashto one, to ask him about his memories of us. Who knows, I thought, maybe an outside observer would have thought we were all terrible. Jordan and I bullshitted for a little while, updated each other on our lives, wondered about the fates of various other DSOs. He allayed my fears, said that while he remembered some drama, that no, we weren't terrible. Toward the end of our conversation, he asked me if I wasn't ultimately thankful for these numbers and all of their associated memories precisely *because* they made me who I am. I told him no, I am in fact not thankful for all those deaths and that I found this argument a little tautological, or at least circular, like "Yes these things are ultimately good because they made me who I am and who I am is good and therefore they are good."

After this initial response, because he's my friend, and because I love him, I actually thought about what he said, instead of just dismissing it like a sarcastic asshole. I had never bothered to think that it was even possible to be thankful for such things. I'd auto-populated his question, or maybe even translated it to the thing I was so used to being asked, "Would you change them?" which I find ridiculous and annoying, because hypotheticals like that are entirely unuseful (I'm fine with considering the impossible, that's often how amazing things get dreamt up, but engaging in this sort of fairy tale wish fulfillment is just frustrating and pointless, as whether I would change them has little to do with their being).

"I think in order to be thankful for the things that made you who you are, you have to be happy with who you are."

"Aren't you?"

"I . . . Sometimes. But not usually, no."

"Oh. Why not?"

"Fuck, man, I don't know."

It's not that I'm necessarily unhappy with who I am, though that is sometimes, and sometimes even more than sometimes, the case. I'm not as suggestable, though. I have firmly held beliefs, things that I've decided are True. I'll listen to others' opinions about these things, but I'm not all that likely to change what I know. I spent so long not knowing what was true, and trying to forget what I eventually did know, that I'm not willing to risk my reality anymore.

So when I said "I don't know" to my friend, it was the truth. I didn't have a good answer as to why I'm not happy with who I am, in part, I think, because answering that question would run the risk of expanding my reality. But I suspect that realities are like the universe, constantly expanding, and so I've begun to wonder: If I'm right, and that in order to be thankful for certain experiences that made you who you are, you have to be happy with who you are, then it follows that you have to *know* who you are (I suppose it's possible to be "happy" without any self-awareness, but I don't believe that ignorance is in fact bliss). And maybe, more than simple unhappiness, more than the routine malaise, more than even clinical depression, this is my problem. I have these titles I can fall back on, things like physician, and scientist, and writer, and so on and so forth, but I don't feel that any of these things are definitional. They don't provide me with form, or substance. They don't tell me who I am.

Only the Taliban could do that.

ACKNOWLEDGMENTS

TO THOSE WHO TAUGHT ME how to write, in chrono-logical order: Diane Ellis, Tara Diercks, Tara Gallagher, Jerry Mathis, Maura Spiegel, Pip Lipkin, Gaetan Sgro, Peter Trachtenberg.

To my agents, Frank Weimann and Claudia Cross; my editor at Simon & Schuster, Robert Messenger; my editor at the *Atlantic*, Brendan Vaughan; and to Kevin Maurer for telling Frank to find me.

I can't list all the names of the men and women I worked alongside in the Air Force, for reasons of both brevity and security, but thank you to all of my language instructors, everyone I flew with, and to the myriad DSOs and TSOs who taught me about work and, more importantly, life. To all the Pashto DSOs, I hope you can recognize yourselves in the text. FTJ.

To Karen, for supporting me through the writing process, and reading so very many drafts of dubious quality. To Taylor, for the memories. And to all of my friends, whether we've spoken in the last few days, or in the last ten years. e.e. I am not, but I will always carry all of you in my heart.

NOTES

LISTEN

3   **"translate intelligence communications or data"**: UAF Recruiting Quincy MA, August 20, 2020. https://www.facebook.com /watch/?v=596647881212645.

3   **"a lot of the things we do"**: Ibid.

FLYING, OR THE VALLEY OF DEATH

11   **Each Griffin is $127,233**: "AGM-176 Griffin," Wikipedia, August 25, 2022. https://en.wikipedia.org/wiki/AGM-176_Griffin.

13   **twelve of the fourteen Medals of Honor**: "N2kl," Wikipedia, August 21, 2021. https://en.wikipedia.org/wiki/N2KL.

15   **the Taliban's preferred method of communication**: Ben Makuch, "Why the Taliban and Criminal Organizations Have Gone Low Tech," *VICE*, November 14, 2017. https://www.vice.com/en /article/evb87z/why-the-taliban-and-criminal-organizations-have -gone-low-tech.

20   **biggest battle since Vietnam**: James Clark, "5 Incredible Firefight Photos from One of Afghanistan's Deadliest Provinces," *Task & Purpose*, September 13, 2016. https://taskandpurpose.com

/history/5-incredible-firefight-photos-one-afghanistans-dead
liest-provinces/.

22   **"develop observable, achievable, and reasonable measures"**:
CJCSI 3162.02, *Methodology for Combat Assessment* (Joint Staff,
Washington, D.C., March 8, 2019), B-2. https://www.jcs.mil
/Portals/36/Documents/Doctrine/training/jts/cjcsi_3162_02
.pdf?ver=2019-03-13-092459-350.

BEFORE, OR HOW TO BECOME A LINGUIST

34   **"measures developed abilities and helps predict"**: ASVAB,
March 26, 2021. https://www.officialasvab.com/.

SAPIR-WHORF, OR NEXT TO MY HEART

41   **differentiate between shades of blue:** Jonathan Winawer,
Nathan Witthoft, Michael C. Frank, Lisa Wu, Alex R. Wade,
and Lera Boroditsky, "Russian Blues Reveal Effects of Language
on Color Discrimination," *Proceedings of the National Academy
of Sciences* 104, no. 19 (2007): 7780–85. https://doi.org/10.1073
/pnas.0701644104.

41   **turning left or right:** "Guugu Yimithirr Language," Wikipedia,
June 10, 2022. https://en.wikipedia.org/wiki/Guugu_Yimithirr
_language.

50   **a billion-dollar spy plane:** "British Air Force Gets RC-135 Rivet
Joint Surveillance Plane," *Stars and Stripes*, September 4, 2015.
https://www.stripes.com/news/british-air-force-gets-rc-135
-rivet-joint-surveillance-plane-1.366430.

60   **spent a quarter million dollars:** Thomas Manacapilli, Carl F.
Matthies, Louis W. Miller, Paul Howe, P. J. Perez, Chaitra M.
Hardison, H. G. Massey, Jerald Greenberg, Christopher Beighley,

and Carra S. Sims, "Reducing Attrition in Selected Air Force Training Pipelines" (Santa Monica, RAND Corporation, February 2, 2012), 27. https://www.rand.org/pubs/technical_reports /TR955.html.

66   **"a person who uses unlawful violence":** "Terrorist," *New Oxford American Dictionary*, 3rd ed., accessed February 23, 2023. https://www.oxfordreference.com/display/10.1093 /acref/9780195392883.001.0001/m_en_us1297922?rskey= ijRRkg&result=85611.

BULLSHIT, OR YOU'LL ONLY DIE TIRED

73   **"so lacking in originality":** "Banal," Encyclopedia.com, September 18, 2022. https://www.encyclopedia.com/literature-and -arts /language-linguistics-and-literary-terms/english-vocab ulary-d/banal.

75   **"up to a month":** Mark Memmott, "At Scene of Battle in Afghanistan, IEDs 'Are Everywhere,'" NPR, February 14, 2010. https://www.npr.org/sections/thetwo-way/2010/02/at_scene _of_battle_in_afghanis.html.

75   **"bleeding ulcer" by General Stanley McChrystal:** Jeff Muskus, "McChrystal: Marjah a 'Bleeding Ulcer' in Afghan Campaign," *HuffPost*, May 25, 2011. https://www.huffpost.com/entry /mcchrystal-marjah-bleeding-ulcer_n_587949.

85   **reported the incident to higher-ups:** Anna Mulrine, "Sexual Assault in the Military: What Happens When the Victim Is a Man?," *Christian Science Monitor*, May 5, 2014. https:// www.csmonitor.com/USA/Military/2014/0505/Sexual -assault-in-the-military-What-happens-when-the-victim -is-a-man.

HOME, OR YOU LOOK LIKE MORE OF A MAN

136   **All night I lay on my pillow:** The National, "Baby We'll Be Fine," Val Jester Music, 2005.

139   **"Process intelligence information in an airborne environment":** AFSC 1A8X2, *Airborne Intelligence, Surveillance, and Reconnaissance (ISR) Operator Specialty Career Field Education and Training Plan* (Washington, D.C., Department of the Air Force, 2020), 9. https://static.e-publishing.af.mil/production/1/af_a2_6 /publication/cfetp1a8x2/cfetp1a8x2.pdf.

KANDAHAR, OR LISTENING TO AFGHANS

176   **"the mere fact that a combatant":** "Practice Relating to Rule 47. Attacks against Persons Hors De Combat," Customary IHL, accessed September 13, 2022. https://ihl-databases.icrc.org /customary-ihl/eng/docs/v2_rul_rule47_sectionb.

176   **can be considered a violation of:** Ibid.

FEAR, OR YOU CAN'T GO HOME AGAIN

182   **primarily used as an anti-aircraft weapon:** Sebastien Roblin, "How a Deadly Russian World War II .50 Caliber Machine Gun Blasted Its Mark into History," *National Interest*, November 10, 2018. https://nationalinterest.org/blog/buzz/how -deadly-russian-world-war-ii-50-caliber-machine-gun-blasted -its-mark-history-35762.

183   **without the billions of dollars:** Evan Koslof, "VERIFY: No, the U.S. Government Did Not Directly Fund the Taliban as Claimed Online," wusa9.com, August 17, 2021.

https://www.wusa9.com/article/news/verify/no-the-us
-government-did-not-directly-fund-the-taliban-fact-check
-afghanistan-cia-reagan-carter/65-fa07d053-aa77-4998-ad13
-950bc6dc007e.

189   **somewhere around six a day:** Spencer Ackerman, "Petraeus'
Commando Raids Killed Lots of Taliban. So?," *Wired*, July 19, 2011.
https://www.wired.com/2011/07/commando-killed-taliban-so/.

ANGER, OR YOU CAN'T KILL AN IDEA

207   **"I don't want to be threatening":** Hanif Abdurraqib, *The
Crown Ain't Worth Much* (Minneapolis, MN: Button Poetry,
2016), 9.

219   **"We checked with the legal team":** Fintan O'Toole, "The Lie of
Nation Building," *New York Review of Books*, October 11, 2021.
https://www.nybooks.com/articles/2021/10/07/afghanistan
-lie-nation-building/.

219   **"not a war":** Matthew C. Brand, *General McChrystal's Strategic
Assessment Evaluating the Operating Environment in Afghanistan in
the Summer of 2009* (Alabama: Air University Air Force Research
Institute, 2011), 2–3. https://media.defense.gov/2017
/Jun/19/2001765050/-1/-1/0/AP_BRAND_MCCHRYSTALS
_ASSESSMENT.PDF.

219   **"the conventional sense":** Julian Borger, "The Afghanistan
Papers Review: Superb Exposé of a War Built on Lies,"
Guardian, September 5, 2021. https://www.theguardian.com
/books/2021/sep/05/the-afghanistan-papers-review-craig
-whitlock-washington-post.

220   **"You're never going to eradicate that.":** Elisabeth Bumiller,

"Soldier, Thinker, Hunter, Spy: Drawing a Bead on Al Qaeda," *New York Times*, September 3, 2011. https://www.nytimes.com/2011/09/04/world/04vickers.html.

INFINITY, OR WHAT I WISH I HADN'T HEARD

223   **"Moral injury is the damage":** "What Is Moral Injury," The Moral Injury Project, accessed September 13, 2022. https://moralinjuryproject.syr.edu/about-moral-injury/.

225   **"cognitive combat intimacy":** Eyal Press, "The Wounds of the Drone Warrior," *New York Times*, June 13, 2018. https://www.nytimes.com/2018/06/13/magazine/veterans-ptsd-drone-warrior-wounds.html.

232   **"strong affection for another":** "Love," definition and meaning, Merriam-Webster, accessed September 13, 2022. https://www.merriam-webster.com/dictionary/love.

234   **"There is but one truly serious":** Albert Camus, *The Myth of Sisyphus* (New York: Vintage Books, 2018), 3.

235   **it was a survival skill:** Jonathan Shay, *Achilles in Vietnam: Combat Trauma and the Undoing of Character* (New York: Scribner, 2003), 175.

236   **"when a man has seen so many":** Erich Maria Remarque, *All Quiet on the Western Front* (New York: Little, Brown and Company, 1929), 187.

TINNITUS, OR YOU SEEM FINE NOW

241   **nightmared us for so long:** Brian Turner, *Here, Bullet* (Farmington, ME: Alice James Books, 2005), 56.

244   "the truth does not instruct": Tim O'Brien, *The Things They Carried* (New York: Penguin, 2009), 65.

245   12 percent of Americans: *"The First Measured Century*: Book: Section 11.9," Public Broadcasting Service, accessed September 13, 2022. https://www.pbs.org/fmc/book/11government9.htm.

246   only 7 percent of the population: Katherine Schaeffer, "The Changing Face of America's Veteran Population," Pew Research Center, April 5, 2021. https://www.pewresearch.org/fact-tank/2021/04/05/the-changing-face-of-americas-veteran-population/.

REAPING, OR FUCK 'EM

255   killed at least 170 people: Jim Garamone, "U.S. Central Command Releases Report on August Abbey Gate Attack," U.S. Department of Defense, February 4, 2022. https://www.defense.gov/News/News-Stories/Article/Article/2924398/us-central-command-releases-report-on-august-abbey-gate-attack/.

256   entitled "The Other Afghan Women": Anand Gopal, "The Other Afghan Women," *New Yorker*, September 6, 2021. https://www.newyorker.com/magazine/2021/09/13/the-other-afghan-women.

256   quiet that pervaded the countryside: Jim Huylebroek, "This Is Life in Rural Afghanistan After the Taliban Takeover," *New York Times*, September 15, 2021. https://www.nytimes.com/2021/09/15/world/Afghanistan-rural-life-under-Taliban.html.

262   the Taliban reclaimed Afghanistan: Ruhullah Khapalwak and Carlotta Gull, "20-Year U.S. War Ending as It Began, with Taliban Ruling Afghanistan," *New York Times*, August 29, 2021. https://www.nytimes.com/live/2021/08/15/world/taliban-afghanistan-news.

262   **Whatever delusions existed about:** Mike Jason, "What We Got
       Wrong in Afghanistan," *Atlantic*, August 12, 2021. https://www
       .theatlantic.com/ideas/archive/2021/08/how-america-failed
       -afghanistan/619740/.

262   **how long it might take:** Gordon Lubold and Yaroslav Trofimov,
       "WSJ News Exclusive | Afghan Government Could Collapse
       Six Months After U.S. Withdrawal, New Intelligence
       Assessment Says," *Wall Street Journal*, June 23, 2021. https://
       www.wsj.com/articles/afghan-government-could-collapse
       -six-months-after-u-s-withdrawal-new-intelligence-assessment
       -says-11624466743.

AFTER, OR YOU CAN'T UNKILL THEM

277   **the routine malaise:** Grizzly Bear, "Two Weeks," Warp Records,
       2009.

ABOUT THE AUTHOR

IAN FRITZ was an airborne cryptologic linguist in the United States Air Force from 2008 to 2013. He became a physician after completing his enlistment.

Now, he writes.